# A HANDBOOK
## on
# LAMENTATIONS

The Handbooks in the **UBS Handbook Series** are in-depth commentaries providing valuable exegetical, historical, cultural, and linguistic information on the books of the Bible. They are prepared primarily to assist practicing Bible translators as they carry out the important task of putting God's Word into the many languages spoken in the world today. The text is discussed verse by verse and is accompanied by running text in at least one modern English translation.

Over the years church leaders and Bible readers have found the UBS Handbooks to be useful for their own study of the Scriptures. Many of the issues Bible translators must address when trying to communicate the Bible's message to modern readers are the ones Bible students must address when approaching the Bible text as part of their own private study and devotions.

The Handbooks will continue to be prepared primarily for translators, but we are confident that they will be useful to a wider audience, helping all who use them to gain a better understanding of the Bible message.

# UBS Helps for Translators

**Handbooks:**

A Handbook on . . .

Leviticus
The Book of Joshua
The Book of Ruth
The Book of Job
The Book of Psalms
Lamentations
The Book of Amos
The Books of Obadiah and Micah
The Book of Jonah
The Books of Nahum, Habakkuk,
    and Zephaniah
The Gospel of Matthew
The Gospel of Mark
The Gospel of Luke
The Gospel of John

The Acts of the Apostles
Paul's Letter to the Romans
Paul's First Letter to the Corinthi-
    ans
Paul's Letter to the Galatians
Paul's Letter to the Ephesians
Paul's Letter to the Philippians
Paul's Letters to the Colossians
    and to Philemon
Paul's Letters to the Thessalonians
The Letter to the Hebrews
The First Letter from Peter
The Letter from Jude and the
    Second Letter from Peter
The Letters of John

**Guides:**

A Translator's Guide to . . .

Selections from the First Five
    Books of the Old Testament
Selected Psalms
the Gospel of Mark
the Gospel of Luke
Paul's Second Letter to the Corin-
    thians

Paul's Letters to Timothy and to
    Titus
the Letters from James, Peter, and
    Jude
the Revelation to John

**Technical Helps:**

Old Testament Quotations in the
    New Testament
Short Bible Reference System
New Testament Index
The Theory and Practice of Trans-
    lation
Bible Index

Fauna and Flora of the Bible
Marginal Notes for the Old Testa-
    ment
Marginal Notes for the New Testa-
    ment
The Practice of Translating

# A HANDBOOK ON

# Lamentations

by William D. Reyburn

UBS Handbook Series

United Bible Societies
New York

Books in the series of **Helps for Translators** may be ordered from a national Bible Society, or from either of the following centers:

United Bible Societies
European Production Fund
W-7000 Stuttgart 80
Postfach 81 03 40
Germany

United Bible Societies
1865 Broadway
New York, New York 10023
U.S.A.

**L.C. Cataloging-in-Publication Data**

Reyburn, William David
   A handbook on Lamentations / by William D. Reyburn.
       p.      cm.  —  (UBS helps for translators) (UBS handbook series)
   Includes bibliographical references and index.
   ISBN 0-8267-0124-8
   1. Bible.    O.T. Lamentations—Translating.    2. Bible.   O.T. Lamentations—Criticism, interpretations, etc.   I. Title.   II. Series. III. Series: Helps for translators.
BS1535.2.R49  1992
224'.3077—dc20                                            92-22755
                                                              CIP

ABS-1992-750-EB-1-104975

# Contents

Preface . . . . . . . . . . . . . . . . . . . . . . . . . . . . . . . . . . . . . . vii

Abbreviations Used in This Volume . . . . . . . . . . . . . . . . . . . . ix

Translating Lamentations . . . . . . . . . . . . . . . . . . . . . . . . . . . 1
  Title . . . . . . . . . . . . . . . . . . . . . . . . . . . . . . . . . . . . . . 10
  Chapter 1 . . . . . . . . . . . . . . . . . . . . . . . . . . . . . . . . . . 10
  Chapter 2 . . . . . . . . . . . . . . . . . . . . . . . . . . . . . . . . . . 41
  Chapter 3 . . . . . . . . . . . . . . . . . . . . . . . . . . . . . . . . . . 72
  Chapter 4 . . . . . . . . . . . . . . . . . . . . . . . . . . . . . . . . . . 106
  Chapter 5 . . . . . . . . . . . . . . . . . . . . . . . . . . . . . . . . . . 129

Selected Bibliography . . . . . . . . . . . . . . . . . . . . . . . . . . . . . 147

Glossary . . . . . . . . . . . . . . . . . . . . . . . . . . . . . . . . . . . . . 151

Index . . . . . . . . . . . . . . . . . . . . . . . . . . . . . . . . . . . . . . . 163

Illustrations:
  Wine Press . . . . . . . . . . . . . . . . . . . . . . . . . . . . . . . . . . 33
  Small Millstones . . . . . . . . . . . . . . . . . . . . . . . . . . . . . . 139

# Preface

This Handbook, like others in the series, concentrates on exegetical information important for translators, and it attempts to indicate possible solutions for translational problems related to language or culture. The authors do not consciously attempt to provide help that other theologians and scholars may seek but which is not directly related to the translation task. Such information is normally sought elsewhere. However, many church leaders and interested Bible readers have found these Handbooks useful and informative, and we hope that this volume will be no exception.

In *A Handbook on Lamentations,* special attention has been given to the poetic structure so that the translator will be able to understand the movement and the logical progression of the sections of this book, and how they contribute to the message of the whole.

The Revised Standard Version (RSV) and Today's English Version (TEV) translations are shown at the beginning of each chapter, so that the translator may see models of how the poetry may be presented in the receptor language, with added line spacing to show divisions in the discourse. RSV and TEV are then reproduced again at the beginning of the discussion of each verse or smaller group of verses. When RSV is quoted in the discussion, the words are printed in **boldface**, while quotation marks are used when TEV and other translations are quoted, or when a passage of RSV is quoted other than from the verse being discussed.

Toward the end of the project the Revised English Version and the New Revised Standard Version became available, but it is to be regretted that it was too late to use them in any systematic fashion. Translators may wish to have these new versions available during the translation of Lamentations, because they provide many good models of possible translations.

A limited bibliography is included for the benefit of those interested in further study. The glossary explains technical terms according to their usage in this volume. The translator may find it useful to read through the glossary in order to become aware of the specialized way in which certain terms are used. An index gives the location by page number of some of the important words and subjects discussed in the Handbook, especially where the Handbook provides the translator with help in rendering these concepts into the receptor language.

The original author who prepared an exegetical draft for this Handbook was the Reverend Brynmor F. Price, who served at the time on the staff of the British and Foreign Bible Society. He has since retired, and in the meantime the base and model approach to our Handbooks has changed radically, and new insights are available, not only about the content and meaning of this book, but about the forms of the Hebrew poetry that comprise the major section of the book. It was therefore necessary to begin the drafting anew. The author, however, found that the original draft did serve as a good resource, and both credit and thanks are due to Mr. Price for his work on the project.

The editor of UBS Helps for Translators continues to seek comments from translators and others who use these books, so that future volumes may benefit and may better serve the needs of the readers.

# Abbreviations Used in This Volume

## General Abbreviations, Bible Versions, and Other Works Cited
(For details see Bibliography)

| | | | |
|---|---|---|---|
| AB | Anchor Bible | Mft | Moffatt |
| B.C. | Before Christ | NAB | New American Bible |
| BDB | Brown-Driver-Briggs lexicon | NEB | New English Bible |
| BJ | *Bible de Jérusalem* | NIV | New International Version |
| FRCL | French common language version | NJB | New Jerusalem Bible |
| | | NJV | New Jewish Version |
| GECL | German common language version | RSV | Revised Standard Version |
| | | SPCL | Spanish common language version |
| HOTTP | Hebrew Old Testament Text Project | | |
| | | TEV | Today's English Version |
| K-B | Koehler-Baumgartner lexicon | TOB | *Traduction œcuménique de la Bible* |
| KJV | King James Version | | |

## Books of the Bible

| | | | |
|---|---|---|---|
| Exo | Exodus | Neh | Nehemiah |
| Lev | Leviticus | Psa | Psalms |
| Deut | Deuteronomy | Matt | Matthew |
| 1,2 Sam | 1,2 Samuel | | |

# Translating Lamentations

## Message and purpose

The book of Lamentations poetically depicts the horrible atrocities that struck the city of Jerusalem and its inhabitants when the city was invaded by the Babylonian army in 587 B.C. It does so in part by contrasting the greatness and glory of the past with the abject misery of the present, which is the result of the defeat of Judah and the destruction of its capital city. But Lamentations is much more than a recital of sufferings; it is a confession which accepts God's word that he would destroy the nation and punish its people for their iniquity.

The events which the poet describes came as a crushing blow to Israel. For more than four hundred years direct descendants of King David had ruled, and so the words spoken to David by the prophet Nathan (2 Sam 7.16) appeared as solid as stone: "And your house and your kingdom shall be made sure for ever before me; your throne shall be established for ever." Now, however, there was no more kingdom, king, or throne. Everything that was believed to be permanent and guaranteed by God had been swept away by pagans, and it was an angry God who had used these foreigners to bring judgment on his people.

In spite of the total loss of everything held sacred and dear, the poet does not urge survivors to find consolation in Israel's glorious past. He recognizes clearly that the greatness of the past has ended in horrible judgment. Neither does he look forward to a happy tomorrow when Israel will again reclaim her position among the nations. Instead he shows us, in the very heart of the book (chapter 3), an ordinary man who has known the depths of suffering and who, in spite of it all, remembers that the steadfast love of the LORD never ceases, that the LORD's mercies are new every morning (3.22-23); and so he says "Therefore I have hope" (3.21). This individual who asks "Why should a living man complain . . . about the punishment of his sins?" (3.39) knows that it is not God's final will for people to suffer and to be crushed (3.34-36).

## The alphabetical pattern

The book of Lamentations is unique among the poetic books of the Old Testament: it is the only book which is entirely in poetic form. Psalms has prose headings, and Job has a prose introduction and ending; only Lamentations is without any prose element. Lamentations consists of five poems, each being a separate and individual unit, and yet each poem or chapter flows into the same stream of thought discussed above under "Message and purpose."

Moreover, each chapter has twenty-two verses, except chapter 3, which has sixty-six verses arranged in twenty-two groups of three. The arrangement into twenty-two verses or groups of verses in chapters 1–4 is to accommodate the verses to the twenty-two letters of the Hebrew alphabet. In chapters 1, 2, and 4, the first word in

1

each verse begins with the successive letter of the alphabet. That is, the first word in 1.1 begins with *alef,* the first word in 1.2 begins with *beth,* the first word in 1.3 with *gimel,* and so forth through the twenty-two letters of the alphabet.

When we come to chapter 3, we find twenty-two groups of three verses, and in each group the first word in each of the three verses begins with the same letter. For example, the first word in each of the verses 3.1, 3.2, and 3.3 begins with *alef,* the first word in 3.4, 3.5, and 3.6 begins with *beth,* and so on. In this way the twenty-two letters of the alphabet are accommodated to sixty-six verses.

Chapter five also has twenty-two verses but does not follow the alphabetical pattern described for chapters 1–4.

It is not certain why a poet should begin each line with the next letter of the alphabet, a scheme which is called acrostic or alphabetic acrostic, but it may have been a challenge to the Hebrew poet's use of the language. Some interpreters have suggested that it served as a help for memorizing, and others think it gave a sense of completeness to the poem, something like covering every point "from A to Z," or "from beginning to end."

It is no doubt the case that the ancient Hebrew poets strained the usage of their language to write poetic acrostics, because the first word in the line had to be forced into a mold. Translators who attempt to follow this pattern will soon find how unnatural their translation becomes. Therefore translators using this Handbook are advised to refrain from carrying over this poetic device into their translations.

There is no question that the acrostic form makes it possible to divide the Hebrew lines pretty much as the original poets intended. Consequently most scholars are agreed on the line divisions in the printed editions of the Hebrew Bible. However, the matter of meter or rhythm within the line presents a radically different picture.

**Meter in the lines**

Views on meter (the number of stressed syllables in a line) in Hebrew poetry in general, and concerning Lamentations in particular, are commonly presented as linguistic facts, but they are in reality little more than personal opinions. This is because scholars do not know, and do not have the means of knowing, how biblical poetry sounded when it was written. No one is entirely sure where the accents and stresses fell. The indications of stress and vocalization of the Hebrew Masoretic text were written down more than a thousand years after the poems themselves. It follows, therefore, that what is said about meter here must be taken in the light of these cautions.

One view that has been given considerable recognition is that the typical poetic line in Lamentations consists of a line made up of two parts with a break in sense between them. The first half-line is said to be slightly longer, containing one more beat (stress) than the second half-line. In this view, if the first half-line has 4 beats, the second half-line has 3 beats; and these patterns are written as 4 + 3, 3 + 2 and so forth. The assumption is often made that exceptions to such unbalanced patterning mean that there are sometimes variants or that the text is corrupt at that point. Budde, who formulated this view, found the same patterning in other laments in the Old Testament, and so named this stress system *Qinah* meter, from the Hebrew word meaning "lament."

Budde claimed that this unbalanced stress system held true for every line in chapters 1, 2, and 4, and for a great part of chapter 5. Since Budde's work, others have found Budde's unbalanced lines to be balanced with the same number of stresses in both half-lines. They conclude that, while the *Qinah* meter line is a dominant pattern, the first four chapters have a great mixture of other metric patterns, and that correcting the text on the basis of exceptional meter is not a useful undertaking. In fact even the term *Qinah* is not very useful, because the same stress patterns referred to by this term are found in Hebrew poems having no relation to laments for the dead. Moreover, other funeral songs such as David's lament over Saul and Jonathan (2 Sam 1.17-27) are not in *Qinah* meter.

It should become clear by now to the translator why the Handbook will not call attention to the so-called meters of particular lines. Not only is the entire subject built on very questionable linguistic assumptions, but the task of translators is not to imitate Hebrew stress patterns—rather it is to produce the poetic devices and style in their own languages that are suitable for the subject matter of the poems in Lamentations.

## Parallelism

Translators are referred to the discussions on parallelism in *A Handbook on the Book of Psalms* and *A Handbook on the Book of Job*. The present treatment is for the purpose of giving translators a view of some of the ways parallelism operates in Lamentations. It is assumed in this Handbook that translators will have translated the Psalms before undertaking Lamentations, and will have worked out the ways in which different kinds of parallelism will be translated. Accordingly, in the treatment of parallelism in this Handbook, our purpose is to illustrate some typical kinds of parallelism found in Lamentations and to discuss the relationships between their parts. A detailed discussion of the parallelism in every verse would make this Handbook far too long. However, the Handbook discusses particularly significant examples of parallelism in the text. It is hoped that translators will use the presentations here, plus the information in the other Handbooks cited, to make their own analysis of parallelism in the verses in Lamentations.

Parallelism is the very heart of Hebrew poetry. It forms the basic structural unit throughout Lamentations. Using Kugel's notation, parallelism consists of a first clause (half-line), a short pause, a second clause (half-line), a longer pause. This may be displayed as:

_____ / _____ //

All the poems or chapters of Lamentations are made up of these structural units of parallelism. For example, in chapters 3 and 5 each verse consists of one such unit:

_____ / _____ //

Each verse in chapter 4 has two units:

_____ / _____ //

_____ / _____ //

3

Each verse in chapters 1 and 2 has 3 units (except 1.7 and 2.19, which have 4):

———————————— / ———————————— //

———————————— / ———————————— //

———————————— / ———————————— //

      The relationship between the two halves of a unit of parallelism or between two or more units, in terms of meaning, may be so close that the two say almost the same thing, or be so loose that they bear almost no sense relationship. The two parts may stand in some logical relationship to each other, or they may individually contribute information to a larger theme. In other words their relations can be as varied as the poet wishes to make them.

      Before considering some examples of parallelism in Lamentations, it may be helpful to call attention to the matter of printed poetic lines. Translators using a number of translations will notice that there is little uniformity in the way in which poetic lines are printed. However, in order to show that the text is in poetic form, the practice is to use various levels of line indentation. Since we are speaking of half-lines and parallel units, we need to look closely at the way in which these are laid out in RSV and TEV.

      Both RSV and TEV use two levels of indentation, but not in the same manner. For example, in 1.1 RSV has:

(Unit 1)                How lonely sits the city
                          that was full of people!

Many editions of RSV have either a large number "1" or a large letter "H" at the beginning of the first chapter, and so the printed lines may have been forced to move to the right of this large figure. But if large letters or numbers are not used, the two lines will appear as seen above. RSV will then reflect the printed Hebrew line division: **that** in the second half-line is placed at the first level of indentation, and thus it is linked closely to the first half-line. Therefore an initial half-line followed by a half-line at first level indentation make up a unit of parallelism, or:

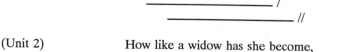

(Unit 2)                How like a widow has she become,
                          she that was great among the nations!

As is true of Unit 1, many editions of RSV will not print Unit 2 exactly as seen here. If the columns of print are too narrow, one or more words at the end of the line may have to be printed on the following line, but indented further to a second indentation. In this unit **become** and **the nations** are sometimes placed at the second level of indentation to show that they each belong to the end of the previous half-line, but would make the line too long for printing if placed there.

(Unit 3)                        She that was a princess among the cities
                                has become a vassal.

What was said of **become** and **the nations** may apply to **among the cities**. **Has** is placed at the first level, like **that** and **she** in Units 1 and 2. The first word in the first half-line of each unit is capitalized in this instance, because in RSV each begins a new sentence.

In a slightly different line arrangement, TEV treats each unit as if it were a single line. Unit 1 is positioned at the left, and Units 2 and 3 are placed at the first level of indentation. The portion of each line that does not fit within the column is then indented to the second level of indentation. This means that TEV will not always show parallelism clearly within a unit, and in fact TEV often combines two parallel portions into a single clause so that parallelism disappears.

It is hoped that this discussion will help the translator to understand how the idea of half-lines and parallel units are applied to the RSV and TEV texts. In some cases in the text, reference will be made to the "line," and in such cases "line" and "unit" are used interchangeably. This is done in preference to assigning letters to each half-line (in chapters 1 and 2 these would be "a" to "f"), which would be still more complicated.

The examples that follow begin with the single-unit parallelism (chapters 3 and 5) and go on to the more complex kinds in chapter 4, and then to the three-unit verses in chapters 1 and 2. The examples are taken from RSV, and the end of the first half-line is indicated with / and the second half-line with //.

3.15                        He has filled me with bitterness/
                            he has sated me with wormwood//

The two half-lines of this verse are not only parallel in their word order (in Hebrew and English), but each clause also says approximately the same thing. The second half-line matches the first in both form and meaning. The major difference is that the verb in the second half is more narrowly defined in meaning, with the sense "make someone drink" or "force someone to swallow." **Wormwood** translates a more vivid example of bitter-tasting poison. The net effect in this example is that the second half-line reproduces the meaning of the first half-line in more dramatic, picturable terms and thus sharpens the impact. Translators must see that this sharpening of effect is intended by the poet's selection and placement of the matching terms. Other devices may be available in their languages to reproduce the same effect.

5.11                        Women are ravished in Zion/
                            virgins in the towns of Judah//

Here there is parallelism of structure, in that in Hebrew **Women . . . in Zion** is matched by **virgins in the towns of Judah**. The one verb **ravished** (equivalent to "raped" in current English) serves for both halves and thus binds the two halves. **Virgins**, which is a specific class of "women," matches **Women** and has the effect of sharpening the picture in the second part. However, **towns of Judah** is more general than **Zion**. In this way the poet has combined in the second line elements making the meaning both more particular and more general. In no case does the

5

poet expect us to think of two separate events, women raped in one area and virgins in a different area.

3.4          He has made my flesh and my skin waste away/
                  and broken my bones//

In this example the lack of parallelism of form is evident in the translation. The first half-line is much longer, and only the first half-line has a subject. Nevertheless **made . . . waste away** is matched by **broken**, and **my flesh and my skin** is matched by **my bones**. However, **bones** is not any more particular, dramatic, or picturable, and so the second half does not intensify or sharpen the images in the first half.

3.48          My eyes flow with rivers of tears/
                  because of the destruction of the daughter of my people//

In this verse the second half-line stands in a logical relation to the first. It gives the reason for the statement in the first half-line. There is no matching of meaning or similarity of images, just an addition to or a continuation of the thought.

3.46                  All our enemies/
                        rail against us//

This verse is literally "They have opened their mouths against us/ all our enemies//." The second half-line simply makes clear who "they" represents in the first line.

As the units of parallelism increase in number within a verse, their relationships also become more complex.

4.1                  How the gold has grown dim/
                        how the pure gold is changed//
                  The holy stones lie scattered/
                        at the head of every street//

The RSV wording makes the parallelism of form in the first two half-lines more matching than the Hebrew, where **how** is only implied in the second half-line. There is very clear matching in which the more particular **pure gold** matches **gold** in the first half-line. However, the same cannot be said for **changed** as matched with **dim** (meaning "tarnished"). The second unit, by contrast, has no matching elements. Its second half-line merely gives the location of the scattered stones referred to in the first half-line.

4.5                  Those who feasted on dainties/
                        perish in the streets//
                  those who were brought up in purple/
                        lie on ash heaps//

In this example the parallelism of meaning is between those described in the first half-line of each unit (the rich, and royalty) and their present status seen in the second half-line of each. However, there is little poetic movement between the matching lines, so that the second one fails to heighten the intensity of the first, unless **lie on ash heaps** may be considered as narrower in meaning than **perish in the streets**. The main point is that the matching is not between the half-lines within a unit, but between the corresponding half-lines in the two units.

4.16
> The LORD himself has scattered them/
> he will regard them no more//
> no honor was shown to the priests/
> no favor to the elders//

Here the parallelism of meaning is seen in each unit. The parallelism between the two parts of the first unit is not as strong as in the second unit, where the two units have closely matching terms, and both halves depend upon the single verb in the first half-line. There is no attempt by the poet to make the second half-lines more specific or dramatic.

The parallel units in chapters 1 and 2 are the most complex. Here are two examples:

1.20
> Behold, O LORD, for I am in distress/
> my soul is in tumult//
> my heart is wrung within me/
> because I have been very rebellious//
> In the street the sword bereaves/
> in the house it is like death//

In the first unit the more general **distress** is matched by the Hebrew metaphor "my intestines ferment" (**my soul is in tumult**). This clearly has the effect of shifting the whole unit to a higher emotional pitch. This is followed in the first half-line of the second unit with another less dramatic metaphor of emotion (literally "my heart is turned within me"). The second half-line does not match the first with a more forceful figure but simply gives the reason for it all. By the time we reach the third unit, the focus is no longer on the poet's personal experience (I–me) but rather on death. However, instead of placing the metaphor in the second half-line, the poet places it in the first. The sword, which is only the instrument in the hand of the killer, becomes the focus of slaying, not of the poet but of people generally. **In the street**, or "outdoors," is matched in the final half-line by **in the house**, and these matching pairs together give the sense of "everywhere."

2.5
> The LORD has become like an enemy/
> he has destroyed Israel//
> he has destroyed all its palaces/
> laid in ruins its strongholds//
> and he has multiplied in the daughter of Judah/
> mourning and lamentation//

In the first unit the second half-line is metaphorical, with **destroyed Israel** (Hebrew "swallowed") spelling out concretely what it means to **become like an enemy**. But more than this, the poet uses the next unit to say what it means in particular to destroy Israel. And so **palaces** are swallowed, and **strongholds**, or forts, are ruined. The two half-lines of the second unit are fully parallel in meaning, but their function is to carry further the thought of the first unit, **he has destroyed Israel**. The third unit serves the same purpose as the second; however, here there is no parallelism between the two half-lines, and **mourning and lamentation** are again more general descriptions and effects of human destruction.

## Jerusalem and other personifications

A common device used by poets is to give human qualities to things that are not human and so make the reader feel for them emotionally as he feels about real human beings. Jerusalem and its people are called "daughter of Jerusalem," "daughter of my people," "daughter of Zion," and "virgin daughter of Zion." The entire country and its people are also referred to as "daughter of Judah," "Judah," and "virgin daughter of Judah." In their contexts these designations call to mind a suffering female figure.

Personification is particularly evident in the first two chapters of Lamentations, in which Jerusalem, Judah, Zion, or some part of Jerusalem such as the roads, gates, or altar, are depicted as:

(A) belonging to a class of women; for example, "she/her," "widow," "princess," "slave" (1.1);

(B) participating in human actions: she sees the nations invade (1.10), she weeps bitterly, she is betrayed by her lovers and friends (1.2), she suffers bitterly (1.4), she remembers (1.7), she sinned, became filthy, was despised, was shamefully exposed, she groans, turns her face (1.8), stretches out her hands (1.17), calls to her lovers (1.19);

(C) having human qualities: lonely (1.1), afflicted (1.9), stunned (1.13), faint 1.13), comfortless (1.17), distressed (1.20), forgotten (2.1), dishonored (2.2), mocked (2.15) destroyed (2.16), pitiless (2.17).

Translators must examine the various designations to determine if these expressions may be meaningfully used in their own languages. Since, for example, "daughter of Jerusalem" is a figurative expression, it may in translation mean nothing more than "a young girl who lives in Jerusalem." In the same way a literal rendering of "daughter of Zion," "virgin daughter of Zion," and "daughter of my people" may suggest that these are all different young women, when in reality they are all expressions meaning Jerusalem and its people. Accordingly TEV does not use "daughter of . . ." or "virgin daughter of . . ." but replaces these poetic expressions with nonpoetic ones. Translators may find it necessary to do likewise.

In some languages personifying or humanizing inanimate objects signals that a text is a folk-tale, since in those languages that device is used only in such stories. In those cases it may be necessary to make greater use of similes and say, for example, "Jerusalem is like a woman who . . . ," "the roads to Zion are like people who . . . ," "the gates of the city are like . . . ." Alternatively it is possible to replace "she" and "daughter of Jerusalem" with "the people of Jerusalem," and sometimes with "they."

Some translators may find it convenient to provide a footnote explaining the personification, or to include that information in the heading.

## God in Lamentations

Only in 3.41 is there a term translated "God" in RSV and TEV. The word is *'el,* a general word for God, which occurs commonly in poetic books such as Psalms and Job. A second term found in 3.35 and 38 is *'elyon,* translated by RSV as "the Most High" and by TEV as "he" and "his" respectively.

The most common term referring to God, found in every chapter of Lamentations, is written as "LORD" in RSV and TEV. "LORD" translates in English the four Hebrew letters *YHWH,* which represent the personal name of the God of the Israelites. The approximate pronunciation of the name is "Yahweh." In order to avoid pronouncing the sacred name, this was later written with the vowels of *'adonai* "my lord" and pronounced "adonai." The early Greek translators translated the sacred name by the Greek word for "lord," *kurios,* and many English translators have followed this tradition, spelling it "LORD."

Most translators will probably have arrived at a satisfactory translation of the sacred name. However, for those who have not, the following guidelines should be taken into account: firstly, *Yahweh* is a proper name and not a title; secondly, there is no generally-agreed meaning which can be assigned to this name, but such meanings as "he who is" or "he who always will be" are frequently mentioned. Accordingly the translation of the name may differ from language to language. The usual solutions are the following: (a) Transliterate, that is, write *Yahweh* by adapting it to the sound system of the translator's language. (b) Translate one of the suggested meanings; for example, "the one who is eternal." (c) Use the same term that has been chosen to translate *'adonai,* and make an orthographic or writing distinction between *Yahweh* and *'adonai,* as is done in RSV and TEV. However, the use of large or capital letters is meaningless to the listener, who will hear "LORD" and "Lord" alike. Furthermore, many languages do not use capital letters. In some languages it may be necessary to follow the Septuagint pattern and represent *Yahweh* by a term meaning "master, ruler, chief."

The only other term for the deity in Lamentations is *'adonai,* which occurs only in chapters 1, 2, and 3. *'Adonai,* which is written as "Lord" in both RSV and TEV, is an honorific title whose meaning is "master, owner, lord." It is a title used to show respect to a superior. In Old Testament practice this title was used for human beings as well as for God. For example, in Genesis 19.2-18 the two angels who appeared at Sodom are addressed as *'adonai.* In the later Old Testament period *'adonai* was always substituted for *YHWH* whenever the text was being spoken or read aloud.

# Title

In the Hebrew Bible the title of the book *Lamentations* is the first word of the first verse and means "How" ("How deserted lies the city . . ."). See also 2.1 and 4.1. This practice in naming books was used in the literature of other ancient languages in the Middle East. The English title *Lamentations* is based on the Greek translation, the Septuagint, where the title is taken from other early Jewish writings.

Some translations add ". . . of Jeremiah" or ". . . of Jeremiah the prophet" to the title. This tradition probably arose from the way Jeremiah spoke and acted at the time of the fall of Jerusalem; but there is no evidence that Jeremiah was the author.

The term *Lamentations* refers to the weeping and sorrow caused by the destruction of the city of Jerusalem by the Babylonian army in 587 B.C. It is thus an appropriate title for the content of the poetic laments which make up the book.

Languages often distinguish between various kinds of weeping or crying, particularly as associated with physical pain, grief, and death. In some languages weeping from grief, whether caused by death or other causes, is done in the form of a chant or dirge. Accordingly translators should use a title that is appropriate for a lament brought about by the tragic conditions described throughout the book. In some languages it will be necessary to use a full sentence as a title; for example, "The people of Jerusalem weep because of the destruction of their city," "This is a death chant when Jerusalem is destroyed," "Jerusalem is destroyed, and so the people weep."

# Chapter 1

Chapter one is the first of five poetic laments or poems which express deep sorrow. There are twenty-two verses in the chapter, and each verse begins with the succeeding letter of the Hebrew alphabet. See "The alphabetical pattern" in "Translating Lamentations" at the beginning of this Handbook, page 1.

The chapter is divided into two equal halves. In the first eleven verses the poet speaks of the pitiful conditions of the city of Jerusalem by contrasting its present destruction to its past glories. Jerusalem is pictured as a woman in these descriptions.

In the second half the point of view changes. Now Jerusalem speaks of herself in the first person, except in verse 17, where there is a change back to the third person. Verse 11 marks this shift in viewpoint. In verses 20 and 21 Jerusalem pleads for the LORD's mercy, and the chapter closes with a call to the LORD to punish Jerusalem's enemies in the same way as he has punished her.

## 1.1-22

REVISED STANDARD VERSION

TODAY'S ENGLISH VERSION
*The Sorrows of Jerusalem*

1  How lonely sits the city
       that was full of people!
    How like a widow has she become,
       she that was great among the nations!
    She that was a princess among the cities
       has become a vassal.

2  She weeps bitterly in the night,
       tears on her cheeks;
    among all her lovers
       she has none to comfort her;
    all her friends have dealt treacherously
          with her,
       they have become her enemies.

3  Judah has gone into exile because of
          affliction
       and hard servitude;
    she dwells now among the nations,
       but finds no resting place;
    her pursuers have all overtaken her
       in the midst of her distress.

4  The roads to Zion mourn,
       for none come to the appointed feasts;
    all her gates are desolate,
       her priests groan;
    her maidens have been dragged away,
       and she herself suffers bitterly.

5  Her foes have become the head,
       her enemies prosper,
    because the LORD has made her suffer
       for the multitude of her transgressions;
    her children have gone away,
       captives before the foe.

6  From the daughter of Zion has departed
       all her majesty.
    Her princes have become like harts
       that find no pasture;
    they fled without strength
       before the pursuer.

7  Jerusalem remembers
       in the days of her affliction and bitter-
          ness
    all the precious things
       that were hers from days of old.
    When her people fell into the hand of the
          foe,
       and there was none to help her,
    the foe gloated over her,

1  How lonely lies Jerusalem, once so full of
       people!
    Once honored by the world, she is now
       like a widow;
    The noblest of cities has fallen into
       slavery.

2  All night long she cries; tears run down
       her cheeks.
    Of all her former friends, not one is
       left to comfort her.
    Her allies have betrayed her and are
       all against her now.

3  Judah's people are helpless slaves, forced
       away from home.
    They live in other lands, with no place
       to call their own—
    Surrounded by enemies, with no way
       to escape.

4  No one comes to the Temple now to
       worship on the holy days.
    The girls who sang there suffer, and
       the priests can only groan.
    The city gates stand empty, and Zion
       is in agony.

5  Her enemies succeeded; they hold her in
       their power.
    The LORD has made her suffer for all
       her many sins;
    Her children have been captured and
       taken away.

6  The splendor of Jerusalem is a thing of
       the past.
    Her leaders are like deer that are
       weak from hunger,
    Whose strength is almost gone as they
       flee from the hunters.

7  A lonely ruin now, Jerusalem recalls her
       ancient splendor.
    When she fell to the enemy, there was
       no one to help her;
    Her conquerors laughed at her down-
       fall.

8  Her honor is gone; she is naked and held
       in contempt.
    She groans and hides her face in
       shame.

mocking at her downfall.

8   Jerusalem sinned grievously,
        therefore she became filthy;
    all who honored her despise her,
        for they have seen her nakedness;
    yea, she herself groans,
        and turns her face away.

9   Her uncleanness was in her skirts;
        she took no thought of her doom;
    therefore her fall is terrible,
        she has no comforter.
    "O LORD, behold my affliction,
        for the enemy has triumphed!"

10  The enemy has stretched out his hands
        over all her precious things;
    yea, she has seen the nations
        invade her sanctuary,
    those whom thou didst forbid
        to enter thy congregation.

11  All her people groan
        as they search for bread;
    they trade their treasures for food
        to revive their strength.
    "Look, O LORD, and behold,
        for I am despised."

12  "Is it nothing to you, all you who pass by?
        Look and see
    if there is any sorrow like my sorrow
        which was brought upon me,
    which the LORD inflicted
        on the day of his fierce anger.

13  "From on high he sent fire;
        into my bones he made it descend;
    he spread a net for my feet;
        he turned me back;
    he has left me stunned,
        faint all the day long.

14  "My transgressions were bound into a
        yoke;
    by his hand they were fastened togeth-
        er;
    they were set upon my neck;
        he caused my strength to fail;
    the Lord gave me into the hands
        of those whom I cannot withstand.

15  "The Lord flouted all my mighty men
        in the midst of me;
    he summoned an assembly against me
        to crush my young men;
    the Lord has trodden as in a wine press

Jerusalem made herself filthy with
    terrible sin.

9   Her uncleanness was easily seen, but she
        showed no concern for her fate.
    Her downfall was terrible; no one can
        comfort her.
    Her enemies have won, and she cries
        to the LORD for mercy.

10  The enemies robbed her of all her trea-
        sures.
    She saw them enter the Temple itself,
    Where the LORD had forbidden Gen-
        tiles to go.

11  Her people groan as they look for some-
        thing to eat;
    They exchange their treasures for food
        to keep themselves alive.
    "Look at me, LORD," the city cries;
        "see me in my misery."

12  "Look at me!" she cries to everyone who
        passes by.
    "No one has ever had pain like mine,
    Pain that the LORD brought on me in
        the time of his anger.

13  "He sent fire from above, a fire that
        burned inside me.
    He set a trap for me and brought me
        to the ground.
    Then he abandoned me and left me in
        constant pain.

14  "He took note of all my sins and tied
        them all together;
    He hung them around my neck, and I
        grew weak beneath the weight.
    The Lord gave me to my foes, and I
        was helpless against them.

15  "The Lord laughed at all my strongest
        soldiers;
    He sent an army to destroy my young
        men.
    He crushed my people like grapes in a
        wine press.

16  "That is why my eyes are overflowing
        with tears.
    No one can comfort me; no one can
        give me courage.
    The enemy has conquered me; my
        people have nothing left.

17  "I stretch out my hands, but no one will

the virgin daughter of Judah.

16 "For these things I weep;
    my eyes flow with tears;
for a comforter is far from me,
    one to revive my courage;
my children are desolate,
    for the enemy has prevailed."

17 Zion stretches out her hands,
    but there is none to comfort her;
the LORD has commanded against Jacob
    that his neighbors should be his foes;
Jerusalem has become
    a filthy thing among them.

18 "The LORD is in the right,
    for I have rebelled against his word;
but hear, all you peoples,
    and behold my suffering;
my maidens and my young men
    have gone into captivity.

19 "I called to my lovers
    but they deceived me;
my priests and elders
    perished in the city,
while they sought food
    to revive their strength.

20 "Behold, O LORD, for I am in distress,
    my soul is in tumult,
my heart is wrung within me,
    because I have been very rebellious.
In the street the sword bereaves;
    in the house it is like death.

21 "Hear how I groan;
    there is none to comfort me.
All my enemies have heard of my trouble;
    they are glad that thou hast done it.
Bring thou the day thou hast announced,
    and let them be as I am.

22 "Let all their evil-doing come before thee;
    and deal with them
as thou hast dealt with me
    because of all my transgressions;
for my groans are many
    and my heart is faint."

help me.
The LORD has called enemies against
    me from every side;
They treat me like some filthy thing.

18 "But the LORD is just, for I have diso-
    beyed him.
Listen to me, people everywhere; look
    at me in my pain.
My young men and women have been
    taken away captive.

19 "I called to my allies, but they refused to
    help me.
The priests and the leaders died in the
    city streets,
Looking for food to keep themselves
    alive.

20 "Look, O LORD, at my agony, at the
    anguish of my soul!
My heart is broken in sorrow for my
    sins.
There is murder in the streets; even
    indoors there is death.

21 "Listen to my groans; there is no one to
    comfort me.
My enemies are glad that you brought
    disaster on me.
Bring the day you promised; make my
    enemies suffer as I do.

22 "Condemn them for all their wickedness;
Punish them as you punished me for
    my sins.
I groan in misery, and I am sick at
    heart."

## Section Heading

Today's English Version (TEV) has as its heading "The Sorrows of Jerusalem."
If this is followed, the translator may need to shift to something like "This is the way
the people of Jerusalem suffered" or "Jerusalem is like a widow who suffers." In
some languages it will be helpful to retain the word "city" in the title in order to

make clear that the descriptions which follow refer to the city of Jerusalem and not to a person by that name. Some other headings are: "Jerusalem, like an abandoned widow" (*La Bible en français courant,* or French Common Language version [FRCL]), "Sorrows of captive Zion" (New English Bible [NEB]), "City without love" (*Traduction œcuménique de la Bible* [TOB]), "First lament," (*Dios Habla Hoy,* or Spanish Common Language version [SPCL]).

**1.1**  RSV

How lonely sits the city
   that was full of people!
How like a widow has she become,
   she that was great among the
      nations!
She that was a princess among
   the cities
has become a vassal.

TEV

How lonely lies Jerusalem, once
   so full of people!
Once honored by the world,
   she is now like a widow;
The noblest of cities has fallen
   into slavery.

As was pointed out in the section entitled "Parallelism," in "Translating Lamentations" (page 3 and following), all verses in chapter 1 have three units of parallelism (except 1.7, which has four). The first half-line of each unit is identified in both RSV and TEV by its initial capital letter: **How, How, She**, and "How," "Once," "The."

In all three units of verse 1, the poet contrasts the condition of Jerusalem as it is now, with what the city formerly was. In the first two units the present condition is described in the first half-line, and the former condition in the second half-line. However, in the third unit that order is reversed, with the former status (**was a princess**) described in the first half-line, and the present condition (**become a vassal**) in the second half-line. Not only is the poet contrasting "now" with "then," but by reversing the order in the last unit, a structural contrast is created within the verse. Moreover there is a good bit of matching of meaning between **like a widow has she become** and **has become a vassal**, also between **great among the nations** and **princess among the cities**. This parallelism of meaning, it should be noticed, occurs between the half-lines of different units rather than between half-lines within the same unit. TEV follows the same order, except in the second unit, where the past condition is placed first; TEV does this apparently for stylistic reasons.

In some languages it may be clearer to reverse the "now . . . then" order in the first two units so that they conform to the pattern of the third unit. In this way all three units depict the past as occurring before the present. For example:

Jerusalem that was once full of people is now lonely;
   she who was once great among the nations is now like a widow;
   she who was like a princess is now like a slave.

**How . . . that was: How** is the first Hebrew word in the first sentence and serves as the title for the whole book in its Hebrew form. The same word occurs also at the beginning of chapters 2 and 4 and is found in Jeremiah 48.17c and in Isaiah 1.21, where Jerusalem is also described as a woman. The expression serves here to stress the contrast between the past and the present. In many languages this exclamation must be rendered by a clause. For example, "Look, how awful it is" or "It is a very terrible thing." The same expression may sometimes be rendered idiomatically; for example, "I say this with tears" or "I say this with my heart failing." In some languages it may be clearer to mark the contrasts between the present sufferings and the past glories by saying, for example, "In earlier times," "In the past," or "Before Jerusalem was defeated."

**Sits the city** makes the city appear as a person. In some languages it is possible to employ a verb such as **sit** only with an animate subject. Therefore it may be necessary to say "The city is very empty" or "There are no people in the city."

The term **lonely** refers here to the lack of people, or to being deserted by those who once lived there. It may sometimes be translated figuratively; for example, "having only one word left," "with no one to talk to," "with only one dog for a friend."

**City** refers to the city of Jerusalem, which in modern terms would be more like a village or town. Although today most people are acquainted with noisy modern cities, it may be better to speak of the "town," if such a category exists in the translator's language. TEV says "How lonely lies Jerusalem." This is to make clear that **city** refers only to the city of Jerusalem and not to some other city.

The expression **full of people** makes it clear that a population center is in focus. **Full of people** is an expression of relative degree. A term used in translation should not give the idea that it was so full that there was no space not taken up by people. The sense is "with very many people" or "having a large number of people."

The expression **like a widow** compares Jerusalem to a wife who has lost her husband. This may imply that Yahweh has deserted her—a thought that is expanded in verse 2. The picture of a widow is used to emphasize the misery of Jerusalem compared with her previous greatness. The same is true in the last unit of verse 1, where Jerusalem is compared to a slave. If the term **widow** must be replaced by a descriptive phrase, it may be possible to say "like a miserable woman whose husband has died." If a nonfigurative expression must be used in place of **widow**, it may be possible to say, for example, "Jerusalem was a great city, but now is as miserable as a woman whose husband has died." A further translation decision is whether to keep the third person reference or to change to a more personal second person. If the second person is preferred, the translator should use it consistently.

**She that was great among the nations**: **nations** translates the Hebrew term *goyim*, a word that is sometimes applied to the gentiles or pagan people. For example, in Exodus 34.24, "I will cast out nations (*goyim*) before you, and enlarge your borders." The term is also used to refer to the descendants of Abraham in Genesis 12.2, "I will make of you a great nation . . . ." In verse 1 there is no attempt to contrast Israel with the non-Israelites, and so **nations** refers to all the political groupings, among which Israel was one. TEV "honored by the world" expresses this well.

**Princess among the cities** refers to the high status of Jerusalem in contrast with the servant status of **vassal** in the following half-line. The term does not mean the daughter of a king but rather a noble lady, or the wife of a noble or leader among the people. TEV "noblest of cities" may need to be reworded to say, for example, "Before you were like a princess" or, as FRCL says, "Yesterday a princess ruling the provinces, but now reduced to . . . ."

**Vassal** translates a word which suggests forced labor imposed upon a conquered people, and so TEV "fallen into slavery." NEB has "now put to forced labour." In some languages it is possible to maintain the figurative language of this unit by saying, for example, "You were like the rich daughter of the chief, but now you have become like the poorest slave" or "You who were like a great princess have now become like a poor servant."

**1.2**       RSV                                    TEV

> She weeps bitterly in the night,          All night long she cries; tears
>     tears on her cheeks;                        run down her cheeks.
> among all her lovers                       Of all her former friends, not
>     she has none to comfort her;               one is left to comfort her.
> all her friends have dealt treach-        Her allies have betrayed her
>     erously with her,                          and are all against her now.
>     they have become her enemies.

In this verse the imagery of weeping and tears continues the theme of sorrow. The first two half-lines of the verse are parallel in meaning. The verb **weeps** is sometimes followed in the second line by the verb "shed tears"; see Jeremiah 13.17, "run down with tears." Here the second half-line contains only the noun **tears**. However, the sense is the same as if "shed tears" was used. This movement from a general verb in the first half-line to a more precise expression in the second half-line gives a sense of increasing the force or intensity of the first unit. Translators who seek to translate in poetic terms should follow the rules of poetic style in their own language to provide for intensification within the second half-line, if such intensification is not expressed adequately by the particular selection of words.

**She weeps bitterly in the night**: **bitterly** refers to the resentful nature and intensity of her weeping. **In the night** refers to the extent of her weeping. That is, "she weeps throughout the entire night" or, as TEV says, "all night long she cries."

**Tears on her cheeks** represents the picturable or dramatic rephrasing of the first half-line. In simple prose terms the whole unit says "She weeps bitterly all night long so that tears are on her cheeks." If the translator is unable to retain the repetition of parallelism, it may be possible to replace it here by relating the two similar statements by a logical connective; for example, "Because she cries all night long, her cheeks are wet with her tears."

The remaining units in verse 2 provide the reason for Jerusalem's weeping. In some languages it may be necessary to introduce them with "this is because" or "this is the reason."

**Among all her lovers**: **lovers** translates a word which carries the sense of an irregular relation a man has with a woman to whom he is not married. It is used in Ezekiel 16.33 with reference to Jerusalem's political allies, and in Hosea 2.5 with reference to Israel's worship of Baal. In the present context it draws attention to Jerusalem's faithlessness to the LORD, her true husband. **Lovers**, which is used figuratively, emphasizes Jerusalem's female image, as is pointed out in "Jerusalem and other personifications" in "Translating Lamentations" at the beginning of this Handbook, page 8. In some languages it will be necessary to make it clear that **lovers** refers to a temporary relationship. This may sometimes be expressed as, for example, "her male friends" or "those who made love to her."

It is also possible to translate **lovers** as "allies, friends, friendly nations." If the translator follows TEV "allies," this may be expressed sometimes as "friendly countries" or "other tribes who were friendly to her."

**None to comfort her**: **comfort** refers to the act of encouraging or cheering someone who has become discouraged or saddened. The thought is sometimes expressed as "strengthen, cheer up, cause to recover." In many languages **to comfort** someone who is distressed is expressed idiomatically; for example, "to give them back their heart," "to make their heart strong again," "to quiet the shaking of their insides." This unit may sometimes be rendered "None of her former lovers is able to cheer her up" or "None of those who made love to her will give her new courage."

**All her friends** is parallel in meaning with **all her lovers** and refers to her political allies. Those, of course, are **friends** she used to have but who are no longer friends, and this may need to be made clear in translation. **Dealt treacherously** translates a Hebrew verb meaning "to deal faithlessly with" and is used in relation to Israel's unfaithfulness to the LORD in Hosea 8.9-10; Ezekiel 16.28-29. TEV translates "Her allies have betrayed her." "Betray" refers to being handed over to someone else's authority or control, against a person's own wishes and through a breach of trust. "Betray" is sometimes expressed as "to sell a friend to his enemy" or "to turn one's face away from a friend." The poet's allusion to **enemies** is probably to 2 Kings 24, in which the LORD sent Babylonians, Syrians, Moabites and Ammonites against King Jehoiakim to destroy Judah.

**Her enemies**: **enemies** refers to those who are opposed to Jerusalem. These include those who made war against her as well as those who opposed her more passively. Languages do not lack for terms for **enemies**, but sometimes they express the idea idiomatically; for example, "those who fight against her" or "those who turn away from her."

| 1.3 | RSV | TEV |
|---|---|---|
| | Judah has gone into exile be-<br>cause of affliction<br>and hard servitude;<br>she dwells now among the na-<br>tions,<br>but finds no resting place;<br>her pursuers have all overtaken<br>her<br>in the midst of her distress. | Judah's people are helpless<br>slaves, forced away from<br>home.[a]<br>They live in other lands, with<br>no place to call their own—<br>Surrounded by enemies, with<br>no way to escape. |

[a] are helpless . . . home; *or* fled from home, from the misery of slavery.

**Judah has gone into exile: Judah** serves to widen the perspective. It is the entire nation or kingdom that suffers exile, not just the city of Jerusalem. The reference is to the people of Judah, as in TEV. In translation it is important to avoid the impression that the poet has left off speaking of Jerusalem and has begun a new subject called **Judah**. Accordingly it may be advisable to speak of "Jerusalem in the region of Judah" or "Judah, the region around Jerusalem." In many languages it will be necessary to speak of the people of the area. In that case we may say, for example, "The people of Judah, where Jerusalem is." The same principle will apply in verse 4, where Zion refers to Jerusalem.

Translators will notice a difference in translation between RSV **gone into exile because of affliction** and TEV "helpless slaves, forced away from home." The reason for this difference is that the Hebrew verb translated **gone into exile** may be understood as either active or passive. RSV takes it to be active and consequently gives the impression that Judah went voluntarily into exile because of the afflictions she suffered at home. This interpretation agrees with the alternative given in the TEV footnote but does not accord with the rest of chapter 1. The TEV text rendering is to be preferred.

**Gone into exile** may be expressed as in TEV, "forced away from home"; or we may say, for example, "The people were taken as prisoners to other countries" or "Their enemies forced them to go and live in other lands."

**She dwells among the nations** means that Judah is living, not in her own land, but rather in the lands of foreigners. Here **nations**, in contrast to its use in verse 1, refers to the non-Israelite peoples. FRCL and others translate "pagans." *Die Bibel in heutigem Deutsch* (German Common Language version [GECL]) says "and must live among foreign people." Another interpretation, which is followed by the Anchor Bible (AB), is that this is a reference to the time before the exile, when Judah was an independent nation like other nations. However, it seems preferable to understand this statement as describing Judah's present situation, and so a rendering such as TEV, FRCL, and GECL is to be preferred.

**Finds no resting place**: for many years Judah had been the battleground between Assyria, Egypt, and Babylon, who all threatened her independence. Judah had therefore failed to enjoy the security or "rest" to which she looked forward, having, as TEV says, "no place to call their own." The poet uses the idea of "the rest" which Israel had been promised in Deuteronomy 12.9, "you have not as yet come to the rest . . . which the LORD your God gives you" (RSV), as well as the lack of "rest" mentioned in Deuteronomy 28.65. The focus is on the absence of peace and security experienced by the people of Judah even before the capture of Jerusalem, and this situation is also summarized in the last unit of the verse. In some languages **resting place** may be rendered "a place where people farm their own lands," "a place where people eat from their own gardens," or "a place where people's hearts are always cool."

**Her pursuers have all overtaken her**: **pursuers** refers to her "enemies, persecutors." The picture is of her enemies chasing Judah in order to catch her and strike her down. They have been successful and have **overtaken her**, that is, "caught her, seized her," and all of this **in the midst of her distress**. This last expression translates what is literally "between the straits." This expression is used only here, and so the meaning is not fully certain. The reference is probably to a military pursuit, in which a fleeing army is driven into a narrow pass where movement is slow and difficult, and this results in its capture and defeat. Translators may follow RSV, but TEV, which speaks of "no way to escape," is probably more accurate.

RSV                                            TEV

| | |
|---|---|
| The roads to Zion mourn, <br>    for none come to the appointed <br>        feasts; <br> all her gates are desolate, <br>    her priests groan; <br> her maidens have been dragged <br>        away,[a] <br>    and she herself suffers bitterly. | No one comes to the Temple now <br>    to worship on the holy days. <br> The girls who sang there suf- <br>    fer, and the priests can only <br>    groan. <br> The city gates stand empty, <br>    and Zion is in agony. |

[a] Gk Old Latin: Heb *afflicted*

Verse 4 expands the picture of Jerusalem's suffering by focusing now on the disappearance of worship in the Temple. The Hebrew text, as represented by RSV, says **The roads to Zion mourn**. The thought is that the roads that were once filled with worshipers are now desolate and empty. These roads led to the holy hill of Zion, where the Temple stood.

It may be necessary to modify the description of roads mourning and say, for example, "The roads to Zion are as people who mourn for their dead." In some languages this would imply that the roads are noisy places filled with wailing mourners. However, as the second half-line points out, it is the absence of people walking along the roads on their way to the Temple that makes even the roads mourn. TEV says "no one comes to the Temple." Accordingly it may be necessary to say, for example, "The empty roads that lead to the Temple at Mount Zion are sad, like mourners at a burial."

The names "Zion," "Jerusalem," and "Temple" are used interchangeably in Lamentations. Translators should make clear that **Zion** is the same as Jerusalem, or more exactly the Temple in Jerusalem; in fact they may wish to replace **Zion** with "Temple," as in TEV. "Temple," as used here, is the place where God is worshiped in Jerusalem, and is considered to be his dwelling or building. In some languages "Temple" may be translated "the holy house," "the holy building," "house of God," or "house where people worship God."

**Appointed feasts** is literally "appointed," but the reference is to the great festival times in the Old Testament. TEV calls these "holy days," and NEB "sacred feasts." In languages in which **appointed feasts** would simply mean "scheduled eating and drinking," it will be necessary to provide the idea of worship; for example, "the days when people came to worship" or "on the special days when people thanked God in the Temple."

**All her gates are desolate**: it is not certain whether these are the gates of the city wall or the entrances to the Temple. TEV and others make it clear that these are the "city gates." Others translating more formally keep **her gates**. During the celebration of the great festivals of Israel, the worshipers would come crowding through both the city gates and the Temple entrances. FRCL takes **her gates** to refer to the meeting area inside the city gates and translates "her public squares." The word **gates** may sometimes be translated as "the entry place" or "where people went in and out of the city." The word translated **desolate**, when used in reference to land or a place, means to be empty, without people, deserted.

**Her priests groan**: in a similar passage in Joel 1.9, the priests mourn at the destruction of the countryside. Since the priests are no longer present in the Temple, it may be assumed that they **groan** in captivity. A **priest** is one who is primarily engaged in leading the rituals of religion. In some societies where there are no priests, it may be necessary to substitute a local term, if it is acceptable. Whether or not this can be done successfully depends on the reaction of the people and their association with men of these professions. If it is felt that local terms designating the leader of the religious cult give a wrong impression, translators may sometimes speak of "the one who makes sacrifices," where such practice is known, or say "the officer of the Temple" or "the one who functions in the house of God."

**Her maidens have been dragged away**: **maidens** is literally "virgins," but in English and many other languages the word "virgin" focuses upon a girl's lack of sexual experience. Accordingly a more general term such as TEV "girls" is more satisfactory. Like the priest these young women had a part to play in the regular Temple worship, as suggested in Psalm 68.25. RSV assumes the Hebrew verb translated "afflicted" was originally **dragged away**, and so changes the verb on this basis. See RSV footnote. TEV does not change the word and so has "The girls . . . suffer." TEV "who sang there" further identifies these girls, who would otherwise have no expressed association with the Temple.

**And she herself suffers bitterly**: **suffers** has been supplied by RSV but is required in the context. Just as "her" in the previous unit refers to "Zion" (the Temple), so also does **she** in the final half-line. FRCL translates the final half-line as a summary statement, "How bitter all that is for Zion," which may be recommended to translators. **Suffer** is sometimes translated "to have pain" or "to hurt with grief."

TEV has rearranged the second and third pair of half-lines of the Hebrew in verse 4 so as to bring together the description of the "girls who sang" and "the priests," both of whose activities are related to the act of worship. The final line of TEV then puts together "the city gates" and "Zion." The effect of this reordering of the lines is to give greater coherence to the related parts of the verse.

| 1.5 RSV | TEV |
|---|---|
| Her foes have become the head, her enemies prosper, because the LORD has made her suffer for the multitude of her transgressions; her children have gone away, captives before the foe. | Her enemies succeeded; they hold her in their power. The LORD has made her suffer for all her many sins; Her children have been captured and taken away. |

The first two units of verse 5 contrast Jerusalem's powerful enemies with the suffering of the defeated city. **Her** occurs five times with reference to Jerusalem (or, Zion). TEV makes this reference to Zion clear by placing that name in the final line of verse 4. The translator must examine the repeated use of the pronoun **her** and decide whether or not it will be clearer in some cases to say "Jerusalem's" or "of Jerusalem."

**Her foes have become the head** is a literal translation of the Hebrew. The meaning is that Jerusalem's enemies have triumphed and defeated her. TEV "succeeded" implies that her enemies have succeeded in conquering her. FRCL translates "Her enemies have got the upper hand," GECL "The enemies are at the peak of their fortune," and NEB "Her adversaries have become her masters." This use of **head** may be picking up the thought of Deuteronomy 28.44, which RSV translates "He shall be the head and you shall be the tail."

**Her enemies prosper** translates the Hebrew for "her enemies are at ease," which NEB renders "her enemies take their ease." This means that they scarcely need to exert themselves to conquer Jerusalem, since their victory is given to them by God. The poet clearly looks at the conquest of Jerusalem as a fulfillment of the warnings of the prophets. This half-line may also be rendered, for example, "It is easy for Jerusalem's enemies to win their battles."

**Because the LORD has made her suffer** provides the reason why **her enemies prosper**. In some languages "to cause to suffer" is expressed as "because the LORD punished her." For the translation of **suffer** see verse 4.

**LORD** translates in English the four Hebrew letters *YHWH*, which represent the personal name of the God of the Israelites. There is a section in "Translating Lamentations" at the beginning of this Handbook that deals with this matter, with the heading "God in Lamentations," page 9.

**For the multitude of her transgressions** gives the reason for Jerusalem's suffering. The word translated **transgressions** and "sins" (TEV) carries a strong element of disobedience and willful rebellion and is sometimes used to refer to political rebellions. If the idea of rebellion is to be stressed, we may sometimes say, for example, "because the people of Jerusalem disobeyed God" or "because Jerusalem turned away from God." Some languages say idiomatically "The people of Jerusalem made their livers hard toward God." It may be necessary in translation to make the cause–effect relation clearer than in TEV; for example, "God has made Jerusalem suffer because she has sinned" or "Jerusalem suffers because of her sins. God makes her suffer."

**Her children** is taken by nearly all translations to refer to the young offspring of the inhabitants of Jerusalem. To speak of **her children . . . gone away** gives the impression that they have left voluntarily, which is hardly the case. TEV "have been captured and taken away" may suggest the picture of children being pursued and caught. TEV translates a similar Hebrew expression in Deuteronomy 28.41, "they will be taken away as prisoners of war," which is also a good model for translation in this verse. In languages which do not have a general term for **children**, it is usually possible to say "her sons and daughters" or "Jerusalem's sons and daughters."

**Captives before the foe**: in Deuteronomy 28.36,63-68 it is the LORD who leads the rebellious nation of Israel away into captivity for breaking the covenant. The last pair of half-lines of verse 5 depict the children of Jerusalem being led away by their captors. The final half-line seems to indicate that these **children** are forced to march off into captivity, perhaps like sheep driven before their captors. This suggests that the children are old enough to be led away. **Captives** are persons captured, seized, imprisoned by conquering armies. We may translate "Her children have become prisoners of war and have been taken away" or "The enemy has taken away the children of Jerusalem as prisoners of war."

**1.6**

| RSV | TEV |
|---|---|
| From the daughter of Zion has departed <br> all her majesty. <br> Her princes have become like harts <br> that find no pasture; <br> they fled without strength <br> before the pursuer. | The splendor of Jerusalem is a thing of the past. <br> Her leaders are like deer that are weak from hunger, <br> Whose strength is almost gone as they flee from the hunters. |

The expression **daughter of Zion** expands again the poet's terms referring to the city of Jerusalem. This expression is found throughout Lamentations and also in Isaiah 1.8; 10.32; Jeremiah 4.31. The parallel expressions "daughter of Judah" and "daughter of my people" are also used in Lamentations. All of these expressions serve poetically to picture Jerusalem as a woman. A literal rendering of **daughter of Zion** must usually be avoided so as not to confuse the reader. In such cases it is better to say "Jerusalem," as in TEV.

**Her majesty** and TEV "splendor of Jerusalem" appear to refer to the glory of the former rulers and not particularly to Jerusalem's external beauty. However, the latter meaning may also be included, since the term is very general. It is often translated by words meaning "pomp," "honor," "glory," and "beauty." The honor, splendor, glory of Jerusalem is gone. She has it no longer because she has been conquered and defiled by a pagan nation. TEV "The splendor of Jerusalem is a thing of the past" is a good translation model. We may also say, for example, "All the things that made Jerusalem great have gone," "The greatness of Zion exists no longer," "Zion no longer has any greatness."

**Her princes** refers to the rulers or leaders of Jerusalem who held civil authority. This may sometimes be translated, for example, "the chiefs of Jerusalem" or "those who ruled the city."

**Have become like harts**: Jerusalem's leaders are compared to male "deer" (TEV). The point of the comparison is that they are hunted down, are weak and exhausted. In some areas the translation of **harts** or "deer" will require substituting another wild animal that eats grass and is hunted. In areas where pastures are unknown, it will often be necessary to say, for example, "They are like deer that are weak and have no grass to eat" or "They are weak and hungry, like an animal that finds no food."

**They fled without strength: they** refers to the **princes** or rulers who have been compared to deer. **Before the pursuer** is parallel in meaning and form to "before the foe" in the final half-line of verse 5. **Pursuer**, in the context of the deer, refers to "hunters," as in TEV. The children are led away, perhaps like sheep, while the rulers are hunted down to be killed like deer.

**1.7**

| RSV | TEV |
|---|---|
| Jerusalem remembers <br> in the days of her affliction | A lonely ruin now, Jerusalem recalls her ancient splendor. |

| | |
|---|---|
| and bitterness<sup>b</sup> | When she fell to the enemy, |
| all the precious things | there was no one to help |
| that were hers from days of | her; |
| old. | Her conquerors laughed at her |
| When her people fell into the | downfall. |
| hand of the foe, | |
| and there was none to help | |
| her, | |
| the foe gloated over her, | |
| mocking at her downfall. | |

<sup>b</sup> Cn: Heb *wandering*

This verse is exceptional in that the Hebrew text has eight half-lines instead of the six half-lines in each of the other verses in this chapter. Accordingly some scholars propose deleting one pair; however, there is little agreement on which pair should be dropped. RSV and TEV retain all the lines. TEV's first line corresponds to the whole of the first half of the verse in Hebrew. Most modern translations retain all eight half-lines, and users of this Handbook are encouraged to do the same.

**Jerusalem remembers . . . :** Jerusalem is pictured as a person recalling the past. In languages in which **Jerusalem remembers** is not natural, it will be necessary to say, for example, "The people of Jerusalem remember" or "Those who lived in Jerusalem remember." In some languages it will be necessary to place the subordinate clause first; for example, "During the time of her suffering and wandering . . ." or "While the people of Jerusalem suffered and wandered . . . ."

**In the days . . . bitterness** refers to the time when the thoughts of the people turn to the **days of old** or the former great times. RSV has changed the Hebrew word for "wandering" to **bitterness**. See RSV footnote. The Hebrew Old Testament Text Project (HOTTP) gives "wandering" an "A" rating, meaning that this word is without doubt the original sense, and so recommends "and of her wandering."

**All the precious things that were hers from days of old** are the things the people of Jerusalem remember. These things are not specified, but she has had them for a very long time. FRCL translates "Jerusalem remembers all that was precious from a long time ago." TEV shortens the expression and calls these "her ancient splendor," in order to relate this line to the first half-line in verse 6.

**When her people fell into the hand of the foe** states the event that caused these precious things to become memories. **Fell into the hand of the foe** is a figure of speech meaning to be conquered, defeated by the enemy. This expression may sometimes be translated "When the enemies conquered them," "When they were defeated by their enemies," or "When the enemies defeated Jerusalem's people."

**None to help her:** that is, there was no nation to help Jerusalem; this may also be understood in a general sense that not even God helped her, and so we may translate "there was no one to help fight against Jerusalem's enemies."

**The foe gloated over her: gloated** translates the verb "see," which is also used in Psalm 22.17, "they stare and gloat over me." In the context this is a special way of seeing or staring at the defeated enemy. **Gloat** means to stare with joy at someone who is suffering. The one who stares in this way experiences evil satisfaction. In some languages this may be translated "the enemy smiled when they saw how the people of Jerusalem suffered" or "Jerusalem's enemies laughed when they saw how she suffered."

**Mocking at her downfall: mocking** translates the Hebrew for "they laughed." This laughter, like the gloating in the previous half-line, is a wicked laughter that rejoices at the sight of someone else's misfortune. TEV "Her conquerors laughed at her downfall" is a good translation model. **Downfall** means "defeat," "destruction," "loss." Another model is "those who defeated Jerusalem laughed at her."

| 1.8 | RSV | TEV |
|---|---|---|

<table>
<tr><td>

Jerusalem sinned grievously,
   therefore she became filthy;
all who honored her despise her,
   for they have seen her naked-
     ness;
yea, she herself groans,
   and turns her face away.

</td><td>

Her honor is gone; she is naked
   and held in contempt.
She groans and hides her face
   in shame.
Jerusalem made herself filthy
   with terrible sin.

</td></tr>
</table>

Verse 8 has undergone considerable rearrangement in TEV. TEV's first line corresponds to the second unit in Hebrew, the second line in TEV corresponds to the third unit in Hebrew, and TEV's third line is the first unit in Hebrew. The purpose of this reordering of units is to set forth the conditions which describe Jerusalem's present status. The past act which caused the condition is kept for the final line. It is equally possible, however, to give an accurate picture by following the Hebrew line order as seen in RSV.

**Jerusalem sinned grievously: sinned** does not translate the word rendered "transgressions" in verse 5. Here the term is general and means to do evil or wrong, to err by being opposed to God. **Grievously** translates a word indicating sorrowful extent and may be translated "greatly," "terribly," "gravely." See TEV's final line "with terrible sin."

**She became filthy:** the word translated **filthy** is taken by some interpreters to refer to an object of scorn, and so AB translates "people shake their heads at her." This ties in well with the last unit of verse 7. Gordis agrees and translates "Therefore she is scorned." However, most modern translations understand the word to signify the ceremonial uncleanliness of a woman during her period of menstruation, as indicated in Leviticus 12.2,5; 15.19-24. In view of the context the word is probably to be understood as a variant spelling of the word translated "filthy thing" in verse 17. This line clearly links verse 8 with verse 9.

In many languages **she became filthy** will refer only to physical dirtiness. In some cases the real meaning may be clear. However, it is unlikely that the reader will understand how sin can result in a person becoming "dirty." Accordingly in many languages it will be more meaningful to shift to the idea of defilement, and in some languages we may say, for example, "no one would touch her because her sins had made her defiled" or "no one would go near her because she had sinned and was taboo."

**All who honored her despise her:** that is, all those nations who formerly respected Jerusalem now hate her. Still speaking of Jerusalem as a woman, the next half-line gives the reason for despising her: **for they have seen her nakedness,** which TEV renders "she is naked and held in contempt." Those who honored her are her former allies, as in verse 2. In Ezekiel 16.37 Jerusalem is again represented as a woman and is stripped naked in the sight of her "lovers." Nakedness was a disgrace, and stripping off the clothing was a punishment for faithless women, as in Hosea 2.3.

**Yea, she herself groans: yea** translates the Hebrew for "also" and may not require translating. It is because of her shame that she **groans** (same verb as in verse 4). **Turns her face away** is her reaction to the public shame of exposure. TEV "hides her face in shame" expresses the idea well in English. FRCL says "She can only withdraw and utter sighs." Translators should use the common expression suitable for the context. In some languages this is "she covers her head with her hands," "she places her hands over her eyes," or "she drops to the ground."

| 1.9 | RSV | TEV |
|---|---|---|
| | Her uncleanness was in her skirts; | Her uncleanness was easily seen, but she showed no concern for her fate. |
| | she took no thought of her doom; | Her downfall was terrible; no one can comfort her. |
| | therefore her fall is terrible, she has no comforter. | Her enemies have won, and she cries to the LORD for mercy. |
| | "O LORD, behold my affliction, for the enemy has triumphed!" | |

The first two units are a continuation of the poet's description of Jerusalem as a woman and are closely connected with verse 8.

**Her uncleanness** represents the sins she has committed, and these are perhaps symbolized by referring to menstrual blood which has stained her clothing. The consequence is that all can see it. Jerusalem's sins render her unclean just as menstruation renders a woman ritually unclean (Lev 12.2). The poet uses such language as this to emphasize the full horror of Jerusalem's sinfulness. In many languages there are specific terms referring to **uncleanness,** or "taboo" as some cultures call it, resulting from menstruation. However, caution must be taken that the expression is not offensive or objectionable for public reading. **Skirts** refers to the lower part of a woman's dress, not to a number of different dresses called "skirts."

**Took no thought of her doom:** in her unfaithfulness to the LORD, Jerusalem had overlooked the possibility of punishment. Isaiah 47.7 uses similar language with regard to Babylon, also pictured as a woman. The expression **no thought of her doom** or "fate" may in some languages require saying, for example, "she did not think about where she would finally end," or idiomatically, "she closed her eyes and did not see where she could come out."

**Therefore her fall is terrible** is the consequence of failure to take thought for her future in the previous half-line. **Fall** refers to Jerusalem's downfall or defeat.

**She has no comforter: comforter** translates the same verb used for "comfort" in verse 2. See there for comments.

**O LORD, behold my affliction** is a cry to the LORD for mercy as voiced by suffering Jerusalem.

RSV has placed its final two lines in quotes, while TEV keeps the third person. Here TEV and others have accepted an alternative wording of the Hebrew as "her affliction." But HOTTP supports RSV with **my affliction**. In translation it will often be clearer to show, as in RSV, that the final unit of verse 9 is an utterance of Jerusalem itself; for example "Jerusalem says, 'Help me, LORD, see how I am suffering because my enemies have defeated me,'" or "Jerusalem says, 'My enemies have beaten me; see how I am suffering. Help me, LORD.'"

**For the enemy has triumphed: triumphed** means "won the battle," "been victorious," or, in this context, "defeated me."

---

**1.10**              RSV                                    TEV

The enemy has stretched out his          The enemies robbed her of all
   hands                                      her treasures.
   over all her precious things;          She saw them enter the Tem-
yea, she has seen the nations                ple itself,
   invade her sanctuary,                  Where the LORD had forbidden
those whom thou didst forbid                 Gentiles to go.
   to enter thy congregation.

In verse 10 the focus switches to the invading enemy that has robbed the Temple.

**The enemy has stretched out his hands over . . .** is a figure of speech when the object is something like **all her precious things.** The meaning is "rob, plunder, carry off." While some languages are able to retain a similar figure of speech, most will find it necessary to substitute a different figure or to employ a nonfigure.

**All her precious things** is the same expression used in verse 7, and here refers to the Temple treasures, which the Babylonians carried away (2 Kings 25.13-17). **Precious things** is often translated "wealth," "objects of great value," "rich treasures."

**Yea, she has seen the nations: yea** translates the Hebrew *ki*, which emphasizes the fact that **she**, referring to the people of Jerusalem, has been a witness to these events. It may be translated into English as "indeed," "truly." **Nations** translates the Hebrew *goyim* and refers to all non-Israelites; it is sometimes translated as "pagans, Gentiles, those who do not worship the LORD." See comments on verses 1 and 3.

**Her sanctuary** is the first use of a term for the Temple in this chapter. **Her sanctuary** translates the Hebrew for "her holy place." For comments see verse 4. Translators should avoid giving the impression that entire nations were invading the Temple. The reference is to the soldiers and rulers of the pagan or Gentile nations. We may say, for example, "the soldiers of nations that did not worship the LORD."

The final pair of half-lines in verse 10 defines further these pagan nations. Deuteronomy 23.3 says "No Ammonite or Moabite shall enter the assembly of the LORD; even to the tenth generation . . . ." This prohibition has been extended by the poet to include all foreigners, just as Ezra and Nehemiah later applied this command to forbid intermarriage with all non-Israelites (see Neh 13.1-3). The word translated **congregation** refers to the place where the people are assembled, and so is parallel in meaning to **sanctuary** or "Temple."

Translators may find it necessary or helpful to reorder the sequence of lines in verse 10, particularly in order to relate clearly the final two half-lines to the middle pair. For example, we may begin with the final unit:

> The LORD had forbidden foreigners to enter the Temple,
>     but the people of Jerusalem saw them go in.
> They went in and robbed the Temple of its treasures.

**1.11**                RSV                                                      TEV

| | |
|---|---|
| All her people groan<br>  as they search for bread;<br>they trade their treasures for<br>    food<br>  to revive their strength.<br>"Look, O LORD, and behold,<br>  for I am despised." | Her people groan as they look for<br>  something to eat;<br>They exchange their treasures<br>  for food to keep themselves<br>  alive.<br>"Look at me, LORD," the city<br>  cries; "see me in my mis-<br>  ery." |

The final line of the Hebrew text, which is in quotes in both RSV and TEV, marks the transition to the second half of the chapter. From this point on Jerusalem speaks of herself in the first person, except in verse 17, as noted above, page 10.

**All her people groan: groan** is the same word used in verses 4 and 8. The groaning in this case is due to the pains of starvation. **Bread** translates a word whose ordinary meaning is "bread," but in the context of starving people the meaning is food in general, and therefore as in TEV, "something to eat." In some languages there is no general word for food, but many specific words depending upon the nature of the food, whether, for example, its form is solid or liquid, cooked or uncooked.

**They trade their treasures for food: treasures** translates the same Hebrew word used in verses 7 and 10, "precious things." TEV and others consider these to be literally "treasures," meaning objects of great value, personal possessions. However, the same expression is used in Hosea 9.16, referring to people's offspring, and TEV there translates "the children so dear to them." In Lamentations 2.4 TEV translates this expression as "those who were our joy and delight." Here in this verse AE says "They gave their darlings for food . . . ," and Gordis agrees with this rendering. Because there is no certain solution to this problem, translators may take **treasures** to mean either "offspring" or "wealth." The point in exchanging their children or their personal possessions is to obtain **food** in order to **revive their strength** or, as TEV says, "to keep themselves alive."

In verse 9 Jerusalem was depicted as crying out to the LORD for help. The final unit of verse 11 is again a cry addressed to the LORD. By themselves the quotation marks used in RSV are not sufficient to indicate who cried to the LORD. TEV makes clear that it is "the city" (meaning the people of the city) that cries out, and this is probably correct. **Look, O LORD, and behold** is a close formal rendering of the Hebrew "See, *Yahweh*, and look." The use of two verbs of similar meaning serves to make the plea stronger.

**For I am despised**: **despised** translates a word meaning "lowered, demeaned, disgraced." In some languages this may be translated "Look at me, God, and see how little I have become" or ". . . how I have become a nobody."

**1.12**           RSV                                    TEV

"Is it nothing to you,[c] all you
  who pass by?
  Look and see
if there is any sorrow like my
  sorrow
  which was brought upon me,
which the LORD inflicted
  on the day of his fierce anger.

[c] Heb uncertain

"Look at me!" she cries to everyone who passes by.[b]
"No one has ever had pain like
  mine,
Pain that the LORD brought on
  me in the time of his anger.

[b] Look . . . by; *or* May this not happen
to you that pass by; *or* Does this mean
nothing to you that pass by?

Verses 12-14 contain several textual problems, and each will be dealt with briefly in its own context.

**Is it nothing to you, all you who pass by?** translates what appears to be literally "No/not to you all passing by the way." The RSV footnote says "Hebrew uncertain," while TEV provides one interpretation in its text and two more in the footnote. The traditional rendering found in RSV, NEB, and others follows the last interpretation in the TEV note. NJV translates "May it never befall you," which is the first of the TEV variant interpretations. FRCL changes the text to read "Come, all you who pass . . ." and gives in its footnote "Come: probable text; Hebrew 'May this (the misfortune described in verse 11?) not happen to you (plural)!'"

The most convincing treatment of this expression comes from HOTTP, which gives a "B" rating to the awkward Hebrew "no/not to you" and recommends to translators "(It is) not your concern." So in the Handbook we recommend taking as a statement essentially what is a question in RSV: "It is nothing to you who pass by" or "You who pass by don't care."

**You who pass by** is an idiomatic expression for "anyone, an ordinary person." A very similar expression in English is "the man in the street." The same Hebrew expression is used in Psalm 80.12; 89.41; and Lamentations 2.15.

These people are invited to **Look and see**. What they are to observe is whether or not there is **any sorrow like my sorrow**. Some scholars prefer to translate this as a question; for example, NEB has "Is there any agony like mine . . . ?" The answer to this question is clearly "No," and so TEV translates as a negative statement: "No one has ever had pain like mine." In translation it may be necessary to modify **any sorrow** and **my sorrow** to say, for example, "Is there anyone who suffers as much as I suffer? Of course not."

**Which was brought upon me** is expressed in TEV's translation of the third unit. The sentence is in the passive in Hebrew, and it is followed by a statement in the active in which the LORD is the agent. It seems to emphasize that Jerusalem's suffering is no chance happening but the LORD's doing.

**Which the LORD inflicted**: this half-line is parallel to the previous one and serves to sharpen the focus on the LORD.

RSV translates the final half-line as **on the day of his fierce anger**, and TEV as "in the time of his anger." In other words, there is here the first of several references in Lamentations to the "Day of the LORD," the others being in verse 21 and in 2.1,16,21,22. The "Day of the LORD" is usually an event which the Old Testament prophets expected to take place in the future, as in Amos 5.18-20. In Lamentations **the day** has already come. It is not a day when the LORD wins a victory over Israel's enemies, as popular opinion expected it to be. It is, however, a day on which the LORD's activity was directed against Israel and Israel's sins. The poet saw in the enemies' conquest of Jerusalem a proof of the LORD's anger against his own people.

The translation of **day of his fierce anger** must sometimes be rendered in figurative language; for example, "the day when God shows the heat of his stomach," "the time when God's heart burns like fire," or "the day when God's eyes are very red."

| 1.13 | RSV | TEV |
|---|---|---|
| | "From on high he sent fire;<br>into my bones<sup>d</sup> he made it<br>descend;<br>he spread a net for my feet;<br>he turned me back;<br>he has left me stunned,<br>faint all the day long. | "He sent fire from above, a fire<br>that burned inside me.<br>He set a trap for me and<br>brought me to the ground.<br>Then he abandoned me and<br>left me in constant pain. |

<sup>d</sup> Gk: Heb *bones and*

The poet uses metaphors in verse 13 to describe the way in which the LORD had been dealing with Jerusalem. The LORD is the subject of the verbs in each unit, as though to emphasize that Jerusalem's sufferings were deliberately brought about by him.

**From on high he sent fire** gives the picture of fire coming down from heaven, or "from above" (TEV), perhaps as in the destruction of Sodom and Gomorrah in Genesis 19.24. It is the LORD who sent down the fire on Jerusalem. This may be taken as the literal fire which destroyed the city, or, in accordance with **into my bones he made it descend**, it may be taken figuratively as a fever burning the very bones of Jerusalem. Translators will notice that the versions differ in their interpretation of this half-line. The Hebrew text has "From on high he sent fire into my bones. He is the master of it." The Septuagint translates "From on high he has sent fire; he has brought it into my bones." The Hebrew word translated **descend** is understood by some as causative, and so RSV has **he made it descend**, and the Septuagint "He has brought it." It is also possible that this word is based on the verb meaning "to tread upon," which is found in Joel 3.13, where TEV translates it as "crush them as grapes are crushed." So here the meaning can be "God sent down fire and trampled it into my bones," that is, the bones of Jerusalem.

HOTTP gives a "B" rating to the Hebrew and recommends "in my bones, and it masters them," that is, the fire masters the bones. This is far from clear in English, but it appears to be an attempt to say "the fire subdued the bones of Jerusalem."

Because the understanding of figurative language is such a problem in translation, the Handbook suggests "a fire that burned inside me," "a fire that burned up my bones," or ". . . destroyed my bones." Some translators may prefer to express the thought in a simile and retain the idea of fever; for example, "God sent down a fire that burned in me like a hot fever" or "God burned me with a fever that was as hot as fire."

**He spread a net for my feet**: nets were used in biblical times to catch birds, animals, and fish. The word used here is also used to describe the action of the psalmist's enemies in Psalm 57.6. See also Job 18.8; Proverbs 1.17.

In translation, as seen in TEV "trap," it is necessary to use the word for a device that can be applied to the catching of people. In languages where such things as nets, snares, pitfalls, and traps are unknown, the translator may say, for example, "He has caused me to fall," "He has caught me like an animal is caught," or "He has tripped my feet and caught me."

**He turned me back** refers to God's action of preventing the walker from going any further. He is unable to go forward and to reach his destination, because God refuses to let him pass. The result of spreading the net and preventing him from going any further leaves the speaker **stunned**, which translates the same verb rendered "desolate" in verse 4. TEV is better with "he abandoned me."

**Faint all the day long** is an expression which is parallel to **stunned**, and it concludes the verse without a verb. **Faint** translates a word meaning "sick, miserable." Jerusalem complains that God has left her desolate and sick. **All the day long** means all the time, constantly. This unit may be translated, for example, "God has abandoned me, and I am always in pain."

---

1.14          RSV                                    TEV

"My transgressions were bound[e]              "He took note of all my sins and
   into a yoke;                                   tied them all together;
by his hand they were fastened                He hung them around my
   together;                                      neck, and I grew weak be-
they were set upon my neck;                      neath the weight.
   he caused my strength to fail;             The Lord gave me to my foes,
the Lord gave me into the hands                  and I was helpless against
   of those whom I cannot with-                  them.
   stand.

[e] Cn: Heb uncertain

The Hebrew text of verse 14 is somewhat uncertain, and HOTTP mentions no fewer than five places where the text is in dispute.

**My transgressions were bound into a yoke: transgressions** translates the same noun as in verse 5. See there for comments. **Bound** is uncertain, according to the RSV footnote, and HOTTP gives the Hebrew text a "B" rating, which means there is a little doubt about its validity. However, HOTTP recommends translating the Hebrew text with **bound**, as RSV has done. **Yoke**, which does not occur as a word in TEV, is also disputed. NEB understands the Hebrew base for **yoke** to mean "upon me"; this is due to the similarity between the word for **yoke** and the common preposition "upon or against." The adjustments required for translating the yoke metaphor will be dealt with below.

**By his hand they were fastened together**: the Hebrew expression translated **they were fastened together** is also considered a "B" text by HOTTP. A variant form of this text meaning "He fastens me" is rejected by HOTTP in favor of RSV's translation base. Consequently we have so far, following HOTTP, "He (God) tied up my sins into a yoke. He fastened them (my sins) together with his hands."

In the third half-line **they were set upon** translates a verb meaning "they came up." By changing the vowels it is possible to get "his yoke," which some scholars prefer. However, HOTTP prefers "they came up" or **they were set upon**, as in RSV. The place they are set upon is **my neck**, which all interpreters seem to agree on.

**He caused my strength to fail** may be understood as the consequence of having this burden (yoke) laid upon Jerusalem's neck.

Finally, from the textual point of view, there remains the problem of **into the hands of those whom** . . . . Some scholars suggest changing the Hebrew to get "into their hand" or "into his/its hand." HOTTP classifies this Hebrew text as a "B" reading and supports RSV's translation.

So in brief HOTTP favors RSV's translation of verse 14 and supports it in each of the five places where the text is disputed. The Handbook encourages translators to do the same. However, considerable adjusting will be needed in translation to make the verse clear.

Translators may find that it will be clearer to begin with the second line of RSV; for example, "The LORD took my sins, and with his hands made them into a yoke." "With his hands" calls attention to the fact that it is the LORD who acts; that is, "The LORD himself took my sins . . . ." A yoke is a wooden frame placed on the heads or necks of working animals to enable them to work together to pull a cart or plow. The expression is used figuratively here more in the sense of a burden than of an instrument of work.

In languages where the yoke is unknown, it will be necessary to say, for example, "God took my sins and made a heavy burden of them" or "God fastened my sins together and made something like a heavy rope from them." In areas where the yoke is known and used, it may be necessary to say, for example, "God put my sins on my neck the way a yoke is put on work animals" or "God put a yoke on my neck. This yoke was my sins."

The third line of RSV may be rendered, for example, "then he placed that burden around my neck" or "then he tied it to my neck. In this way he made me weak."

In the final unit the word translated **Lord** is the Hebrew *'adonai*. See comments on the names and titles of God in "God in Lamentations," found in "Translating Lamentations" at the beginning of this Handbook, page 9.

**Gave me into the hands of** means "caused me to be defeated by," "let my enemies defeat me," and so "The Lord let my enemies defeat me."

**Whom I cannot withstand** is literally "I am not able to rise," that is, "to stand up against," or as TEV says, "I was helpless against them." We may also say "against whom I could do nothing."

| 1.15 | RSV | TEV |
|---|---|---|

| | |
|---|---|
| "The Lord flouted all my mighty men<br>  in the midst of me;<br>he summoned an assembly<br>  against me<br>  to crush my young men;<br>the Lord has trodden as in a<br>  wine press<br>  the virgin daughter of Judah. | "The Lord laughed at all my<br>  strongest soldiers;<br>He sent an army to destroy my<br>  young men.<br>He crushed my people like<br>  grapes in a wine press. |

Jerusalem is here still speaking in the first person about the fate of its inhabitants.

**The Lord flouted all my mighty men: The Lord** is the Hebrew *'adonai*, as in verse 14. **Flouted** translates a verb whose meaning is not immediately clear. It is used in Psalm 119.118 with the sense of to spurn or reject. The idea is to treat someone or something as worthless. Accordingly many translators use words signifying rejection, expulsion, discarding. AB finds this sense unsuitable, due to **in my midst**, which follows. It changes the Hebrew word slightly to give a form that means "to heap up," which is a term used of preparation for threshing out grain—an image of God's judgment. This change of the Hebrew text has not found much acceptance. It seems best to understand this verb as meaning God's rejection of Jerusalem's **mighty men**, namely her "soldiers" (TEV).

**In the midst of me** or "in my midst" means "in Jerusalem." FRCL translates "The Lord has despised and rejected all the brave soldiers I had," SPCL "The Lord has thrown far from me all the brave ones who defended me." In both these translations **in the midst of me** is translated not by reference to a position or place, but rather by possession, "that I had (with me)," or by action, "who defended me," and these are recommended to translators.

**He summoned an assembly against me** is literally "he called a meeting against me." The sense is clearly given by FRCL "He mobilized an army against me," and TEV "He sent an army to destroy . . . ."

**To crush my young men: crush** translates the verb used, for example, in Isaiah 63.3. Here, as in Isaiah, the Lord is pictured as crushing or trampling upon people as though they were grapes in a wine press. In Isaiah it is the enemy nations that are crushed. Here in verse 15 it is the people of Judah.

**The Lord has trodden as in a wine press**: as in the first line, **the Lord** translates the Hebrew title *'adonai*. **Trodden** is not the same Hebrew verb which translates "crush" in the previous verse. However, the sense is the same. Both refer to trampling with the feet. **Wine press** refers to a tank or hollowed rock with a hole at the bottom through which the juice from the crushed grapes flows out. Grapes were placed in the wine press, and workers stamped on them with their bare feet to squeeze out the juice. See Amos 9.13.

WINE PRESS

The expression **trodden as in a wine press** will require adjustments in many languages, even in areas where grapes are grown. Basically the translator has three options: (1) Keep the figure, if it is known, and express the idea as a simile, as in RSV and TEV. (2) Substitute an equivalent figure, if one exists. For instance, we may say "God crushed my people as with a pestle in a mortar." The important thing is that the expression should be known and used in the language, and not simply be a fanciful image that will puzzle the reader. (3) Replace the figure by a nonmetaphor. In this case the translator may simply say "God completely destroyed my people."

**The virgin daughter of Judah** refers to Jerusalem and its inhabitants, translated "my people" in the illustrations in the paragraph before. In verse 6 Jerusalem was referred to as a female figure, "daughter of Zion." The word for **virgin** is the same as that translated "maidens" in verse 4. See there for comments. Readers should not be led to think that **virgin daughter of Judah** refers to a particular daughter whose father is called Judah. Therefore it will most often be best to translate "my people," as in TEV.

**1.16**         RSV                                        TEV

"For these things I weep;                    "That is why my eyes are over-
   my eyes flow with tears;                        flowing with tears.
for a comforter is far from me,              No one can comfort me; no
   one to revive my courage;                    one can give me courage.

| | |
|---|---|
| my children are desolate,<br>    for the enemy has prevailed." | The enemy has conquered me;<br>    my people have nothing left. |

The first unit of this verse is a good example of Hebrew parallelism, in which the second half-line enlivens and makes picturable the general remark in the first half-line. That is, **weeps** in the first half-line is matched in the second by **eyes flow with tears**. The two half-lines mean essentially the same thing, but the poetic imagery in the second half-line sharpens the feeling expressed in the first.

**For these things** refers back to the previous two or three verses as the reasons for Zion's tears. The city had been pictured as a weeping woman in verse 2, and here a further explanation is given for her tears. Just as in verse 2, where Jerusalem's "cheeks" were part of the total imagery, so here her **eyes** are mentioned to give added vividness to her grief. In Hebrew the word translated **my eyes** is repeated, and various reasons have been suggested for this. TOB translates "my two eyes," but it is unlikely that the poet intended that meaning. NEB changes one of the two words for eye to mean "my plight," but the Septuagint and other translations ignore the repetition. It is best to translate as do RSV and TEV.

As in verses 2 and 9, it is emphasized that Jerusalem has no one to comfort her. **A comforter is far from me** does not mean that Jerusalem has a comforter at some great distance, but that she has no one to comfort her. **Comforter** translates the same verb root as in verse 2. See there for comments.

**One to revive my courage** adds little that is new to the meaning but parallels the half-line before. Such close parallelism may not serve to emphasize the thought in some languages, and so adjustments may have to be made. For example, instead of repeating the same words, it may be necessary to say "truly, I have no one to comfort me," "I have no one to comfort or encourage me," or "I say this, 'I have no one to comfort me.'" The thought of this pair of parallel half-lines will sometimes be translated idiomatically; for example, "there is no one to make my heart cool" or ". . . to strengthen my insides."

**My children are desolate: children** continues the imagery appropriate for the female speaker who is Jerusalem. The meaning of **children** may be the inhabitants of Jerusalem spoken of as children, or the term may refer literally to the children who lived in Jerusalem. Most translations which attempt to retain the poetic imagery prefer to translate as "children" or "sons." **Desolate** translates the same Hebrew word as in verses 4 and 13 ("stunned"). Here, however, it is because the enemy has prevailed, or triumphed, that the children and people have no hope. GECL says "my children no longer have a future." This serves as a good translation model.

**For the enemy has prevailed: prevailed** here means that the enemy has been too strong for Jerusalem to resist, and so the enemy has been victorious. The same thought is expressed in verse 9. Note that TEV has reversed these two half-lines so that "the enemy has conquered me" is the cause leading to the consequence, "my people have nothing left."

| **1.17** | RSV | TEV |
|---|---|---|
| | Zion stretches out her hands,<br>    but there is none to comfort | "I stretch out my hands, but no<br>    one will help me. |

> her;
> the LORD has commanded
>     against Jacob
>   that his neighbors should be
>     his foes;
> Jerusalem has become a filthy
>   thing among them.

> The LORD has called enemies
>   against me from every side;
> They treat me like some filthy
>   thing.

As in verses 1-11, the speaker in verse 17 is again the poet and not Jerusalem. Therefore the point of view is shifted to the third person. TEV has kept the first person point of view in order not to interrupt the sequence which began with verse 12. In order to show that verse 17 does not fit the structure of the neighboring verses, FRCL places added white space and an asterisk before and after verse 17. Such a practice is not recommended unless the majority of readers are entirely familiar with it.

**Zion stretches out her hands: stretches** translates the same Hebrew verb used in verse 10, where the expression meant "to rob" when used with the preposition "over." Here the sense is "to beg for help," as is made clear in the next half-line. Nevertheless it is sometimes necessary to say in the first half-line "Zion stretches . . . ," "Jerusalem stretches . . . ," or "I stretch out my hands and beg for help" or "I need help and so I stretch out my hands." If translators prefer to retain Zion or Jerusalem as the subject, it may be necessary to use a simile and say, for example, "Zion is like a beggar who stretches out her hands for help."

**None to comfort her** is nearly the same expression as used in verse 9. See there for comments.

**The LORD has commanded against Jacob**: for LORD see comments on the same name of God in verse 5. **Jacob** introduces a third name for the city and its inhabitants. Here **Jacob** may be taken to mean all of Israel, and so FRCL translates "Israel." In this half-line and what follows, it is clear that the poet recognizes the present situation to be the result of orders given by God. These orders are taken by RSV to be given to the **neighbors** who then became Israel's enemies. The word translated **his neighbors** is literally "around him," thus "around him should be his foes," and TEV, which is only slightly different, translates the expression as "from every side." And so it is the LORD who calls these neighboring tribes to become Israel's enemies. FRCL is similar to RSV and provides a good translation model: "On the command of the LORD, the neighbors of Israel became her enemies." This may also be expressed, for example, "The LORD orders Israel's neighbors to become her enemies" or "The LORD commands those who live near Israel to attack her."

**Jerusalem has become a filthy thing among them: filthy thing** translates the same Hebrew word used in verse 8. See there for comments. Surrounded by her enemies, Jerusalem has become an object of disgust, or as NEB says, "a filthy rag." Jerusalem has, as it were, been degraded in the eyes of her enemies from the status of a woman to that of something which represents a woman's impurity. A translation of **filthy thing** should not suggest merely being dirty. The meaning is that of taboo or defilement, and this can be rendered in some languages as "My enemies treat me like a tabooed thing and will not touch me" or "My enemies stay away and will not touch me because I am defiled."

**1.18**    RSV    TEV

| | |
|---|---|
| "The LORD is in the right,<br>   for I have rebelled against his<br>     word;<br>but hear, all you peoples,<br>  and behold my suffering;<br>my maidens and my young men<br>   have gone into captivity. | "But the LORD is just, for I have<br>   disobeyed him.<br>Listen to me, people every-<br>   where; look at me in my<br>   pain.<br>My young men and women<br>   have been taken away cap-<br>   tive. |

From here to the end of chapter 1, Jerusalem is once again the speaker.

**The LORD is in the right** is a confession made by Jerusalem and its people. **In the right** means that God was right, justified in bringing about the downfall of Jerusalem. Similarly in Nehemiah 9.33 the people confess "You have done right to punish us" (TEV), where the word translated "have done right" is the same as the word used here. The translation of **right** and "just" (TEV) requires considerable adjustment in some languages. We can sometimes use a clause; for example, "God has done the right thing to me" or "What God has done to me is right." This may be expressed idiomatically in some languages; for example, "The LORD has been straight with me" or "The LORD has cut my affairs in the right way."

**For I have rebelled against his word: rebelled** is the same word used in Exodus 23.21, ". . . hearken to his voice, do not rebel against him . . . ." **Rebel** means to resist or oppose authority, which in this case is God and his laws. **His word** is literally "his mouth" and refers to God's commands. TEV "I have disobeyed him" is more general than the Hebrew suggests. A better model is SPCL, "I have opposed his commands." In some languages to rebel is expressed idiomatically; for example, "I have laughed at what God commanded people to do" or "what God commanded I have thrown over my shoulder."

The middle unit of the verse is a call to the people as a warning. RSV supplies **but** at the beginning of this unit as a contrast between the confession in the first unit and the warning in the second. A transition may well be required; however, "but" in English is hardly satisfactory.

**All you peoples** is everyone, not just the "nations" or non-Israelites. Jerusalem's plea is for everyone to **behold**, that is, "look at my suffering" or "see how badly I suffer."

**My maidens and my young men: maidens** translates the Hebrew for "virgins," as in verse 4. See there for comments. **Young men** is the same expression used in verse 15. There **young men** is used in parallel with "mighty men" and refers to soldiers. In verse 18 **maidens and young men** refers to the youth, the young people who are the future of Jerusalem.

For **captivity** see the discussion at verse 5. In languages which require an active construction, it may be necessary to say, for example, "the enemy has captured my young men and women and taken them away to other countries."

**1.19**             RSV                                          TEV

"I called to my lovers                    "I called to my allies, but they
   but they deceived me;                        refused to help me.
my priests and elders                     The priests and the leaders
   perished in the city,                        died in the city streets,
while they sought food                    Looking for food to keep them-
   to revive their strength.                    selves alive.

**I called to my lovers**: **lovers** is as in verse 2. In translation it may be necessary
to make clear the purpose of calling to her **lovers**, that is, to her "allies," "friends."
For example, "I called to my friends to help me" or "I asked my allies to help me."

**Deceived me** is the literal translation of the Hebrew verb. However, in this
context the sense is more like "disappointed me." These **lovers** failed to come to
give Jerusalem support. Accordingly TEV has "refused to help me." The New
International Version (NIV) has "betrayed me."

**My priests and elders**: for **priests** see verse 4. **Elders** refers to "leaders,
counselors" and in some languages is translated "my old men" or "my wise old
men." This category of persons complements the maidens and young men at the end
of verse 18 to give the picture of people at both ends of the social and age scale as
being deported or dead.

**Perished in the city** most likely represents the best Hebrew text. Some
scholars have modified the Hebrew to say, with NEB, "went hungry and could find
nothing." HOTTP recommends "They died in the city."

**While they sought food to revive their strength**: **food** translates the general
term here and not the word for "bread" used in verse 11. **To revive their strength**
is literally "to bring back their soul," which TEV translates well as "to keep
themselves alive."

**1.20**             RSV                                          TEV

"Behold, O LORD, for I am in              "Look, O LORD, at my agony, at
   distress,                                     the anguish of my soul!
my soul is in tumult,                     My heart is broken in sorrow
my heart is wrung within me,                 for my sins.
   because I have been very rebel-        There is murder in the streets;
   lious.                                     even indoors there is death.
In the street the sword bereaves;
   in the house it is like death.

In verse 20 the first two half-lines are parallel in meaning. The second pair are
related logically, and the final pair are again parallel in meaning.

**Behold, O LORD, for I am in distress**: **Behold** translates the Hebrew for
"see" and is a plea for God to look, as TEV translates. **Distress** translates a different
word than the one used in verse 3, but the sense is the same: "agony, anguish,
suffering, trouble." In some languages **distress** is expressed idiomatically; for
example, "trouble has seized me" or "bad has fallen on me."

**My soul is in tumult** translates the Hebrew, which is literally "my intestines ferment." A literal translation of the Hebrew into English would only suggest an upset bowel. This is a clear case in which the second half-line in Hebrew says in figurative language what the first half-line says literally. The literary effect is to increase the vividness of the unit. Translators may be able to follow the Hebrew pattern and employ a vivid metaphor in the second half-line. If not, the translator should not sacrifice meaning in an attempt to imitate the Hebrew.

**My heart is wrung within me** is literally "My heart is turned over within me." A similar expression is found in Hosea 11.8. The sense is that the speaker experiences troubling sadness, or as TEV says, "My heart is broken."

**Because I have been very rebellious** gives the reason for the condition in the previous half-line. **Rebellious** translates the same root used in verse 18. See there for comments. In some languages the reason may have to be placed before the consequence; for example, "I have rebelled against God, and therefore my heart does not rest well within me."

**In the street the sword bereaves**: **in the street** is literally "outdoors" as contrasted with "indoors." The places are expressed as singular, but the sense is collective, that is, "everywhere outside," and "inside the houses." **Bereaves** translates a word in Hebrew that gives the sense that the sword takes someone away from loved ones by killing that person. Many translations take the loss to refer to the death of children. If the symbol of the **sword** is used in translation, we may sometimes say, for example, "Outside the enemy kills my children with the sword." If the translator feels it is better to be general, as in TEV "murder," it may be possible to say, for example, "In the streets of Jerusalem the enemy is killing people" or "The enemy slaughters people out in the streets." Translators should probably use a term for "killing" which is used for the killing of human beings during war.

**In the house it is like death**: **in the house** gives a particular location, whereas the contrasting "outside" can be almost anywhere. **Like death** suggests that indoors there is not really the experience of death, but only something like it. Various comments have been made by interpreters regarding this expression. AB alters the text to mean "inside, it was famine," and so implies a similar situation to the one described in the first part of Jeremiah 14.18. Some scholars point out that in Hebrew a preposition is sometimes left out if it is preceded by the word meaning "like." The word translated **death** can sometimes mean "the world of the dead," namely "Sheol," as in Psalm 6.5. TOB, for example, treats the expression as a person by saying "Inside it is like in the house of Death." NJV, Mft, and GECL interpret the expression to refer to the plague.

In translation it will often be necessary to reword **like death** as something which is more precise. TEV "there is death" may have to be rendered, for example, "people are dying." If it is necessary to give a reason for the dying in the houses, it may be possible to say "because they have no food to eat" or "because disease (or, the plague) has struck them down."

| 1.21 | RSV | TEV |
|---|---|---|
| | "Hear[f] how I groan; there is none to comfort me. | "Listen[c] to my groans; there is no one to comfort me. |

| All my enemies have heard of my trouble; | My enemies are glad that you brought disaster on me. |
|---|---|
| they are glad that thou hast done it. | Bring<sup>d</sup> the day you promised; make my enemies suffer as I do. |
| Bring thou<sup>g</sup> the day thou hast announced, and let them be as I am. | |

<sup>c</sup> *One ancient translation* Listen; *Hebrew* They listened.

<sup>f</sup> Gk Syr: Heb *they heard*

<sup>g</sup> Syr: Heb *thou hast brought*

<sup>d</sup> *One ancient translation* Bring; *Hebrew* You brought.

**Hear how I groan: Hear**, a command, is noted in the footnotes of RSV and TEV as being "They heard (or, listened)" in the Hebrew text. HOTTP recommends translating "They heard how I groan." However, HOTTP gives the Hebrew only a "C" rating, meaning that there is considerable doubt about it. The context of the first unit as well as the unit beginning with **Bring thou** favor interpreting these as imperatives, as in RSV and TEV. The question then becomes whether the command "hear, listen" is in the singular or plural. In view of the other singular imperatives in the context, it is preferable to understand these ("hear" and "bring") as addressed to the LORD, as they are in the Syriac version. Therefore the Handbook recommends that translators follow RSV and TEV. "Listen (you singular—*Yahweh*) to my groans."

**There is none to comfort me** is nearly the same expression used in verse 2.

**All my enemies have heard of my trouble: have heard** is the same verb translated **hear** in the unit before. However, here there is no need to modify the Hebrew text. **My trouble** translates a general term meaning "evil, misfortune." This is not the evil or trouble that Jerusalem does, but rather the trouble that has been forced on her. In some languages it will be clearer to say, for example, "All my enemies have heard how I am troubled" or ". . . the misfortune that has happened to me."

**They are glad that thou hast done it: they** refers to Jerusalem's enemies and **thou** to the LORD. In some languages it will be necessary to say, for example, "All my enemies have heard how you have made me suffer, and they are glad."

**Bring thou the day thou hast announced: Bring thou**, as pointed out above, is in Hebrew "You (singular) have brought" (see also the footnotes of RSV, TEV). If the translator has followed the Handbook recommendation for the first unit of verse 21, the same should be done here; that is, the translator should follow RSV and TEV. HOTTP, however, supports the unchanged Hebrew text here also (a "B" rating) and recommends "You have brought . . . ."

In 1.12; 2.1,21-22, **the day** refers to the time when God judged and punished Israel, without regard to the length of time this required. However, here that expression refers to the coming event of God's judgment of Israel's enemies. In some languages it is not possible to speak of "bringing a day" as if a day were a material object to be carried. Accordingly the translator must often say something like "Make the day dawn which you promised" or "You promised to make a certain day. Now keep your promise."

**And let them be as I am: them** refers to Jerusalem's enemies. And so this half-line may be translated, for example, "Let my enemies suffer as I have suffered."

**1.22**        RSV                                           TEV

> "Let all their evil-doing come
>     before thee;
> and deal with them
> as thou hast dealt with me
>     because of all my transgres-
>         sions;
> for my groans are many
>     and my heart is faint."

> "Condemn them for all their
>     wickedness;
> Punish them as you punished
>     me for my sins.
> I groan in misery, and I am
>     sick at heart."

Verse 22 continues Jerusalem's plea for the LORD to punish her enemies just as he is punishing Jerusalem.

**Let all their evil-doing come before thee** shows Jerusalem pleading to God that her enemies be punished for their wickedness. This expression is idiomatic and means "Look at, examine, observe for the purpose of judging." In some languages it will be necessary to translate, for example, "Look at the evil deeds they have done" or "Punish them for their wicked deeds." TEV "Condemn them . . ." expresses the idea well.

**Deal with them as thou hast dealt with me**: **deal** translates a general verb meaning "to treat"; that is, "treat them as you have treated me." A translation which spells out the sense of the general verb may be, for example, "make them suffer the way you have made me suffer."

**Because of my transgressions**: **transgressions** is the same as in verse 5. See there for comments. In some languages it may be clearer to place this expression before the plea; for example, "You have made me suffer because I rebelled against you. Now make my enemies suffer too."

**For my groans are many**: the final unit is introduced by the Hebrew particle *ki*, which normally introduces a clause of reason, and therefore RSV has **for**. In some languages it will be necessary to make the relation between these final two half-lines and those before them clearer by saying, for example, "I say all of this as I groan in suffering."

The speaker closes the chapter by adding **my heart is faint**, which translates "my heart (is) faint." Here the **heart** stands for the whole person. This expression is often rendered idiomatically; for example, "my insides tremble" or "my liver has vanished."

# Chapter 2

Chapter 2 is an acrostic poem similar in form to chapter 1. The normal order of the letters in the Hebrew alphabet is reversed in verses 16 and 17 of this poem, but this has no significance for the translator.

This chapter describes the destruction of Jerusalem. The content is not built on an evenly-balanced arrangement of verses as in chapter 1. The major division is between the first nine verses and the remaining thirteen. Verses 1-9 focus on the LORD's acts as he systematically destroys the city.

As was pointed out in the section entitled "Parallelism" in "Translating Lamentations," page 4, each verse in chapter 2 is made up of three units of parallelism (except verse 19, which has four). In verses 1-9 many units picture an angry LORD in destructive action against Jerusalem, its people, the Temple, Israel, Judah, the rulers. There is a sense of destruction that is ever increasing, in which the units of verse 1 begin with Zion under a threatening cloud, the loss of Israel's splendor, and the LORD forgetting about his Temple. Then in verse 2 the physical destruction begins, as each verse in turn beats with the rhythm of hammer blows as the LORD strikes down his people. Verse follows verse as the destruction increases. Many times a parallel unit echoes the one before it or enlarges upon it. Step by measured step everything is taken away, and by the time we reach verse 9, even "the law is no more." From the middle of verse 9 the destructive acts cease, and in verse 10 the silence of death, with old men in mourning, settles over the devastated scene.

The remainder of the chapter does not have a uniform structure but rather contains a mixture of themes. Verse 10 shows the dejection of Jerusalem's people, old and young. In verse 11 the poet speaks in the first person as he describes his grief. In verse 12 attention is focused on the starving and dying children. The poet finds nothing to compare Jerusalem's sufferings with in verse 13. In verse 14 the false prophets are blamed for Jerusalem's collapse, and this is followed in verses 15 and 16 by the mockery of Jerusalem by her enemies. In verse 17 the poet returns to the theme of verses 1-9, showing how the LORD has kept his word by destroying the city. Verses 18-20 call on Jerusalem to cry out to the LORD for mercy. The final two verses combine the poet's description of suffering with comments on the LORD's role in that suffering. Chapter 2 closes, as it opened, with a reference to "the day of his anger."

**2.1-22**

| RSV | TEV |
|---|---|
| | *The Lord's Punishment of Jerusalem* |
| 1  How the Lord in his anger has set the daughter of Zion under a | 1  The Lord in his anger has covered Zion with darkness. |

41

cloud!
He has cast down from heaven to earth
   the splendor of Israel;
he has not remembered his footstool
   in the day of his anger.

2   The Lord has destroyed without mercy
      all the habitations of Jacob;
   in his wrath he has broken down
      the strongholds of the daughter of
         Judah;
   he has brought down to the ground in
         dishonor
      the kingdom and its rulers.

3   He has cut down in fierce anger
      all the might of Israel;
   he has withdrawn from them his right
         hand
      in the face of the enemy;
   he has burned like a flaming fire in Jacob,
      consuming all around.

4   He has bent his bow like an enemy,
      with his right hand set like a foe;
   and he has slain all the pride of our eyes
      in the tent of the daughter of Zion;
   he has poured out his fury like fire.

5   The Lord has become like an enemy,
      he has destroyed Israel;
   he has destroyed all its palaces,
      laid in ruins its strongholds;
   and he has multiplied in the daughter of
         Judah
      mourning and lamentation.

6   He has broken down his booth like that
         of a garden,
      laid in ruins the place of his appointed
         feasts;
   the LORD has brought to an end in Zion
      appointed feast and sabbath,
   and in his fierce indignation has spurned
      king and priest.

7   The Lord has scorned his altar,
      disowned his sanctuary;
   he has delivered into the hand of the
         enemy
      the walls of her palaces;
   a clamor was raised in the house of the
         LORD
      as on the day of an appointed feast.

8   The LORD determined to lay in ruins
      the wall of the daughter of Zion;
   he marked it off by the line;

Its heavenly splendor he has turned
   into ruins.
On the day of his anger he abandoned
   even his Temple.

2   The Lord destroyed without mercy every
      village in Judah
   And tore down the forts that defended
      the land.
   He brought disgrace on the kingdom
      and its rulers.

3   In his fury he shattered the strength of
      Israel;
   He refused to help us when the enemy
      came.
   He raged against us like fire, destroy-
      ing everything.

4   He aimed his arrows at us like an enemy;
   He killed all those who were our joy
      and delight.
   Here in Jerusalem we felt his burning
      anger.

5   Like an enemy, the Lord has destroyed
      Israel;
   He has left her forts and palaces in
      ruins.
   He has brought on the people of
      Judah unending sorrow.

6   He smashed to pieces the Temple where
      we worshiped him;
   He has put an end to holy days and
      Sabbaths.
   King and priest alike have felt the
      force of his anger.

7   The Lord rejected his altar and deserted
      his holy Temple;
   He allowed the enemy to tear down its
      walls.
   They shouted in victory where once we
      had worshiped in joy.

8   The LORD was determined that the walls
      of Zion should fall;
   He measured them off to make sure of
      total destruction.
   The towers and walls now lie in ruins
      together.

9   The gates lie buried in rubble, their bars
      smashed to pieces.
   The king and the noblemen now are in
      exile.
   The Law is no longer taught, and the

he restrained not his hand from destroying;
he caused rampart and wall to lament,
they languish together.

9    Her gates have sunk into the ground;
he has ruined and broken her bars;
her king and princes are among the nations;
the law is no more,
and her prophets obtain
no vision from the LORD.

10   The elders of the daughter of Zion
sit on the ground in silence;
they have cast dust on their heads
and put on sackcloth;
the maidens of Jerusalem
have bowed their heads to the ground.

11   My eyes are spent with weeping;
my soul is in tumult;
my heart is poured out in grief
because of the destruction of the
daughter of my people,
because infants and babes faint
in the streets of the city.

12   They cry to their mothers,
"Where is bread and wine?"
as they faint like wounded men
in the streets of the city,
as their life is poured out
on their mothers' bosom.

13   What can I say for you, to what compare
you,
O daughter of Jerusalem?
What can I liken to you, that I may com-
fort you,
O virgin daughter of Zion?
For vast as the sea is your ruin;
who can restore you?

14   Your prophets have seen for you
false and deceptive visions;
they have not exposed your iniquity
to restore your fortunes,
but have seen for you oracles
false and misleading.

15   All who pass along the way
clap their hands at you;
they hiss and wag their heads
at the daughter of Jerusalem;
"Is this the city which was called
the perfection of beauty,
the joy of all the earth?"

prophets have no visions from the
LORD.

10   Jerusalem's old men sit on the ground in
silence,
With dust on their heads and sackcloth
on their bodies.
Young girls bow their heads to the
ground.

11   My eyes are worn out with weeping; my
soul is in anguish.
I am exhausted with grief at the destruction of my people.
Children and babies are fainting in the
streets of the city.

12   Hungry and thirsty, they cry to their
mothers;
They fall in the streets as though they
were wounded,
And slowly die in their mothers' arms.

13   O Jerusalem, beloved Jerusalem, what can
I say?
How can I comfort you? No one has
ever suffered like this.
Your disaster is boundless as the
ocean; there is no possible hope.

14   Your prophets had nothing to tell you but
lies;
Their preaching deceived you by never
exposing your sin.
They made you think you did not need
to repent.

15   People passing by the city look at you in
scorn.
They shake their heads and laugh at
Jerusalem's ruins:
"Is this that lovely city? Is this the
pride of the world?"

16   All your enemies mock you and glare at
you with hate.
They curl their lips and sneer, "We
have destroyed it!
This is the day we have waited for!"

17   The LORD has finally done what he
threatened to do:
He has destroyed us without mercy, as
he warned us long ago.
He gave our enemies victory, gave
them joy at our downfall.

18   O Jerusalem, let your very walls cry out

43

16  All your enemies
        rail against you;
    they hiss, they gnash their teeth,
        they cry: "We have destroyed her!
    Ah, this is the day we longed for;
        now we have it; we see it!"

17  The LORD has done what he purposed,
        has carried out his threat;
    as he ordained long ago,
        he has demolished without pity;
    he has made the enemy rejoice over you,
        and exalted the might of your foes.

18  Cry aloud to the Lord!
        O daughter of Zion!
    Let tears stream down like a torrent
        day and night!
    Give yourself no rest,
        your eyes no respite!

19  Arise, cry out in the night,
        at the beginning of the watches!
    Pour out your heart like water
        before the presence of the Lord!
    Lift your hands to him
        for the lives of your children,
    who faint for hunger
        at the head of every street.

20  Look, O LORD, and see!
        With whom hast thou dealt thus?
    Should women eat their offspring,
        the children of their tender care?
    Should priest and prophet be slain
        in the sanctuary of the Lord?

21  In the dust of the streets
        lie the young and the old;
    my maidens and my young men
        have fallen by the sword;
    in the day of thy anger thou hast slain
        them,
        slaughtering without mercy.

22  Thou didst invite as to the day of an
        appointed feast
        my terrors on every side;
    and on the day of the anger of the LORD
        none escaped or survived;
    those whom I dandled and reared
        my enemy destroyed.

to the Lord!
    Let your tears flow like rivers night
        and day;
    Wear yourself out with weeping and
        grief!

19  All through the night get up again and
        again to cry out to the Lord;
    Pour out your heart and beg him for
        mercy on your children—
    Children starving to death on every
        street corner!

20  Look, O LORD! Why are you punishing
        us like this?
    Women are eating the bodies of the
        children they loved!
    Priests and prophets are being killed in
        the Temple itself!

21  Young and old alike lie dead in the
        streets,
    Young men and women, killed by
        enemy swords.
    You slaughtered them without mercy
        on the day of your anger.

22  You invited my enemies to hold a carnival
        of terror all around me,
    And no one could escape on that day
        of your anger.
    They murdered my children, whom I
        had raised and loved.

## Section Heading

If the translator follows the TEV heading, "The Lord's Punishment of Jerusalem," it will often be necessary to avoid a noun phrase and translate with a full clause; for example, "The Lord causes Jerusalem to suffer," "The Lord punishes

44

Jerusalem," or "Jerusalem sinned and the Lord punishes her." Some other headings used for chapter 2 are: FRCL "The Lord acts as Jerusalem's enemy," NEB "Zion's hope of relief after punishment," New Jerusalem Bible (NJB) "Second lamentation," SPCL "Second lament," TOB "The divine enemy," and GECL "God behaves like an enemy."

| **2.1** | RSV | TEV |
|---|---|---|

| RSV | TEV |
|---|---|
| How the Lord in his anger<br>  has set the daughter of Zion<br>    under a cloud!<br>He has cast down from heaven to<br>  earth<br>  the splendor of Israel;<br>he has not remembered his foot-<br>  stool<br>  in the day of his anger. | The Lord in his anger has cov-<br>  ered Zion with darkness.<br>Its heavenly splendor he has<br>  turned into ruins.<br>On the day of his anger he<br>  abandoned even his Temple. |

**How the Lord in his anger: How,** which introduces an exclamation, translates the same word used at the beginning of chapter 1. **Lord** is *'adonai,* as in 1.14. For discussion of the names of God, see "God in Lamentations" in "Translating Lamentations," page 9. **Anger** translates the same word used in 1.12. See there for translation suggestions.

**Has set . . . under a cloud** translates a single word used only here in the Old Testament, and which is translated in various ways. The literal translation of RSV means either that the Lord is placing them where something threatening is about to happen, or that he is providing them with relief from the heat of the sun. It is apparent that the second meaning does not fit the context. TEV has attempted to give the sense of threatening punishment, with "covered . . . with darkness." FRCL says "The Lord holds very somber clouds over Jerusalem," and NEB "What darkness the Lord in his anger has brought upon . . . ." Another group of translations follows a suggestion based on a similar word in Arabic which means "treat with contempt," and so AB; Mft and NJV also follow this suggestion and translate "The Lord has shamed . . . ." If the translator retains the picture of covering Jerusalem with a cloud, the expression should carry the sense of threat of punishment. If the cloud picture lacks this sense, it is better to speak of placing Jerusalem under darkness. But if this picture only means that night has come, translators are advised to say something like "put Jerusalem under the threat of punishment" or "The LORD . . . threatens to punish Jerusalem."

For **daughter of Zion** see discussion of 1.6.

**He has cast down from heaven to earth** expresses the same poetic imagery used in Isaiah 14.12 and Ezekiel 28.14-17, where the rulers are said to be thrown from great heights to the earth. **He** refers to the Lord. **From heaven to earth** gives a picture of extremes of distance, that is, from the very highest place to the very lowest. Although the imagery is of distance in space, the meaning is still the past of Jerusalem's greatness compared to her present ruin. TEV does not attempt to retain the heaven–earth contrast and so sacrifices the picture of extreme positions, with "turned into ruins." The expression **cast down . . . to earth** must not be translated in such a way that the reader pictures something falling from the sky like a meteor.

**Splendor of Israel** probably refers to the glory, beauty, prestige of Jerusalem and its Temple. It calls attention to its visible greatness. In some languages it will be necessary to shift **splendor** to a more specific idea; for example, "the things which the people of Israel loved," "the things which the people of Israel said were wonderful," or "Israel's treasures." The full idea may then be translated in nonfigurative language; for example, "The Lord has caused to be nothing the things which the people of Israel said were wonderful" or "God has made the treasures of Israel to be worthless."

**He has not remembered his footstool**: the expression **not remembered**, if translated literally, will often mean that God in his anger forgot where he had left his stool. However, the sense of **has not remembered** may be expressed positively as "has abandoned, rejected, turned away from." In Isaiah 66.1 the LORD says "Heaven is my throne, and the earth is my footstool." In our context a particular place is meant, as in Psalm 99.5, ". . . worship at his footstool," where the reference is to the Temple. NEB takes the word to be a reference to Jerusalem itself: "The Lord . . . did not remember . . . that Zion was his footstool." The parallelism in 1 Chronicles 28.2 indicates that the ark of the covenant was also referred to as God's footstool, and that is another possible meaning. In some languages it is possible to retain the image of Jerusalem or the Temple as God's footstool; for example, "In his anger he has rejected Jerusalem as his footstool." If the idea of a footstool must be avoided, it may be possible to say, for example, "In his anger God has abandoned his Temple in Jerusalem."

**On the day of his anger**: for **day** see comments on 1.21. As usual in Lamentations, **day of his anger** refers here to the time when God punishes Israel. This time clause must often come before the main clause; for example, FRCL says "When his anger broke out against Zion, he forgot that it was his footstool."

| 2.2 | RSV | TEV |
|---|---|---|

| RSV | TEV |
|---|---|
| The Lord has destroyed without mercy<br>all the habitations of Jacob;<br>in his wrath he has broken down<br>the strongholds of the daughter of Judah;<br>he has brought down to the ground in dishonor<br>the kingdom and its rulers. | The Lord destroyed without mercy every village in Judah<br>And tore down the forts that defended the land.<br>He brought disgrace on the kingdom and its rulers. |

As suggested in the introduction to this chapter, verse 2 takes up the physical destruction which the Lord inflicts upon his people. The three units of this verse are parallel in meaning: the Lord destroys Jacob, breaks down Judah, and brings down the kingdom and its rulers.

Translators will notice that from verse 2 to verse 7 there is a difference in the English tenses used by RSV and TEV to translate the Hebrew verbs. RSV uses the present perfect tense, which indicates that the action of the verb in the past has consequences or effects in the present. This is very appropriate, since the poet is describing the picture of ruin and destruction all around him which is the result of the Lord's action. And it also prepares the way for the very effective switch to the past tense in verse 8, "The LORD determined . . . ," highlighting the one decisive action of the LORD in the past which set the whole course of destruction in motion. TEV's use of the past tense throughout verses 2-8 suggests that the poet is thinking back to a time in the past when the destruction took place. However, TEV creates a bridge from the past to the present when it introduces "now" at the end of the first half-line in the final unit of verse 8, "The towers and walls now lie in ruins together." Where translators need to be sensitive to the natural and idiomatic use of verb tense and aspect in their own language, and not just follow in a mechanical way the tenses used in one or another of the English versions.

**The Lord has destroyed without mercy**: as in verse 1, the actor is still the Lord. **Destroyed** translates in RSV one of forty-seven different Hebrew verbs used in that sense in the Old Testament. This verb, used five times in Lamentations, literally means "swallow." See similar examples in Job 2.3; 8.18; Isaiah 25.7. In some languages "to swallow" things that are not for eating refers to stealing, embezzling. In others "swallow" means to destroy, as here.

**Without mercy** is commonly translated idiomatically; for example, "without showing a good heart," "without feeling in the intestines," or "with a hard liver."

**Habitations of Jacob** refers to the places where the people of Israel lived. This expression often refers to the territory of the former northern kingdom of Israel. However, at the time of the writing of this book, the name Israel or Jacob could be used when speaking of the southern kingdom as it had been enlarged by King Josiah. In translating **habitations of Jacob** it may be necessary to avoid confusing the reader with too many names for Judah and Jerusalem. In this passage it may be better to say "Israel," since it identifies the whole area; for example, "The Lord has destroyed without mercy the towns of Israel."

**In his wrath** matches **without mercy** in the previous unit. TEV either allows the first instance to serve for both expressions, or allows the sense of "anger" in verse 1 to carry through into the second unit of verse 2, and so does not repeat **in his wrath**.

**He has broken down the strongholds**: **strongholds** means forts or fortifications and very likely refers to the fortified cities of Lachish and Azekah mentioned in Jeremiah 34.7. In some languages **strongholds** must be expressed by a descriptive phrase; for example, "He has torn down the places in Israel where people go for protection" or ". . . the walls that protect the people of Israel from their enemies."

**Daughter of Judah** means the people of Judah. See comments on 1.15.

In the final unit of verse 2, the Lord destroys, disgraces, dishonors the kingdom of Judah and its rulers. **Brought down to the ground** echoes "cast down from heaven to earth" in verse 1. Just as in verse 1, where the poet emphasized the contrast between the height to which Jerusalem had risen and the depths to which it has now fallen, so also here he speaks of **the kingdom** as being brought down to the ground. The Hebrew verb translated in TEV as "brought disgrace on" is the same as that used with reference to the royal crown in Psalm 89.39, where TEV translates it "thrown . . . in the dirt." NEB translates it as "desecrated." In other words, the king is treated as though he is no longer a sacred person, and the promise of an eternal line of succession to David is seen to be broken.

**To the ground in dishonor**, meaning in disgrace or humiliation, is sometimes translated idiomatically; for example, "to cause someone to sit down," "to take away someone's swollen heart," or "to put someone beneath everyone else." Since **kingdom** matches **Jacob** and **daughter of Judah** in meaning, it will often be better to use a pronoun than to search for still another term; for example, "God has taken away their rulers' swollen hearts" or "God has placed their rulers beneath everyone."

### 2.3

| RSV | TEV |
|---|---|
| He has cut down in fierce anger<br>    all the might of Israel;<br>he has withdrawn from them his<br>    right hand<br>in the face of the enemy;<br>he has burned like a flaming fire<br>    in Jacob,<br>    consuming all around. | In his fury he shattered the<br>    strength of Israel;<br>He refused to help us when<br>    the enemy came.<br>He raged against us like fire,<br>    destroying everything. |

Although the units of verse 3 have less parallelism of words than verse 2, the basic pattern of successive destructive events continues.

**He has cut down in fierce anger . . .** : the sense of the word rendered **cut down** is "cut off, shatter, break into pieces." NEB says "hacked down." **In fierce anger** is another expression of the manner in which the Lord destroys Jerusalem, matching "in his anger" in verse 1 and "without mercy" in verse 2.

**All the might** is literally "all the horn," the horn being a symbol of power or pride. See Jeremiah 48.25 "the horn of Moab is cut off"; see also Psalm 75.10; Deuteronomy 33.17. Some translations prefer "pride" as a translation of "horn." NEB retains the term so as to keep the image, and gives at the same time the sense: "In his anger he hacked down the horn of Israel's pride." While this is a good translation principle, there is no relation between horn and pride in English, and the sense remains obscure. SPCL gives a better model to follow: "in one slice he cut off the power of Israel."

Translators may follow either "power" or "pride." However, **cut down** must often be expressed differently; for example, "He took away the power of Israel," "He caused the strength of Israel to fail," or "He made Israel weak and helpless."

In the following unit God's next act is that **he has withdrawn from them his right hand**, which is an idiom meaning "refused to help them," or as NEB says, "he withdrew his helping hand." In other words, when Israel needed God's help, God refused. The **right hand**, according to Psalm 98.1, is the source of victory. In Exodus 15.6 it is God's right hand that defeats the Egyptian army. Now it is held back when Israel needs it the most.

The expression **right hand** has different meanings in different languages. In some cases it is possible to say, for example, "God did not give them his hand" or "God's hand was not with them." In languages where withholding the hand does not convey the idea of holding back from helping, it is better to follow the model of TEV, "refused to help."

**In the face of the enemy** means "when the enemy attacks," or as FRCL translates, "when the enemy has arrived." SPCL has "upon meeting the enemy."

**He has burned like a flaming fire in Jacob**: as in Isaiah 10.17 the LORD is pictured as a destroying fire. There he would burn up Israel's enemies; in this verse, however, he destroys Israel itself. The sense is that God has started a fire in **Jacob**, that is, in Israel. The translation of **Jacob** will depend on the way the same term has been handled in 2.2. TEV says "He raged against us like fire." However, "us" identifies the poet more closely with the people of Israel than the original suggests. A better translation is "his people."

| RSV | TEV |
|---|---|
| He has bent his bow like an enemy,<br>with his right hand set like a foe;<br>and he has slain all the pride of our eyes<br>in the tent of the daughter of Zion;<br>he has poured out his fury like fire. | He aimed his arrows at us like an enemy;<br>He killed all those who were our joy and delight.<br>Here in Jerusalem we felt his burning anger. |

In this verse the first unit pictures the preparation of the archer. The second states the consequence of the first, and the third summarizes it all.

It is not clear how this verse should be divided up. Some translations agree with RSV in making **like a foe** the conclusion of the first unit, and others place those words at the beginning of the next unit: "Like a foe he has slain all who were pleasing to the eye." **Like a foe** is omitted by TEV, since the idea is already expressed by the phrase "like an enemy" in the first line. Whichever way the verse is arranged, it seems to be shorter than usual. It is suggested by some interpreters that one line may be missing from the original poem. The consistent use of parallelism in Lamentations favors a translation along the lines of RSV.

**He has bent his bow like an enemy**: **He** refers to God, the one who is destroying Jerusalem and its people. The word translated **bent** more often means "trod"; however, when this verb has **bow** as its object, it can refer to the archer putting his foot against the bow to steady it when taking aim, or it can mean that he bends it enough to slip the bowstring in place on the end of the bow. In 3.12 the LORD is the subject of the same verb. Job also thinks of himself as the target of God's arrows (Job 6.4; 7.20; 16.12-13). A literal translation of **bent his bow** may not suggest to the reader either aiming the bow or stringing it. In that case the Handbook recommends TEV as a model. In languages where the bow and arrow are unfamiliar, a different weapon of throwing or shooting may be used. Otherwise it may be possible to use a more general word; for example, "God has used his weapon like an enemy."

**With his right hand set like a foe** has caused translators to differ considerably. In the Hebrew text **right hand** is feminine, while **set** is a masculine adjective. Regardless of this grammatical peculiarity, the thought seems to be that the archer has his right hand on the arrow, which is pulled back and ready to be shot. TEV has shortened this unit by taking **bent his bow** to mean "aimed his arrows" and allowing this expression to convey also the sense of **with his right hand set**. FRCL gives a fuller translation, which is a good model: "Like an enemy he has pulled the bow string, keeping his right hand in shooting position."

**Slain all the pride of our eyes** is literally "slain those desirable to the eye." The word translated **pride** is the same as used in 1.7,10,11, where it referred to treasures or precious possessions. In the context of verse 4 it may refer to the most valued people, as in Ezekiel 24.16, where TEV renders the expression "the person you love most." It may also refer to small children, and so Mft has "he slaughters and kills the children, the delight of our eyes." Most translations do not state precisely who is killed, and say something similar to NEB ". . . he slew all those who had been his delight," or NJB ". . . he slaughtered all those who were a delight to see." In some languages this may be rendered, for example, "he killed everyone whom we loved most" or ". . . who were dearest to us."

In RSV **in the tent of the daughter of Zion** states the place of the killing. But TEV, NEB, and most other translations follow the Hebrew in making this expression part of the final unit. **Tent** may refer either to the city of Jerusalem or to the Temple. TEV takes it to mean Jerusalem. Most modern translations keep **tent**, but FRCL translates "the temple of Jerusalem," which is a good compromise. For **daughter of Zion** see comments on 1.6.

**He has poured out his fury like fire** is an expression found also in Psalm 69.24; 79.6; Jeremiah 6.11; 7.20; 10.25; 42.18; 44.6. In this expression we have a picture of "anger" as a hot liquid that can be poured out. But in many languages anger cannot be said to pour. Accordingly translators must adjust this expression to another figure of speech, or use it in the form of a simile; for example, "his anger has burned like fire" or "he has shown the people how his anger can burn like fire." TEV has simply "we felt his burning anger."

**Poured out his fury like fire** may sometimes be expressed by other figures; for example, "God's stomach became white. He destroyed Jerusalem like a fire destroys a house."

| 2.5 | RSV | TEV |
|---|---|---|

| RSV | TEV |
|---|---|
| The Lord has become like an enemy, <br>     he has destroyed Israel; <br> he has destroyed all its palaces, <br>     laid in ruins its strongholds; <br> and he has multiplied in the <br>     daughter of Judah <br>     mourning and lamentation. | Like an enemy, the Lord has <br>     destroyed Israel; <br> He has left her forts and pal- <br>     aces in ruins. <br> He has brought on the people <br>     of Judah unending sorrow. |

For comments on the parallelism of 2.5, see the treatment of this verse under "Parallelism" in "Translating Lamentations," page 7.

**The Lord has become like an enemy**: once again the Lord is said to act as Israel's enemy. TEV has joined the two statements in the first unit to say "Like an enemy, the Lord has destroyed Israel." We may also say, for example, "The Lord acts like our enemy by destroying Israel." **Destroyed** translates the Hebrew for "swallowed," which is used again in **destroyed all its palaces.** For comments see 2.2.

The **palaces** mentioned here in the plural were probably not so much royal residences as large houses inhabited by wealthy people. Such houses were fitted out for defense in time of attack. NEB translates the word here as "towered mansions." **Palaces** may sometimes be translated as "the houses of the chiefs" or "the houses in which the rulers lived."

**Laid in ruins its strongholds**: **laid in ruins** translates another of the numerous Hebrew verbs meaning "destroy, ruin, shatter." **Strongholds** is the same term used in 2.2. See there for comments.

**He has multiplied** means that God has increased the number, that is, caused more people to mourn and lament. The increase in mourning and weeping is due to the deaths of people in Jerusalem and the country round about; here the territory is called **the daughter of Judah.**

**Mourning** is not the same term used in 1.4, but the sense is the same, that is, wailing and weeping as is done at the time of death. **Lamentation** is a noun related to the same verb as **mourning**, and so the two sound nearly alike in Hebrew and are synonyms. Since they have similar sounds in Hebrew, NJV translates them as "Mourning and moaning." If the translator's language has a suitable pair of similar-sounding words to use here, they may add to the poetic effect. In Isaiah 29.2 TEV translates this same pair of words as "weeping and wailing." However, in some languages crying and mourning are not considered as associated activities and are not used in the same context. Accordingly in such cases it may be necessary to say, for example, "God made them mourn for the dead."

| 2.6    RSV | TEV |
|---|---|
| He has broken down his booth<br>    like that of a garden,<br>laid in ruins the place of his<br>    appointed feasts;<br>the LORD has brought to an end<br>    in Zion<br>    appointed feast and sabbath,<br>and in his fierce indignation has<br>    spurned<br>    king and priest. | He smashed to pieces the Temple<br>    where we worshiped him;<br>He has put an end to holy days<br>    and Sabbaths.<br>King and priest alike have felt<br>    the force of his anger. |

The first two parallel units of verse 6 focus on the destruction of the Temple. **Broken down** in the first half-line is matched by **laid in ruins** in the second. **Booth** is matched by **place of . . . feasts**. The second unit is parallel to the first in a more general way in its first half-line, and in its second half-line repeats **appointed feast** and enlarges it by adding **sabbath**. The third unit personalizes what the Lord has done through the rejection of the **king** and the **priest**, who can no longer officiate in the Temple.

The reference to the destruction of the Temple is a reminder that it is no longer a place of refuge, and is no more secure than a temporary hut in a garden.

**He has broken down his booth like that of a garden** is not entirely clear in Hebrew. **Broken down** translates another term for "destroy, lay waste, smash." **Booth** appears to be a variant spelling in Hebrew of the word found in Isaiah 1.8, which TEV translates as "watchman's hut." Another form of the same word is used in Psalm 76.2, where it refers to God's "dwelling place" in Zion, and so refers to the Temple.

**Like that of a garden** is literally "like a garden," and this expression does not fit well with the earlier part of the half-line. Therefore RSV has modified it in translation so that the booth is not "like a garden" but like a booth (hut, shed) found in a garden. NEB and others follow the Septuagint and say "He stripped his tabernacle as a vine is stripped." HOTTP gives two possible translations: "He has broken down its walls, which are like those of a garden" and "He has broken down his hut, which is like one in a garden." The second of these agrees with RSV and may be recommended to translators.

In many areas there is no difference between a **garden** and any other area used for growing crops. People may simply speak of "the field," or they may distinguish between areas used for growing food crops for people and those used for growing food for animals. In some areas temporary huts are put up in fields for people to sleep in while protecting crops from robbers and birds. In such cases it is possible to say, for example, "God tore down the Temple as a man tears down a field hut." If no temporary huts are known, but houses are of fragile construction, it may be possible to say "God tore down the Temple as easily as tearing down a house." It may also be possible to translate without using the picture of a hut: "God broke down the Temple. This was no work for him at all"; or "God destroyed the Temple. He did it very easily."

**The place of his appointed feasts** translates the Hebrew for "his appointed feasts" and is the same word used in 1.4. See there for comments. **The place of** is supplied by RSV because this half-line is parallel to the half-line before, and so refers again to the Temple as the place where festivals were celebrated.

**The LORD has brought to an end in Zion: brought to an end** is literally "caused to forget" and is translated by NEB as "blotted out all memory." GECL says "He lets his people forget . . . ." **In Zion** means "in Jerusalem."

**Appointed feast** repeats the same word used in the first unit. The destruction of the Temple meant that these festivals could no longer take place. **Sabbath** refers to the Jewish day consecrated to God for worship and rest from daily activities. The **sabbath** was the seventh day of the week and began at sundown on Friday (the sixth day) and ended at sundown on Saturday. Translators should not translate **sabbath** by a word meaning "Sunday," the day most Christians worship in church. Likewise "Saturday" will not suggest a day of worship. An expression like "day of rest" may mean nothing more than a holiday or a "day off." Therefore it may be necessary to say "Jewish day of rest," "Jewish day for worshiping God," or "Jewish holy day."

**In his fierce indignation** translates "in the indignation of his anger," which is a way of saying "in the heat of his anger."

**Spurned king and priest: spurned** means "rejected, refused to help," and occurs with this sense in Deuteronomy 32.19; Psalm 107.11. TEV says "King and priest alike have felt the force of his anger." Although **priest** is singular in the Hebrew, it is to be understood as collective and in many languages will have to be translated as a plural: "He has angrily rejected both the king and the priests" or "In his anger he has taken away the honor of both the king and the priests." For discussion of **priest** see comments on 1.4.

| 2.7 | RSV | TEV |
|---|---|---|
| | The Lord has scorned his altar,<br>    disowned his sanctuary;<br>he has delivered into the hand of<br>    the enemy<br>    the walls of her palaces;<br>a clamor was raised in the house<br>    of the LORD<br>    as on the day of an appointed<br>    feast. | The Lord rejected his altar and<br>    deserted his holy Temple;<br>He allowed the enemy to tear<br>    down its walls.<br>They shouted in victory where<br>    once we had worshiped in<br>    joy. |

Verse 6, which continued the subject of verse 5, spoke of the rejection of the ruler and of the priests, who played a key role in the worship in the Temple. The poet now goes on to say that the buildings themselves have become the subject of ridicule.

**Scorned his altar: scorned** is a different word than the one translated "spurned" in verse 6; however, the sense is the same. In some languages "reject" may be expressed negatively as "not to accept"; for example, "The Lord does not accept his altar." Or it may be expressed as direct discourse: "The Lord says, 'I will not receive your offerings from my altar,'" or "The Lord says, 'This altar is not mine.'"

**Altar** refers to the place at the Temple where sacrifices are burned as offerings or gifts for God. In some languages a descriptive equivalent can be "place where gifts are made to God" or "place for burning sacrifices to God."

**Disowned his sanctuary** may sometimes be translated, for example, "the Lord has gone away and abandoned his Temple," "the Lord has turned his back on his Temple," or "the Lord says, 'This Temple is not mine.'" For **sanctuary** see comments on 1.10.

**Delivered into the hand of the enemy** is a widely used idiom meaning "he has turned over to the enemy" or "he has given to the enemy." The objects given are **the walls of her palaces**. This expression is unclear since what **her** refers back to is not stated. However, the parallelism is very strong, and so it is best to take **her palaces** as referring to Zion's Temple. Accordingly a translation such as TEV "He allowed the enemy to tear down its (the Temple's) walls" is recommended to translators.

**A clamor was raised in the house of the LORD** refers to noises made by the enemy, and probably these were battle cries, or as NEB says, "they raised shouts of victory." That noise was as great as **on the day of an appointed feast**. NJB says "From the uproar they made in Yahweh's temple it might have been a festival day," and adds in the footnote "But it was the enemy's war cry." In translation it will often be necessary to make clear that the reason for the shouting is to claim victory; for example, "the enemy shouted when they had defeated us" or "the enemy shouted to show they had captured the Temple."

**2.8**  RSV  TEV

| | |
|---|---|
| The LORD determined to lay in ruins the wall of the daughter of Zion; he marked it off by the line; he restrained not his hand from destroying; he caused rampart and wall to lament, they languish together. | The LORD was determined that the walls of Zion should fall; He measured them off to make sure of total destruction. The towers and walls now lie in ruins together. |

The three units of this verse do not show parallelism of meaning but progression of events. In the first unit God decides to destroy the walls. The second unit shows how he went about it, and the third pictures the tragic results.

Once again the poet emphasizes that the destruction of Jerusalem was part of the LORD's plan. He marked off the walls with a measuring line, not to ensure they were properly built, as in Job 38.5, but to ensure their complete and total destruction. In verse 3 the Lord restrained his hand from taking action to help his people. Here the same expression is used negatively to indicate that God used his power to bring about the destruction.

**The LORD determined to lay in ruins: determined** translates a verb meaning "to make a firm decision." **To lay in ruins** means to destroy, and is the same word used in verses 5 and 6.

**The wall** in Hebrew is singular but refers to the walls that enclose the city. **The daughter of Zion** refers to the city of Jerusalem and should be translated in a manner consistent with the other usages of this expression in 1.6; 2.1,4.

**Marked it off by line** will have little or no meaning in areas where local buildings are put up without using measurements. Even where such lines are used, the expression is used here in regard to destroying the wall, which is not a normal practice. Accordingly it may be necessary to translate using a comparison; for example, "As builders draw a straight line to build a wall, so God used a line to break down the walls of Jerusalem." In areas where the use of a measuring line is unknown, it may be possible to express the deliberate and calculated nature of the destruction by saying, for example, "God took great care to destroy the walls of Jerusalem" or "God measured the walls of Jerusalem by stepping them off, and then broke them down."

**He restrained not his hand from destroying** is literally "he did not turn his hand from swallowing." This half-line parallels the sense of the previous one, in that "did not turn his hand" is an idiom meaning "he did not hesitate" or "he went right ahead." **Destroying** again translates the Hebrew for "swallow." See 2.2.

**He caused rampart and wall to lament** depicts the walls of the city as if they were people crying over their own destruction. **Rampart** refers to a defensive wall beyond the main wall, that is, an outer wall, as mentioned in 2 Samuel 20.15. This outer wall had to be broken through before the invaders could attack the main wall. TEV translates "towers," which suggests a high place used as a look-out.

In many areas of the world, walls built around cities for their defense are unknown. Therefore it is often necessary to employ a descriptive phrase in translation; for example, "the walls that protect the city from its enemies" or "the walls that keep the enemy outside the city." In some languages **wall** will be translated by a word meaning fence or hedge, since walls are only associated with houses. In many areas a fence of brush, branches, earth, or stones is placed around a house or garden to protect it, and the term used for such a protection may be appropriate in this context.

The major translation problem is not in the word for "walls" but in the fact that they are said to **lament**. It is sometimes possible to keep something of the poet's imagery by shifting to a simile; for example, "The LORD destroyed the walls that protected Jerusalem, and the walls were like people weeping." **Languish together** again suggests that these ruined walls are like people who have lost their strength and are dying, and so we may have to say, for example, "and they no longer have any strength" or "together they lie in ruins."

| 2.9 | RSV | TEV |
|---|---|---|
| | Her gates have sunk into the ground; | The gates lie buried in rubble, their bars smashed to pieces. |
| | he has ruined and broken her bars; | The king and the noblemen now are in exile. |
| | her king and princes are among the nations; | The Law is no longer taught, and the prophets have no visions from the LORD. |
| | the law is no more, | |
| | and her prophets obtain no vision from the LORD. | |

The first unit of verse 9 continues the thought of verse 8. The first half-line speaks of the gates generally, and the second half-line of one part of the gate that held it closed. The second unit represents a break with verses 1-9a. Until this point the LORD has been the angry force inflicting destruction. Now we see the effects of the defeat in terms of the leaders who experienced it and the loss of authority in the law and prophets. The same thought continues through verse 10.

**Her gates have sunk into the ground: gates** refers to the huge doors in the walls of Jerusalem through which people and animals went in and out. The picture is not of the gates dropping downward into the ground so they cannot swing; rather the gates have collapsed, fallen off, and are covered with earth, or as TEV says, "lie buried in the rubble."

The idea of a **gate** which opens and closes to let people in and out of a city is foreign to many areas of the world. Unless the picture is made clear, the reader may not understand how the gate is said to have fallen down. Therefore it may sometimes be necessary to say, for example, "The big doors where people entered the city have fallen and lie in the dirt."

**Ruined and broken her bars**: the two verbs intensify the idea of destruction. TEV says it well: "bars smashed to pieces." **Bars** refers to the heavy beams used to fasten the gate closed from the inside, and in translation it is often necessary to say, for example, "the big stick that held the doors closed."

**Her king and princes are among the nations**: the king is not identified by name anywhere in Lamentations. Since this king is said to be **among the nations** or "in exile," the reference is probably to Jehoiachin, who was taken away to Babylon along with "all the royal princes," meaning members of the royal family (2 Kings 24.14-15). Jehoiachin lived on for many years in Babylon and was eventually released from prison, probably long after the book of Lamentations was written. **Princes**, on the other hand, may be a general designation, in which case the word may be used, as it often is in the Old Testament, in reference to leaders, chiefs, noblemen, and officials. It seems that either sense may be suitable. The Hebrew term for **princes** is never used in the Old Testament to refer to sons of the king, unless these sons happen to have a position as a leader or chief. Therefore we may suggest translating "Her king and his noblemen," "Jerusalem's king and other leaders," or "the king and his officers." **Among the nations** may sometimes be rendered "are prisoners of war in a foreign land" or "the enemy has taken the chief and . . . away to other tribes."

**The law is no more** may be linked with the half-line before it, but it seems more clearly associated with **prophets** and **vision** in the final unit. The Hebrew word *torah* is here translated **law**. *Torah* has the broader meaning of instruction or teaching, as in Jeremiah 18.18 and Ezekiel 7.26. In those passages it is associated with the priest as the one who received such revelation and passed it on to the people. Because the central meaning is "instruction," it is often best to avoid the word "law," which may have only the meaning of regulations sent out from local officials. It is better in such cases to say, for example, "instruction from God" or "the teaching which God gave the people." The form given in TEV is passive and must be shifted to an active construction in many languages; for example, "The priests no longer teach the people the words of God" or "The priests no longer teach the people what God wanted them to learn."

**Her prophets obtain no vision from the LORD**: associated with the instruction given by the priest in similar passages are the visions of the prophets. These were "revelations" and not necessarily something seen (Psa 89.19). The poet here sums up the religious situation in Jerusalem at this time in purely negative terms: as TEV says, "The Law is no longer taught . . . no visions from the LORD." But the poet knows the LORD continues to reveal himself in judgment. This is much more than a warning. **Prophets** may often be rendered as "the ones who speak for God" or "the ones who tell the people God's message." **Her prophets obtain no vision from the LORD** must often be modified to a more active construction; for example, "The LORD has not shown the prophets what message to tell the people."

**Visions** translates the same word used in Isaiah 29.7 ". . . like a dream, a vision of the night," and Ezekiel 12.27 ". . . The vision that he sees is for many days hence . . . ." However, the same term is also used with the sense of a message received from God, and is appropriately used with that meaning here.

| **2.10** | RSV | TEV |
|---|---|---|
| | The elders of the daughter of Zion<br>  sit on the ground in silence;<br>they have cast dust on their heads<br>  and put on sackcloth;<br>the maidens of Jerusalem<br>  have bowed their heads to the ground. | Jerusalem's old men sit on the ground in silence,<br>With dust on their heads and sackcloth on their bodies.<br>Young girls bow their heads to the ground. |

There is close parallelism between the first and third units of this verse with their reference to **elders** and **maidens**. The reference to old and young and to men and women suggests that all the survivors of Jerusalem are in mourning.

**The elders of the daughter of Zion: elders** translates the same word used in 1.19, where the elders were associated with priests and were called "leaders, rulers." Here, however, **elders** are more appropriately "old men" in contrast to "young women." For **daughter of Zion** see 1.6.

To **sit on the ground in silence** is an action done to show their sadness.

**Dust on their heads . . . sackcloth:** the attitude of the old men resembles that of Job's sorrowing friends as described in Job 2.12. **Sackcloth** was a coarse type of cloth worn as a sign of mourning and penitence. This was sometimes worn next to the skin, as in the description of the king in 2 Kings 6.30. In some languages it is necessary to state clearly that the purpose of the **dust** on the head and **sackcloth** on the body is a sign of mourning in this context; for example, "The old men . . . have put dust on their heads and coarse cloth on their bodies to show the people they are mourning for the dead." In some cultures mourners use other symbols for the same purpose; for example "The old men . . . have painted their bodies because they are mourning for the dead." Generally it will be preferable to use the Hebrew custom, with a footnote to explain its meaning, or provide the equivalent custom.

**The maidens of Jerusalem:** see comments on 1.4.

**Bowed their heads to the ground** is the way these young girls showed their sorrow and distress. In translation it may be necessary to depict these girls as bowing down on their knees so that they can place their foreheads to the ground. Otherwise they may appear like ostriches. For example, "young girls bow down and place their foreheads on the ground."

| **2.11**     RSV | TEV |
|---|---|
| My eyes are spent with weeping;<br> my soul is in tumult;<br>my heart is poured out in grief[h]<br> because of the destruction of<br> the daughter of my people,<br>because infants and babes faint<br> in the streets of the city. | My eyes are worn out with weep-<br> ing; my soul is in anguish.<br>I am exhausted with grief at<br> the destruction of my people.<br>Children and babies are faint-<br> ing in the streets of the city. |

[h] Heb *to the ground*

Up to this point the poet has been describing the fate of Jerusalem as though he were an observer. Now he speaks in the first person of himself and his sorrow for what has happened. Because of the change of pronouns to first person in verses 11-12, FRCL separates these verses with an asterisk from those before and after it. See comment on 1.17.

**My eyes are spent with weeping**: that is, "My eyes are worn out with weeping" (TEV). This half-line is matched by **my soul is in tumult**, which is literally "my intestines are fermenting." NEB tries to keep the Hebrew image with "My bowels writhe in anguish." See comments on 1.20.

**My heart is poured out in grief** is literally "my liver is poured out on the ground." The RSV footnote shows that it has changed the Hebrew for "on the ground" to **in grief**. RSV and TEV are simply expressing this idiom in English terms, and translators will want to do the same in the forms of their own languages.

**Because of the destruction of the daughter of my people**: **daughter of my people** refers again to the people of Jerusalem. In many languages this half-line will have to be adjusted to say, for example, "because the enemy has killed my people" or ". . . the people of Jerusalem."

**Because infants and babes faint**: RSV translates the final unit as a second cause for the grief referred to in the second unit. However, it is better to treat this as a separate statement, as in TEV, or to make it coordinate with the previous clause; for example, "and infants and babies are . . . ." The cause of the children's fainting is their lack of food and drink, which is expressed at the beginning of verse 12. It may help the reader to shift the cause in verse 12 earlier to verse 11 and say, for example, "Because they have nothing to eat or drink, children and babies are fainting in the streets." If hunger and thirst are introduced in verse 11, they need not be repeated in verse 12.

**Infants** here refers to children of both sexes, probably below the age of puberty. **Babies** refers to children who are being breast-fed, also of both sexes. Languages differ greatly in the way they classify children. However, the distinctions given above should be sufficient to assist translators in the selection of appropriate terms in their own languages.

**Faint in the streets of the city**: **faint** translates a different word than that used in 1.13 and 1.22, but the meaning is the same: "to be weak," and particularly in this context, "dying of starvation." In 1.20 the expression "in the street" translates the Hebrew for "outside, outdoors." Here **in the streets** translates a word meaning "wide place" and probably refers to market areas or the city gate area where people gathered, or as NJV says, "in the squares of the city." Most translators prefer something like "in the streets of the city." In those areas where there are no "city streets," it may be better to say, for example, "outside" or "outside where people gather."

**2.12**      RSV                                             TEV

> They cry to their mothers,              Hungry and thirsty, they cry to
>     "Where is bread and wine?"               their mothers;
> as they faint like wounded men          They fall in the streets as
>     in the streets of the city,              though they were wounded,
> as their life is poured out             And slowly die in their moth-
>     on their mothers' bosom.                 ers' arms.

This verse picks up the theme of the last unit of verse 11, so it may have to be made clear to the reader that those who **cry to their mothers** are the infants and babies already mentioned. **Bread and wine** is literally "grain and wine." These two items are not to be taken in their literal sense, but as an idiom for "food and drink." They are used this way in Hosea. A more natural expression is "something to eat." In the Hebrew text the words spoken by the children are expressed in a form which is the equivalent of direct speech. The unit may be translated, for example, "Those children cry to their mothers and say, 'Give us something to eat.'"

**Faint like wounded men**: the verb translated **faint** is used of children three times in this chapter: here, in verse 11, and in verse 19. The word translated **wounded** most often refers to those who are wounded in battle. **In the streets of the city** is the same expression used in verse 11.

**As their life is poured out**: **life** translates the Hebrew *nefesh*. Here the *nefesh*, which can mean "soul, life, existence," is said to be **poured out**. This is an idiom which means "they slowly die" (TEV), "they expire" (FRCL), "exhaling their last breath" (SPCL).

**On their mothers' bosom**: **bosom** refers to the area of the mothers' breasts. The picture is that of the mothers cradling or holding their dying children against their breasts.

**2.13**      RSV                                             TEV

> What can I say for you, to what          O Jerusalem, beloved Jerusalem,
>     compare you,                             what can I say?
> O daughter of Jerusalem?                 How can I comfort you? No
> What can I liken to you, that I              one has ever suffered like
>     may comfort you,                         this.
> O virgin daughter of Zion?              Your disaster is boundless as
> For vast as the sea is your ruin;            the ocean; there is no possi-
>     who can restore you?                     ble hope.

From a description of the situation in Jerusalem, the poet now turns to Jerusalem herself and addresses her with a series of questions.

**What can I say for you: say** translates a word normally meaning "testify," as in the story of Naboth in 1 Kings 21. Scholars question the use of the term in Hebrew, but TEV and others retain the sense of **say,** meaning "There is nothing I can say that will help you." FRCL translates "I no longer know what to say to you." Some, however, agree with the Vulgate in proposing a change in the Hebrew word to get "To what can I liken you?" (AB), which makes a very close parallel with what follows. HOTTP reports that its members divided, half preferring one form of the Hebrew text and the other half preferring another form, with a rating of "C" in each case. But in either case an interpretation of the text, "to what can I compare you?" is given as a possibility. However, if this option is taken there are then three verbs in verse 13, all with the sense of "compare," and this is rare in Hebrew poetry; consequently "What can I say about you?" is to be preferred.

Since there is no certain solution, the Handbook suggests that the first half-line may be translated "What can I say about you?" or "With what can I compare you?" This question assumes a negative answer. Therefore it may be more natural to say, for example, "There is nothing I can say to help you" or "Nothing that I might say would do you any good."

**O daughter of Zion** is the person addressed in the first half-line. In many languages it will be more natural if this is placed before the question, as in TEV. Note how TEV has moved both Jerusalem and Zion ("beloved Jerusalem") to the beginning of verse 13.

In the next unit the poet asks what comparison or likeness he can use to comfort Zion. The sense is that there is nothing he can compare her suffering to, or no comparison he can find that would comfort her in her distress. TEV has adapted its translation by placing the question of comfort first: "How can I comfort you?" Instead of **What can I liken to you,** TEV drops the idea of a comparison and changes to a statement about her suffering: "No one has ever suffered like this." Perhaps "like you" would have been better. Because this half-line is complex in both meaning and structure, TEV provides a good model for translators.

**O virgin daughter of Zion:** in 1.15 this expression is used in regard to Judah. See there for comments.

The final unit affirms the impossibility of healing or restoring the ruined Jerusalem. **Vast as the sea is your ruin** expresses the extent of the disaster which Jerusalem has suffered. For the Hebrews the sea was a vast, mysterious, and hostile power. Comparing the extent of the destruction and suffering of Jerusalem to the sea will be difficult in many languages. However, it may be possible in some languages to compare the destructive force of the sea to the force that destroyed Jerusalem; for example, "As the sea washes away the shore, so is the ruin of Jerusalem." This comparison may have to be applied to flooding rivers in areas where the ocean is unknown.

**Who can restore you?** assumes a negative reply and so may be translated "no one can restore you," "no one can build you back again," "there is no one who can heal you," or "no one can bring you back to life."

| RSV | TEV |
|---|---|
| Your prophets have seen for you false and deceptive visions; they have not exposed your iniquity to restore your fortunes, but have seen for you oracles false and misleading. | Your prophets had nothing to tell you but lies; Their preaching deceived you by never exposing your sin. They made you think you did not need to repent. |

This verse denounces Israel's prophets for failure to speak the truth. The first unit depicts them as false and deceptive. The second unit specifies how they have been deceptive, and the third is closely parallel in meaning to the first.

**Your prophets have seen for you false and deceptive visions**: the **prophets** spoken of here have been unfaithful to their calling. If they had indeed exposed Jerusalem's sin, as they should have done, the people would perhaps have repented. By deceiving the people, and by thus taking away the opportunity for repentance, these prophets gave Jerusalem no chance to be restored to its former conditions. **Prophets**, as indicated in the discussion of verse 9, is sometimes translated "those who speak God's message to the people." But in this context that expression is hardly appropriate, since the prophets referred to have not been faithful in their function. So it may need to be adjusted to something like "those who were supposed to speak God's message" or "the ones who should have spoken for God."

**Have seen . . . visions** is a single verb in the Hebrew which is used regularly to describe a prophet's experience of receiving a message from God.

**False and deceptive** translates two nouns meaning "emptiness and whitewash." The prophets of Jerusalem are described in similar terms in Ezekiel 13.10-13: ". . . when the people build a wall, these prophets daub it with whitewash . . . ." Covering with whitewash was done to make something appear as good on the surface, while underneath it was ugly and bad; thus whitewash became an image of deception. AB translates "Your prophets saw visions for you that were mere whitewash."

The sense of **seen for you** is "they told you, interpreted their visions to you." This unit may also be translated, for example, "Your prophets had nothing to tell you from their visions but empty lies" or "Your prophets saw visions and interpreted them by lying to you."

**Not exposed your iniquity** must often be shifted in translation to two verb clauses; for example, "they did not make you see that you had done evil things" or "they failed to make you know that you had sinned."

**To restore your fortunes** is literally "to turn back your captivity," which NIV translates "to ward off your captivity." However, most modern translations understand this to mean "restore the fortunes," as in Jeremiah 33.7.

**But have seen for you oracles false and misleading**: **oracles** refers to messages given by a god in response to inquiries. The Hebrew term has the basic meaning of a burden, something heavy; and when used of the messages of the prophets, it usually refers to threatening messages from the LORD. In many languages **oracles** in the sense of "visions" will be translated "dreams." Here we may translate, for example, "they have told you their dreams and made you believe things which were not true." TEV has made the false visions a consequence of the failure to expose the people's sins, and so translates "They made you think you did not need to repent," which is a good model to follow. Another model is FRCL, which has "they did not point out to you your sin, which would otherwise have changed your fate."

In RSV the meaning of the first and last units of the Hebrew is closely similar, and several of the words are the same in both units. **False and misleading** is of uncertain meaning, and NEB suggests alternative translations. According to the NEB text, "The visions that they saw for you were delusions, false and fraudulent." The NEB margin has "The visions . . . were delusions, false and causing banishment." If the second rendering is correct, the poet is making a play on the word in the previous half-line which resembles the word for "captivity." The related verb is found in Jeremiah 27.15, "[The LORD] will drive you out," which is also in a context relating to false prophets. However, it seems best to translate the third unit as in RSV or TEV.

**2.15**

| RSV | TEV |
|---|---|
| All who pass along the way<br>    clap their hands at you;<br>they hiss and wag their heads<br>    at the daughter of Jerusalem;<br>"Is this the city which was called<br>    the perfection of beauty,<br>    the joy of all the earth?" | People passing by the city look at<br>    you in scorn.<br>They shake their heads and<br>    laugh at Jerusalem's ruins:<br>"Is this that lovely city? Is this<br>    the pride of the world?" |

The first two units of this verse are closely parallel in meaning. The third unit highlights mockery in the form of a sarcastic question.

In the first unit the passers-by **clap their hands**. This is a literal translation, but it does not mean to applaud as a sign of appreciation, as it does in many countries today; rather it is an expression of ridicule and scorn. NEB "snap their fingers" is an attempt to give a modern equivalent, but it does not really convey the idea of ridicule very well in English. Gestures in most cultures serve several purposes, and each communicates its intention only in the circumstances in which it is used. Accordingly in many languages it is best to give a description of the gesture and then add its purpose; for example, "People pass by the city and thrust out their lips to scorn you," or "People go by you pulling their fingers and saying, 'You are nothing any more.'" See also TEV.

**They wag their heads** is again a close formal translation of the Hebrew; but in some languages this action may mean "they disagree" or "they say 'No.'" Neither of these meanings is intended here. For the sake of clarity it may be necessary to add a word or two of explanation, as in Psalm 109.25, "They shake their heads in scorn" (TEV). Similarly the word **hiss**, which RSV and NEB use to translate the verb at the beginning of the second unit, may well be understood as the verb which introduces the direct speech in the third unit. So the second unit can be translated "they shake their heads in scorn at Jerusalem and use these words to mock her: . . . ."

**Daughter of Jerusalem** is the object of the scornful gestures in this unit. TEV is correct in making it clear that it is the "ruins of Jerusalem" that are being mocked.

The third unit of this verse in Hebrew is exceptionally long. It includes two quotations describing Jerusalem as it was in the past, and both quotations are included within the words spoken by **all who pass along the way**. The quotations are taken word-for-word from Psalm 50.2 and Psalm 48.2 respectively. These words applied to Jerusalem as she was in the past, but they are no longer true. Jerusalem's "perfect beauty" is also mentioned in Ezekiel 16.14 as a thing of the past. Psalm 48 is an expression of confidence that Jerusalem will always be safe from its enemies, but here these same enemies contrast the past with "the ruins of Jerusalem" as it is now.

**Is this . . . the perfection of beauty** may be rendered "Is this the city which was perfect and beautiful?" **Joy of all the earth** may sometimes be translated, for example, "all the people of the world had joy because of Jerusalem?" or "Jerusalem which gave joy to all the earth's people?"

The questions asked in the third unit of this verse are rhetorical, in that they are not asked in order to get a reply, but rather to make a negative statement: "Jerusalem is no longer a perfectly beautiful city, nor is it the joy of all the earth." Moreover the spirit in which these rhetorical questions are asked is that of sarcasm, contempt, ridicule.

In translation it is important that the ridicule shown in the gestures of the first two units should continue into the third. Accordingly it was suggested above that the second unit introduce the final one: "They shake their heads in scorn at Jerusalem and use these words to mock her . . . ." Or we may translate the third unit, for example, "They make fun of Jerusalem when they ask, 'Is this the city . . . ?'" If a rhetorical question cannot be used in sarcasm, the translator may say, for example, "They ridicule the people by saying, 'This certainly is not a perfect and beautiful city, and it does not give joy to the people of the earth.'"

Some languages require the source of direct speech to be placed either before the quoted material or following it; for example, "This is what the people said"; or following the quote, "Those are the words the people spoke."

| 2.16 | RSV | TEV |
|---|---|---|

| RSV | TEV |
|---|---|
| All your enemies<br>    rail against you;<br>they hiss, they gnash their teeth,<br>    they cry: "We have destroyed<br>    her!<br>Ah, this is the day we longed for;<br>    now we have it; we see it!" | All your enemies mock you and<br>    glare at you with hate.<br>They curl their lips and sneer,<br>    "We have destroyed it!<br>This is the day we have waited<br>    for!" |

Verse 16 continues the description of the attitude and actions of the enemies of Jerusalem, following on from the previous verse. As in verse 15, a description of the enemy's gestures is followed by a quotation of their words.

**All your enemies rail against you** is literally "All your enemies have opened their mouths against you." **Rail** is an English verb meaning to scold, scoff, make fun of with abusive language. Many translators keep the Hebrew expression and add the purpose for opening their mouths; for example, FRCL has "They open their mouths to provoke you."

**Hiss and gnash their teeth** are literal translations referring to actions, which will usually require adjusting to other gestures and expressions in translation. Expressions of derision are not lacking in most languages; for example, "to speak of someone with laughter," "to make funny stories about someone," or by means of gestures, "to put the nose in the air at someone," or "to flap the lips at someone." TEV "glare at you with hate" corresponds to **gnash their teeth,** and "curl the lips" is TEV's equivalent of **rail against.** "Sneer" translates the word rendered **hiss** in RSV. Translators should note that TEV has changed the order for stylistic reasons.

**"We have destroyed her!": destroyed** translates the Hebrew for "swallow," as in verse 2. **Her** refers to Jerusalem.

**Ah, this is the day we longed for: Ah,** an exclamation, translates a word meaning "truly, indeed." The poet no doubt intends this sentence as a reference to the "day of the LORD," which the people of Jerusalem had been longing for as a day of the LORD's victory over Israel's enemies. But as Amos 5.18 had warned, the day of the LORD turned out to be "a day of darkness" for Israel and a day of victory for her enemies. **Longed for** means "waited for," that is, "the day we have looked forward to."

**Now we have it; we see it** translates two Hebrew verbs, "We have found" and "we have seen," which are not really represented in TEV. NEB says "We have lived to see it," SPCL "Finally, we have been able to see it," GECL "Finally, the day we have so long awaited has come!"

In some languages the insertion of direct speech requires an element which indicates that it is direct speech. For example, "saying it like this," or if placed after the quotation, "having said it like that." Here it will sometimes be necessary to add that this is the speech of the enemies; for example, "that is what the enemies said."

**2.17**  RSV | TEV

The LORD has done what he purposed,
  has carried out his threat;
as he ordained long ago,
  he has demolished without pity;
he has made the enemy rejoice over you,
  and exalted the might of your foes.

The LORD has finally done what he threatened to do:
He has destroyed us without mercy, as he warned us long ago.
He gave our enemies victory, gave them joy at our downfall.

In this verse the poet continues to address Jerusalem in the second person. Translators will notice that verse 17 is not divided in the same way in all translations. For example, RSV and TEV divide it into three parts, but NEB and NIV divide it into two, linking **as he ordained . . .** with the clauses before it, and **demolished without pity** with the last part of the verse. The RSV and TEV line divisions reflect the parallel units. The first half-lines of the first and second units are closely parallel in sense, as are the corresponding second half-lines. The third unit makes clear what the first two units refer to.

**The LORD has done what he purposed**: **purposed** translates a word meaning "planned, decided, intended."

**Has carried out his threat**, which is literally "fulfilled his word," is parallel in meaning and more definite than the first clause.

As pointed out above, **as he ordained long ago** is understood by some to be linked with **carried out his threat**. In other words, "He ordered a long time ago that his threat would be carried out." If the translator links this last clause with the ones before it, then the following clauses should be joined to each other. On the other hand, it is also possible to retain the clause linkage as in RSV, so that the flow of ideas may be rendered, for example, "Just as he decided long ago, he has now demolished Jerusalem without pity."

The emphasis here is on the fulfillment of predictions made **long ago**. Just how far back in the past these prophecies were spoken is not indicated. There may be a reference here to the words of such prophets as Amos and Hosea, or possibly to the traditions underlying such passages as Leviticus 26.14-16,25 and Deuteronomy 28.25. In any event the poet is saying that God made up his mind a long time before, and now he is carrying out his plans. In translation it will often be necessary to present the historical order of the events of planning the destruction and then the destruction itself; for example, "Long ago God decided to destroy Jerusalem; now he has done it."

**He had made the enemy rejoice over you** shows how the poet attributes the enemy's success to God. **Over you** may require saying "over your defeat," or more fully, "he has caused the enemy to be glad because you have been defeated," or ". . . because you are a destroyed city."

**Exalted the might of your foes** is literally "he has raised up the horn of your foes." For comments on "horn" as a symbol of power and pride, see verse 3. This expression may be translated, for example, "he has increased the strength of your enemies" or "he has made your enemies stronger and stronger."

| 2.18 | RSV | TEV |
|---|---|---|

| RSV | TEV |
|---|---|
| Cry aloud[i] to the Lord! | O Jerusalem, let your very walls |
| O[j] daughter of Zion! | cry out to the Lord![e] |
| Let tears stream down like a | Let your tears flow like rivers |
| torrent | night and day; |
| day and night! | Wear yourself out with weep- |
| Give yourself no rest, | ing and grief! |
| your eyes no respite! | |

[i] Cn: Heb *Their heart cried*
[j] Cn: Heb *O wall of*

[e] *Probable text* O Jerusalem . . . Lord;
*Hebrew* Their hearts cried out to the
Lord, O wall of Jerusalem.

Whether we accept the textual adjustment of RSV or take the Hebrew form, the word **Cry** in the first half-line is matched in the first half-line of the next unit by a particular and picturable form of crying (**tears stream down like a torrent**). The first half-line of the third unit is a general command to continue without rest, and so has a continuity of thought with **day and night** in the previous half-line. The final half-line returns to the thought of crying, and thus all three units share a common theme.

In **Cry aloud to the Lord**, RSV has changed the Hebrew, which says "Their heart cried to the Lord." It is not at all clear to whom "Their" refers. It can hardly refer to Jerusalem's enemies. Possibly it can refer to the people of Jerusalem rather than to the figure **daughter of Zion**. Many translations, however, like RSV and TEV, modify the Hebrew to express an imperative, which is then parallel to the commands in the middle and final units of the verse. HOTTP gives the Hebrew text an "A" rating and recommends "Their hearts cried out," which is better expressed by NIV "The hearts of the people cry out to the Lord."

Another problem occurs in **O daughter of Zion**, which in Hebrew is "O wall of daughter Zion." RSV and others modify the Hebrew by deleting the word for "wall." However, this should not be done merely on the basis that a wall is asked to cry out to the Lord. In poetic discourse, to regard objects as if they were persons is common. See, for example, "The roads to Zion mourn" and "her gates are desolate" in 1.4; and Isaiah 14.31, "Wail, O gate; cry, O city; melt in fear . . . ." TEV keeps the walls: "O Jerusalem, let your very walls cry out to the Lord!" This is a possibility that translators may wish to follow. Some translations link **O daughter of Zion** to the command **let tears stream down . . .** , and so NIV says "O wall of the daughter of Zion let your tears flow . . . ." The Handbook recommends that "wall" be retained, as in TEV, and that **Cry** be expressed as a command, as in RSV and TEV.

If translators base their translation on TEV, in this case it will often be necessary to make some adjustments, since the resulting figure may not be natural. For example, "Jerusalem, let your walls cry to the Lord, as people cry when in grief," or ". . . let your walls mourn as people mourn for their dead."

The second command (the first in Hebrew) is **Let tears stream down like a torrent day and night**. This simile is a call to Jerusalem to cry, weep, show sorrow for her sins, and is parallel in meaning to the first unit. In some languages it may be necessary to say, for example, "Weep until tears flow like rivers from your eyes day and night (or, all the time)."

**Give yourself no rest** repeats the thought of **day and night**. **Your eyes** translates "the daughter of your eye." This expression is used in Psalm 17.8 and Zechariah 2.8, "apple of the eye," and has the meaning "pupil of the eye." This is a case of the figure of speech in which a part of the eye represents the whole eye, and so the sense is "Don't let your eyes stop crying," or more naturally, "Keep the tears flowing from your eyes," or "Keep crying all the time."

**2.19**

| RSV | TEV |
|---|---|
| Arise, cry out in the night,<br>at the beginning of the watch-<br>es!<br>Pour out your heart like water<br>before the presence of the | All through the night get up<br>again and again to cry out to<br>the Lord;<br>Pour out your heart and beg<br>him for mercy on your chil- |

Lord!
Lift your hands to him
  for the lives of your children,
who faint for hunger
  at the head of every street.

dren—
Children starving to death on
  every street corner!

The first three units of this verse are parallel in that each is a command to the people to pray to the LORD for mercy. The fourth unit is exceptional, as explained in the following paragraph.

The Hebrew commands in this verse are in the feminine singular form. They are addressed, therefore, not to women or people in general, but collectively to Jerusalem pictured as the mother of its inhabitants, as in the latter part of chapter 1. The verse is exceptional in having, like 1.7, four units instead of three. Some translations omit the fourth unit, which they believe may have been added under the influence of 4.1 and Isaiah 51.20. The unit contributes nothing new to what is stated in verses 11 and 12. However, it is present in all Hebrew manuscripts and should be translated.

**Arise, cry out in the night: Arise** in this context probably refers to getting up from sleeping or getting out of bed, although the word often simply introduces another action verb. As is made clear in verse 18, it is to the Lord that she (Jerusalem) cries out. In translation it may be necessary to say, for example, "Get up and cry out to the Lord for help!"

**At the beginning of the watches** is expressed by AB as "as each watch begins." This means at regular intervals during the night. The mention of the middle watch in Judges 7.19 suggests that there were three roughly equal divisions or **watches** in the night in Old Testament times. Many languages have terms to divide the periods of both day and night. If the use of particular time words centers too narrowly on the time involved, it is best to follow something more general such as TEV "again and again."

**Pour out your heart like water** is an idiom that occurs only here and in Psalm 62.8. Compare also 1 Samuel 1.15. The sense of this expression is "Tell what is on your heart," "Express the feelings inside you," "Tell how you feel." **Before the presence of the Lord** means simply "to the Lord." The whole unit may be translated into English as "Pour out your heart to the Lord." However, in languages which do not use this idiom, it may be possible to say, for example, "Tell the Lord what you feel inside you" or "Show your heart to the Lord."

**Lift your hands to him** is a common prayer gesture in the Old Testament. For example, Psalm 28.2 says ". . . as I lift up my hands toward thy most holy sanctuary." See also Psalm 63.4; 134.2; 1 Kings 8.22. TEV does not retain this gesture but says "beg him for mercy." If the translator keeps the Hebrew expression, it may be necessary to make clear that the purpose is for prayer; for example, "Lift your hands to him in prayer." The purpose of the prayer is to plead **for the lives of your children**.

**Who faint for hunger** means "who are dying from starvation," "who are weak from having nothing to eat." See 2.12 for comments on **faint**.

**At the head of every street** is literally "at the head of every open place." This expression is similar to that in verses 11 and 12. The word translated **street** is different from that used in verses 11 and 12 but has the general meaning of "in the open" and the more precise sense of **street**. TEV "on every street corner" is well stated. In language areas where there are no street corners, it may be best to say, for example, "on the roads," "along the paths," or "outside the houses."

**2.20**

| RSV | TEV |
|---|---|
| Look, O LORD, and see!<br>  With whom hast thou dealt<br>    thus?<br>Should women eat their off-<br>  spring,<br>  the children of their tender<br>  care?<br>Should priest and prophet be<br>  slain<br>in the sanctuary of the Lord? | Look, O LORD! Why are you<br>  punishing us like this?<br>Women are eating the bodies<br>  of the children they loved!<br>Priests and prophets are being<br>  killed in the Temple itself! |

In the remainder of chapter 2, the poet continues the thought of the appeal made to Jerusalem to pray in verse 19, by giving the content of Jerusalem's prayer. Jerusalem appeals to the Lord to look at what is happening, as she did in 1.11.

In this verse, after the request to the LORD to look at what is taking place in the first unit, the second and third units are structurally parallel, and each expresses a question of disbelief (RSV).

**Look, O LORD, and see!** opens the plea in which Jerusalem calls out for the LORD to see how he is causing her to suffer.

**With whom hast thou dealt thus?** may mean, as NIV says, "Whom have you ever treated like this?" or in other words, "Have you ever made anyone suffer as I am suffering?" Another interpretation makes a contrast between Israel's position as God's chosen people and the horrors Jerusalem is now going through. In this case the expression can be, for example, "Remember who it is you are doing this to!" AB translates ". . . consider whom you have treated so," and NJV "See . . . To whom You have done this." Lying behind these words is the question of how God's promises to his people can be reconciled with his present treatment of them. That treatment is described in the rest of the verse and takes the form of two questions.

**Should women eat their offspring . . . ?** In Hebrew this expression is made up of a particle followed by the imperfect form of the verb, a construction which translators handle in various ways. AB suggests that these forms may be translated as questions of disbelief, which may be rendered in English, for example, "Can it be that women eat their children?" or "Is it really possible that women can eat their own children?" FRCL translates "Can women go so far as to eat their children?" and SPCL asks "Should mothers have to eat their own children?" In other words these events are looked upon as unbelievable, and translators are encouraged to translate them in this mode.

**Their offspring** translates the Hebrew "their fruit," a general term to be followed by what that term really refers to, **children**. NEB expresses this as "the fruit of their wombs." Translators may be able to use a general term that lends itself to poetry here, but they should not force images that will not be correctly understood.

**The children of their tender care**: **children** matches **fruit** in the previous half-line. For translation notes on **children**, see 1.5. **Of their tender care** means "whom they have raised, cared for, given affection to, loved."

**Should priests and prophets be slain in the sanctuary of the Lord?** This question should follow the construction used in the unit: "Should women eat . . . ?" Here the unbelievable aspect is that priests and prophets who ministered in the Temple were not safe in God's own house, but rather were murdered there. For **priests** see 1.4, and for **prophets** see 2.9. For **sanctuary** see 1.10.

The final unit of this verse may be translated, for example, "Can it be that priests and prophets are killed even in the Lord's Temple?" or in the active voice, "Is it possible that the enemy kills the priests and prophets in the Lord's own Temple?"

| **2.21** | RSV | TEV |
|---|---|---|

| | |
|---|---|
| In the dust of the streets<br> lie the young and the old;<br>my maidens and my young men<br> have fallen by the sword;<br>in the day of thy anger thou hast<br> slain them,<br> slaughtering without mercy. | Young and old alike lie dead in<br> the streets,<br>Young men and women, killed<br> by enemy swords.<br>You slaughtered them without<br> mercy on the day of your<br> anger. |

In this verse the theme of violent death runs through all three units. In the first unit it has taken the youth and old men. In the second unit the order of subject and verb is the reverse from that in the first unit, a device called chiasmus. For a definition of chiasmus, see the Glossary. This is only partially seen in RSV. The thoughts, however, are closely parallel in meaning. The third unit makes clear who has killed the people, and uses different words for "kill" in each half-line. See discussion below.

**In the dust of the streets** is literally "on the ground in open places," where **streets** translates the same word found in the last unit of verse 19, which TEV translates "street corner," and RSV "street." See comments on verse 19.

**Lie the young and the old: the young and the old** refers to people of all ages and both sexes. No one escapes. In order to avoid the picture of people lying down to rest in the streets, it may be necessary to say, for example, "Young people and old people alike lie dead in the streets."

**My maidens and my young men: my maidens** translates "my virgins." See note of explanation on 1.4. **My** is Jerusalem speaking. However, TEV has avoided the first person and thus retains the general sense as in the first unit. Translators may find it is better to do the same rather than introduce **my** in the second unit. **Young men** refers to youths who are mature adults but still not married.

**Have fallen by the sword** is the literal Hebrew text. The Septuagint adds "and by famine," which NEB accepts. HOTTP and most translations follow the Hebrew. **Fallen by the sword** or "killed by enemy swords" (TEV) may require some adjustments in translation, particularly in languages in which the sword is unknown. In some cases an equivalent weapon may be substituted; for example, "The enemy has thrown spears and killed my young men and women." It is also possible to use a verb which requires the use of a weapon; for example, "The enemy has stabbed my young men and women." Of course it is also possible to avoid any reference to weapons and say, for example, "The enemy has killed my young men and women."

**In the day of thy anger thou hast slain them**: for **day of thy anger** see 1.12 and 2.1.

**Slaughtering without mercy**: **slaughtering** is generally used with reference to killing animals to be eaten as food; but it can also be used figuratively to mean killing many people in a brutal manner, massacring (Psa 37.14), and this understanding is reinforced by **without mercy**. Another interpretation is that **slaughtering** as used here is related to the reference in verse 22 to a religious festival. The noun related to this verb is used in Isaiah 34.6, where "sacrifice" and "slaughter" are parallel terms; there the victims are the people of Edom, but here they are the people of Jerusalem. In other words, the poet is saying that the Lord is preparing his sacrificial victims, not bulls or rams, but his own people. Translators may follow either interpretation, and in many languages the translation will not be affected. However, in languages in which **slaughtering** is not used figuratively for the brutal slaying of enemies, we may have to say simply "killing them brutally." If there is a special term for killing enemies in war, that term will be appropriate. If **without mercy** does not indicate a brutal manner, the term may need other descriptive words. For other comments on **without mercy**, see verse 2.

| 2.22 | RSV | TEV |
|---|---|---|

| | |
|---|---|
| Thou didst invite as to the day of an appointed feast my terrors on every side; and on the day of the anger of the LORD none escaped or survived; those whom I dandled and reared my enemy destroyed. | You invited my enemies to hold a carnival of terror all around me, And no one could escape on that day of your anger. They murdered my children, whom I had raised and loved. |

RSV, which attempts to retain the Hebrew form of this verse, is difficult to understand. Part of the problem is that the ones invited to the **feast** in the first half-line are not depicted as people, but as **my terrors on every side** in the next half-line. This same expression is found also in Jeremiah 6.25; 20.3,10; 46.5; 49.29, in which the prophet applies the expression to his opponents. It is not clear how or why the same expression should be used in verse 22. In any event, as AB suggests, the use of **terrors** as a figure of speech here results in a mixture of metaphors which is not typical of Hebrew poetry. AB recommends "attackers" and translates "You invited, as though to a festival, men to attack me from all sides." The speaker appears to be Jerusalem, that is, the people of Jerusalem. **My terrors** are those who cause terror, and so TEV has "my enemies."

**As to the day of an appointed feast** is best understood as a simile. For **appointed feast** see 1.4; 2.6-7. FRCL translates this simile "As for a festival day . . . ." For the entire first poetic unit in Hebrew (the first three printed lines in RSV),

NEB translates "Thou didst summon my enemies against me from every side, like men assembling for a festival." This may also be translated, for example, "You invited my enemies, as people invited to a feast, to attack me on every side." Another choice may be "You invited my enemies to attack me from every side. They came eagerly, as people hurrying to a feast." See also TEV.

**(None) escaped or survived** translates two nouns in Hebrew "(there was no) . . . refugee and survivor." Many languages, like RSV, will prefer to translate these nouns as verbs, or better, as whole clauses. For example, "No one got away and no one lived to tell it."

**Those whom I dandled and reared: those** refers to the children. **Dandled** is a little-used word and translates a Hebrew word meaning "to fondle, cradle in the arms." Translators may wish to express the first word as representing the way a mother holds and caresses an infant. **Reared** expresses the idea of "raising, bringing up, educating" an older child.

In spite of the tender love given to these little ones, **my enemy destroyed** them. RSV uses **destroyed** to translate one of the numerous Hebrew verbs having that general sense. However, in this context it is better to give the particular sense of "murder, kill, slay." See TEV.

# Chapter 3

A glance at the text of RSV or TEV will show the translator that chapter 3 is different in form from any of the other four chapters. The most obvious difference is that chapter 3 has sixty-six verses in contrast to the twenty-two verses in each of the other chapters. However, these verse numbers do not mean that chapter 3 is three times as long. Rather, each unit in chapter 3 is numbered. Then, each group of three units, or verses, is clustered to form a stanza. There are the same number of units in the Hebrew text of chapter 3 as in the others. In chapters 1, 2, 4, and 5, each verse consists of three full units, but only the first letter of the first unit in each verse begins with the succeeding letter of the Hebrew alphabet. By contrast, in chapter 3 the first letter of each unit in a group of three verses begins with the same letter. For example, verses 1, 2, and 3 each begin with *alef,* verses 4, 5, and 6 each begin with *beth,* and so forth through the sixty-six verses. Only Psalm 119 is more detailed in its use of the acrostic pattern.

What is not immediately evident from the form of the chapter is the structure of the content. Chapter 3, in contrast to the rest of the book, says very little about the fall of Jerusalem and the subsequent suffering of the people. Furthermore, the point of view is presented by "the man" who has suffered. Various explanations have been given regarding the identity of this unknown speaker. AB suggests that he is not a person we can identify from history, but rather an ordinary person—a typical sufferer who represents the people of fallen Jerusalem.

To help the translator follow the structure of chapter 3, the following display divides its contents into sections, showing the themes of each section and the way in which the shifting of pronouns from first person singular to third person to first person plural and back to first person singular is related to the themes.

| Verses | Pronouns | Themes |
|---|---|---|
| 1-20 | I, me, my | The suffering of a man |
| 21-24 | I, my | God's mercy gives hope |
| 25-39 | one, he, him, "a man" | God is good even if he punishes |
| 40-47 | we, us, our | Confession and lament |
| 48-54 | I, me, my | Confession and lament |
| 55-63 | I, me, my | Confidence in God's justice |
| 64-66 | (I) | Pleas to curse and destroy |

It will be noticed in verses 26-39 that TEV does not retain the third person perspective as RSV does, but rather shifts to the first person plural (we, us, our). Since TEV follows the Hebrew usage in 40-47, this means TEV has we, us, our (first person plural) from verse 26 to verse 47 before shifting back to I, me, my (first person singular) in verses 48 to 63. See discussion of verse 26 for the recommendation to translators.

## 3.1-66

| RSV | | TEV |
| --- | --- | --- |
| | | *Punishment, Repentance, and Hope* |

| | RSV | | TEV |
|---|---|---|---|
| 1 | I am the man who has seen affliction under the rod of his wrath; | 1 | I am one who knows what it is to be punished by God. |
| 2 | he has driven and brought me into darkness without any light; | 2 | He drove me deeper and deeper into darkness |
| 3 | surely against me he turns his hand again and again the whole day long. | 3 | And beat me again and again with merciless blows. |
| 4 | He has made my flesh and my skin waste away, and broken my bones; | 4 | He has left my flesh open and raw, and has broken my bones. |
| 5 | he has besieged and enveloped me with bitterness and tribulation; | 5 | He has shut me in a prison of misery and anguish. |
| 6 | he has made me dwell in darkness like the dead of long ago. | 6 | He has forced me to live in the stagnant darkness of death. |
| 7 | He has walled me about so that I cannot escape; he has put heavy chains on me; | 7 | He has bound me in chains; I am a prisoner with no hope of escape. |
| 8 | though I call and cry for help, he shuts out my prayer, | 8 | I cry aloud for help, but God refuses to listen; |
| 9 | he has blocked my ways with hewn stones, he has made my paths crooked. | 9 | I stagger as I walk; stone walls block me wherever I turn. |
| 10 | He is to me like a bear lying in wait, like a lion in hiding; | 10 | He waited for me like a bear; he pounced on me like a lion. |
| 11 | he led me off my way and tore me to pieces; he has made me desolate; | 11 | He chased me off the road, tore me to pieces, and left me. |
| 12 | he bent his bow and set me as a mark for his arrow. | 12 | He drew his bow and made me the target for his arrows. |
| 13 | He drove into my heart the arrows of his quiver; | 13 | He shot his arrows deep into my body. |
| 14 | I have become the laughingstock of all peoples, the burden of their songs all day long. | 14 | People laugh at me all day long; I am a joke to them all. |
| 15 | He has filled me with bitterness, he has sated me with wormwood. | 15 | Bitter suffering is all he has given me for food and drink. |
| 16 | He has made my teeth grind on gravel, and made me cower in ashes; | 16 | He rubbed my face in the ground and broke my teeth on rocks. |
| 17 | my soul is bereft of peace, | 17 | I have forgotten what health and peace and happiness are. |
| | | 18 | I do not have much longer to live; my hope in the LORD is gone. |
| | | 19 | The thought of my pain, my homelessness, is bitter poison. |
| | | 20 | I think of it constantly, and my spirit |

18   I have forgotten what happiness is;
so I say, "Gone is my glory,
and my expectation from the
LORD."

19   Remember my affliction and my bitterness,
the wormwood and the gall!

20   My soul continually thinks of it
and is bowed down within me.

21   But this I call to mind,
and therefore I have hope:

22   The steadfast love of the LORD never
ceases,
his mercies never come to an end;

23   they are new every morning;
great is thy faithfulness.

24   "The LORD is my portion," says my
soul,
"therefore I will hope in him."

25   The LORD is good to those who wait
for him,
to the soul that seeks him.

26   It is good that one should wait quietly
for the salvation of the LORD.

27   It is good for a man that he bear
the yoke in his youth.

28   Let him sit alone in silence
when he has laid it on him;

29   let him put his mouth in the dust—
there may yet be hope;

30   let him give his cheek to the smiter,
and be filled with insults.

31   For the Lord will not
cast off forever,

32   but, though he cause grief, he will have
compassion
according to the abundance of his
steadfast love;

33   for he does not willingly afflict
or grieve the sons of men.

34   To crush under foot
all the prisoners of the earth,

35   to turn aside the right of a man
in the presence of the Most High,

36   to subvert a man in his cause,
the Lord does not approve.

37   Who has commanded and it came to
pass,
unless the Lord has ordained it?

38   Is it not from the mouth of the Most
High

---

   is depressed.

21   Yet hope returns when I remember
this one thing:

22   The LORD's unfailing love and mercy
still continue,

23   Fresh as the morning, as sure as the
sunrise.

24   The LORD is all I have, and so in
him I put my hope.

25   The LORD is good to everyone who
trusts in him,

26   So it is best for us to wait in patience—to wait for him to save
us—

27   And it is best to learn this patience
in our youth.

28   When we suffer, we should sit alone in
silent patience;

29   We should bow in submission, for
there may still be hope.

30   Though beaten and insulted, we
should accept it all.

31   The Lord is merciful and will not reject
us forever.

32   He may bring us sorrow, but his
love for us is sure and strong.

33   He takes no pleasure in causing us
grief or pain.

34   The Lord knows when our spirits are
crushed in prison;

35   He knows when we are denied the
rights he gave us;

36   When justice is perverted in court,
he knows.

37   The will of the Lord alone is always
carried out.

38   Good and evil alike take place at his
command.

39   Why should we ever complain when
we are punished for our sin?

40   Let us examine our ways and turn back
to the LORD.

41   Let us open our hearts to God in
heaven and pray,

42   "We have sinned and rebelled, and
you, O LORD, have not forgiven
us.

43   "You pursued us and killed us; your
mercy was hidden by your anger,

44   By a cloud of fury too thick for our

that good and evil come?

39 Why should a living man complain,
a man, about the punishment of his
sins?

40 Let us test and examine our ways,
and return to the LORD!

41 Let us lift up our hearts and hands
to God in heaven:

42 "We have transgressed and rebelled,
and thou hast not forgiven.

43 "Thou hast wrapped thyself with anger
and pursued us,
slaying without pity;

44 thou hast wrapped thyself with a cloud
so that no prayer can pass through.

45 Thou hast made us offscouring and
refuse
among the peoples.

46 "All our enemies
rail against us;

47 panic and pitfall have come upon us,
devastation and destruction;

48 my eyes flow with rivers of tears
because of the destruction of the
daughter of my people.

49 "My eyes will flow without ceasing,
without respite,

50 until the LORD from heaven
looks down and sees;

51 my eyes cause me grief
at the fate of all the maidens of my
city.

52 "I have been hunted like a bird
by those who were my enemies
without cause;

53 they flung me alive into the pit
and cast stones on me;

54 water closed over my head;
I said, 'I am lost.'

55 "I called on thy name, O LORD,
from the depths of the pit;

56 thou didst hear my plea, 'Do not close
thine ear to my cry for help!'

57 Thou didst come near when I called on
thee;
thou didst say, 'Do not fear!'

58 "Thou hast taken up my cause, O
Lord,
thou hast redeemed my life.

59 Thou hast seen the wrong done to me,
O LORD;

prayers to get through.

45 You have made us the garbage
dump of the world.

46 "We are insulted and mocked by all
our enemies.

47 We have been through disaster and
ruin; we live in danger and fear.

48 My eyes flow with rivers of tears at
the destruction of my people.

49 "My tears will pour out in a ceaseless
stream

50 Until the LORD looks down from
heaven and sees us.

51 My heart is grieved when I see what
has happened to the women of
the city.

52 "I was trapped like a bird by enemies
who had no cause to hate me.

53 They threw me alive into a pit and
closed the opening with a stone.

54 Water began to close over me, and I
thought death was near.

55 "From the bottom of the pit, O LORD,
I cried out to you,

56 And when I begged you to listen to
my cry, you heard.

57 You answered me and told me not
to be afraid.

58 "You came to my rescue, Lord, and
saved my life.

59 Judge in my favor; you know the
wrongs done against me.

60 You know how my enemies hate me
and how they plot against me.

61 "You have heard them insult me, O
LORD; you know all their plots.

62 All day long they talk about me and
make their plans.

63 From morning till night they make
fun of me.

64 "Punish them for what they have done,
O LORD;

65 Curse them and fill them with despair!

66 Hunt them down and wipe them off
the earth!"

judge thou my cause.
60    Thou hast seen all their vengeance,
      all their devices against me.

61    Thou hast heard their taunts, O LORD,
      all their devices against me.
62    The lips and thoughts of my assailants
      are against me all the day long.
63    Behold their sitting and their rising;
      I am the burden of their songs.

64    "Thou wilt requite them, O LORD,
      according to the work of their
        hands.
65    Thou wilt give them dullness of heart;
      thy curse will be on them.
66    Thou wilt pursue them in anger and
      destroy them
      from under thy heavens, O LORD."

## Section Heading

The TEV heading "Punishment, Repentance, Hope" may have to be adjusted in translation by switching to verbs; for example, "God punishes a man who confesses and finds hope" or "God makes a man suffer, but he has faith in God." Some other headings are: "In the midst of distress a true reason to hope" (FRCL), "Third lamentation" (NJB), "Hope in spite of the deepest misery" (GECL), "Third lament" (SPCL), "The man of sorrows" (TOB).

| 3.1-3 | RSV | TEV |
|---|---|---|

| | RSV | | | TEV |
|---|---|---|---|---|
| 1 | I am the man who has seen affliction | | 1 | I am one who knows what it is to be punished by God. |
| | under the rod of his wrath; | | 2 | He drove me deeper and deeper into darkness |
| 2 | he has driven and brought me into darkness without any light; | | 3 | And beat me again and again with merciless blows. |
| 3 | surely against me he turns his hand again and again the whole day long. | | | |

**3.1**   Unlike chapters 1 and 2, chapter 3 does not begin with "How." Verse 1 identifies the poet only as the man who has suffered. In contrast with the earlier chapters, in which Jerusalem is depicted as a woman, chapter 3 presents suffering as experienced by a **man**, the Hebrew *geber,* which is often used to emphasize maleness. Here the word serves only to indicate a man as a general description. Its intention is not male as distinct from female. Accordingly TEV "one who" is satisfactory.

In some languages the sudden appearance of **the man** will create an abrupt break with chapter 2, particularly as the reader has seen Jerusalem pictured to this point as a woman. In order to make a satisfactory transition to this new point of view, it may be necessary to do more than supply a section heading. For example, it may be necessary to say "I am the man who now writes this. I am one who knows what it is to have God punish me," or "I am the writer and am a man whom God has made suffer," or ". . . who has suffered under God's anger."

**Seen affliction** is somewhat idiomatic in Hebrew as it is in English. As used here it means "experienced, gone through, endured." In other words "I am a person who has suffered," "I am one who knows what it is to suffer," or "I am the one who has experienced suffering" (SPCL).

**Under the rod of his wrath** may be understood as the condition causing the suffering, as in RSV, or as in NEB's statement, "I have felt the rod of his wrath." **Wrath**, meaning "anger," is the same word as used in 2.2. All references to God are through pronouns in Hebrew until verse 18. Therefore **his wrath** refers to God's anger. **The rod of his wrath** occurs in various forms: Proverbs 22.8 "the rod of his fury"; Proverbs 22.15 "the rod of discipline"; Isaiah 10.5 "the rod of my anger." The expression is idiomatic and refers to God's punishment of someone, or, as SPCL says, "under the blows of the Lord's anger." TEV makes it passive, "to be punished by God."

**3.2** This verse expresses a contrast to the picture of God in Psalms 23 and 80 as the shepherd who leads his people. **Driven** is used in reference to driving cattle in Genesis 31.18. In relation to people it is used in Isaiah 49.10 with the sense of "lead or guide." **Brought** translates a verb meaning "to cause to go, or to walk." So in pastoral terms we may say, for example, "He led me and made me go" or "He guided me and made me walk." The place where God has taken him is **into darkness without any light**, an idiomatic way of saying "into total darkness" or, as NJV has it, "In unrelieved dárkness," that is, darkness which has no light anywhere. We may also say, as in SPCL, "He has led me into dark places and made me walk on paths without light."

**3.3** **Surely against me he turns his hand: surely** translates a Hebrew particle that gives certainty or emphasis to the following statement and is sometimes rendered "certainly, indeed, it is so." However, it can also be restrictive in sense, meaning "only," that is, "only against me . . . ." "Turn his hand against" is an expression not found elsewhere in the Old Testament. However, it is generally thought to be parallel in meaning to Job 19.21: "The hand of God has struck me down" (TEV). See also Psalm 38.2; Isaiah 5.25. GECL translates "His fist always strikes only on me." This may also be rendered, for example, "Certainly his hand strikes me down" or "He lays a heavy hand on me alone." Some languages will not be able to use an expression with **hand** having the meaning here. They may say, for example, "he beat me," "he knocked me down," or "he hit me."

**Again and again** represents the repeated action of striking (turning) and is formed by the use of two verbs meaning to turn, literally "against me he turns and returns his hand all the day." **The whole day long** expresses the extent and emphasizes the continued action of being struck. TEV "beats me again and again with merciless blows" expresses more the manner than the extent.

| | RSV | | TEV |
|---|---|---|---|
| 4 | He has made my flesh and my skin waste away, and broken my bones; | 4 | He has left my flesh open and raw, and has broken my bones. |
| 5 | he has besieged and enveloped me with bitterness and tribulation; | 5 | He has shut me in a prison of misery and anguish. |
| 6 | he has made me dwell in darkness like the dead of long ago. | 6 | He has forced me to live in the stagnant darkness of death. |

**3.4** As a result of the continuous beatings, **my flesh and my skin waste away**. The thought here is that the man's body has been beaten until it is worn out. **Flesh, skin**, and **bones** are to be taken as part of the body representing the whole. Job expresses similar thoughts in Job 7.5; 30.30. Most translations keep the three body parts or modify them to fit the style of their own language; for example, FRCL "He has withered me away from head to foot, he has broken my bones." TEV "left my flesh open and raw" does not mention the skin, but "flesh open" means that the skin too has been affected. The vision of Isaiah concerning Jerusalem is expressed in similar language. See Isaiah 1.5-6.

**3.5** **Besieged and enveloped** (or encircled, surrounded) are military terms used here to depict the man caught and surrounded, unable to escape. Beginning with this verse and continuing to verse 9 there is a series of images expressing various ways in which God has closed the poet in, as in a prison or as if surrounded by a wall.

Instead of besieging with weapons, God attacks the man with **bitterness and tribulation**. **Bitterness** translates a word which means "poison" and refers to a little-known poisonous herb with a bitter taste; see *Fauna and Flora of the Bible,* pages 167-168. Some take the general sense to mean "poverty" (AB). NJV and TEV change the Hebrew slightly to get "misery." Mft and others take the word to mean "head." HOTTP classifies the expression as a "B" reading and translates "bitterness and torment," which supports RSV. **Bitterness** in its extended meaning refers to harsh conditions of life, and so a word meaning "suffering" is an adequate translation. See Jeremiah 8.14, "poisoned water." **Tribulation** here means hardship, trouble, suffering.

In translation it will often be necessary to adjust the relation of the first half-line to the second, since in many languages abstract terms such as bitterness and suffering cannot be used as weapons or instruments. TEV has done this with "a prison of misery and anguish." FRCL says "He has raised around me a wall of bitterness and suffering." We may also say, for example, "He has attacked me and surrounded me so that I live in misery and trouble."

**3.6** This verse is similar to Psalm 143.3: "he has made me sit in darkness like those long dead." In the psalm the jailer is the psalmist's enemy; here the jailer is God himself.

**Made me dwell in darkness: darkness,** as the completion of the unit will show, is a poetic term for Sheol, the place of the dead.

**Like the dead of long ago** refers to the condition in Sheol of those who have been there for a long time, slowly reduced to nothing. TEV is poetic, with "in the stagnant darkness of death," but this is not very close to the form of the original. It may be better to say, for example, "He has made me live in darkness, like the darkness where those long dead live." In many languages there is no necessary connection between death and darkness. However, it is clear that the sufferer is still alive, and it is sometimes possible to say, for example, "He has made me live in a dark place like in the graves of those who died long ago."

| 3.7-9 | RSV | TEV |
|---|---|---|
| 7 | He has walled me about so that I cannot escape; he has put heavy chains on me; | 7 He has bound me in chains; I am a prisoner with no hope of escape. |
| 8 | though I call and cry for help, he shuts out my prayer; | 8 I cry aloud for help, but God refuses to listen; |
| 9 | he has blocked my ways with hewn stones, he has made my paths crooked. | 9 I stagger as I walk; stone walls block me wherever I turn. |

**3.7** The closest parallel to this verse is Job 13.27: "Thou puttest my feet in the stocks, and watchest over all my paths." See also Psalm 88.8. TEV reverses the order of the two halves of verse 7.

**Walled me about** or "built a wall around me" continues the poetic description of the way God torments the man. **Walled . . . about** means imprisoned, or as TEV says, "I am a prisoner." The consequence of the wall about him is **I cannot escape** or "I cannot go free."

Not only does the wall keep him in, God has also **put heavy chains on me,** where **chains** translates the Hebrew for "bronze" (a metal produced from tin and copper). "Bronze" is used here not to refer to the metal as such but to an object which is made from this metal. In this context the object is **heavy chains.**

The expression **heavy chains on me** will often require some adjustments in translation. In some areas chains are not known, and even where they are widely known, they may not be used to bind people. Therefore the translator must often substitute a local material used for binding someone; for example, "He has tied me up with vines," or simply "He has tied me up" or "He has tied my hands and feet."

**3.8** Not only is the prisoner unable to escape from prison, but even his **cry for help** fails to reach God's ears. The most usual Hebrew word for prayer only occurs twice in Lamentations, here and again in verse 44. In both places the poet complains that God is deaf to prayer. The expression **cry for help** must often be rendered in the form of two verb phrases, the second being subordinate to the first; for example, "I cry asking God to help me."

**He shuts out my prayer** may be translated as in TEV, or, for example, "He pays no attention to my prayers," or sometimes idiomatically, "His ears are like stones for my prayers."

**3.9** In this verse the prisoner comes up against the walls and is unable to find his way, as though in a situation where every turn leads to a dead end. Compare Hosea 2.6. This is well expressed in NJV, "He has made my paths a maze." **Hewn stones** refers to stones that have been cut to a proper shape before being used to build a wall. In some areas this must be rendered "mud walls," "earth walls," or "bamboo walls."

**He has made my path crooked** will not mean very much for some readers who know no other kind of path in their area. The Hebrew is literally "he bends (or twists) my paths." The effect is that a person does not arrive at the intended destination; he is lost as he tries to follow the paths. TEV has taken the bending or twisting to refer to the way someone walks, "I stagger as I walk." This may be meaningful, or we may say, for example, "He has made my paths so that they lead nowhere."

| 3.10-12 | RSV | TEV |
|---|---|---|
| 10 | He is to me like a bear lying in wait, like a lion in hiding; | 10 He waited for me like a bear; he pounced on me like a lion. |
| 11 | he led me off my way and tore me to pieces; he has made me desolate; | 11 He chased me off the road, tore me to pieces, and left me. |
| 12 | he bent his bow and set me as a mark for his arrow. | 12 He drew his bow and made me the target for his arrows. |

**3.10** The two half-lines of verse 10 say much the same thing. God is compared to a bear and a lion waiting to pounce on their prey, as in Hosea 13.7-8. In Amos 5.18-19 the bear and the lion are used as images of the Day of the Lord. The translation of **bear** and **lion** will depend upon familiarity with these two animals. Where they are unknown the translator may substitute local animals, provided they are wild and capable of attacking a person. If no such animals exist, it is always possible to shift to a generic term; for example, "He is like a wild animal that waits for me and pounces on me." If this solution is still unsatisfactory, the translator may have to drop the simile of the animal attack and say, for example, "He waited for me to attack me. He kept himself in hiding." In some cases it may be more natural to reverse the order of these two half-lines.

**3.11** **He led me off my way**: **he** refers to God, who is compared to dangerous animals in verse 10. **Led me off** translates a verb whose meaning is not certain. However, the presence of **way** or "path" in the context, plus the context of the previous verse, makes it probable that RSV and TEV express the idea correctly. NIV "he dragged me from the path" is a good translation model. The verb translated

**tore me to pieces** is even less certain, as it occurs nowhere else. NEB derives the verb from the Hebrew word meaning "lame" and so translates "He has lamed me." This translation is based on one of the early Greek versions. The same Hebrew verb is found with a slight difference of spelling in 2 Samuel 4.4. However, most modern translations give something similar to **tore me to pieces**, which suits the context well.

**Made me desolate: desolate** (see 1.4,16) means "abandoned, lonely, helpless" in reference to a person's situation.

---

**3.12** **He bent his bow** is the same as in 2.4. See there for comments. In both passages the sufferer pictures himself as God's victim in the same terms as are used by Job in Job 6.4; 16.12,13. **Set me as a mark** or "made me his target" pictures God as an archer using the poet for his target practice. In areas in which the bow and arrow are not known, a substitute weapon may have to be used. A throwing weapon will retain something of the imagery.

---

**3.13-15**            RSV                                        TEV

13   He drove into my heart                13   He shot his arrows deep into
         the arrows of his quiver;                     my body.
14   I have become the laughing-           14   People laugh at me all day
         stock of all peoples,                        long; I am a joke to them
     the burden of their songs all                    all.
         day long.                         15   Bitter suffering is all he has
15   He has filled me with bitter-                    given me for food and
         ness,                                        drink.
     he has sated me with worm-
         wood.

---

**3.13** This stanza (group of three verses, 13-15) begins with a continuation of the figure of God as one who shoots his arrows into the body of the sufferer so that they penetrate his kidneys (translated **heart** by RSV). Job 16.13 also speaks of Job's kidneys as the target of God's arrows. Translators differ greatly in the handling of the Hebrew for "kidneys." TEV has "deep into my body," SPCL "very deep," FRCL "my kidneys," NJB "deep into me," NJV "my vitals," Mft "driven his shafts home, right into me."

**Arrows of his quiver** is literally "sons of his quiver." The **quiver** as the container for the arrows is not central to the description of God's attack, and translators handle this expression in various ways; for example, TEV omits it as unnecessary when speaking of the action of "his arrows." FRCL has "all his arrows"; GECL, which says "arrow after arrow," also does not mention the **quiver**. However, translators who are translating into poetry may find the expression necessary and may try something like "His quiver gave (produced, bore) arrows that he shot into my heart."

---

**3.14** **I have become the laughingstock of all peoples: laughingstock** means "the object of mockery, ridicule, scorn, or contempt." **Of all**

**peoples** is a textual problem. The Hebrew text has "of my people," but RSV translates an alternative form of the text which is based on a long textual tradition. Modern translators, as well as the ancient ones, have been divided on which form to follow. The difference between the two forms consists of only one letter. If the poet is thinking that the prediction in Deuteronomy 28.37 has now been fulfilled ("the people . . . will make fun of you and ridicule you"—TEV), the form **all peoples** is more likely to be the original. But the HOTTP committee favors "all my people" (a "B" rating), since a scribal change to make the text consistent with Deuteronomy 28.37 explains that variant. There is really no way to know, and consequently translators are free to say "all my people" (which refers to the people of Israel) or "all people" (all the nations that have known of the fall of Jerusalem).

**The burden of their songs all day long** is literally "their song all the day." This refers to songs of ridicule sung to make fun of someone. The use of songs for satire and ridicule is very common in many language areas. Where such songs are common a special term often designates them. Here the songs are said to be sung **all day long**, to emphasize the intensity of the ridicule. **The burden of their songs** may be rendered, for example, "I am the one they ridicule in their songs," "when they sing ridicule songs, they always mention my name," or "the people sing satire songs all day, and they are all about me." TEV "I am a joke to them all" gets the effect of the ridicule but misses the idea of singing.

| **3.15** | The two half-lines of verse 15, as seen in RSV, are fully parallel in meaning. For a discussion of the parallelism of verse 15, see "Parallelism" |

in "Translating Lamentations" at the beginning of this Handbook, page 3. The Hebrew word for the **bitterness** with which the poet is filled is the same as used of "bitter herbs" in Exodus 12.8 (see *Fauna and Flora*, page 98). Similarly, **wormwood** is a plant that yields a bitter-tasting medicinal juice (see *Fauna and Flora*, pages 197-198. Translators may keep the metaphorical use of **filled with bitterness** and **sated with wormwood**, as in both RSV and TEV, or they can shift to a nonfigurative expression. If translators follows the second way, they avoid giving the reader the impression that God is intent on curing the man with foul-tasting medicine. We may translate, for example, "He has caused me to suffer greatly, to suffer more than I am able to endure." It is also possible to combine the figurative expression and the direct meaning by saying, for example, "He has made me suffer like one who is forced to swallow the most bitter liquid."

| **3.16-18** | RSV | TEV |
|---|---|---|
| 16 | He has made my teeth grind on gravel, and made me cower in ashes; | 16 He rubbed my face in the ground and broke my teeth on rocks. |
| 17 | my soul is bereft of peace, I have forgotten what happiness is; | 17 I have forgotten what health and peace and happiness are. |
| 18 | so I say, "Gone is my glory, and my expectation from the LORD." | 18 I do not have much longer to live; my hope in the LORD is gone. |

**3.16** **Made my teeth grind on gravel** is literally "broke my teeth on gravel," which is somewhat ambiguous. The sense can be "He made me chew gravel and so ground down my teeth," or "He pushed my face into the rocks and broke my teeth," or "He hit me in the teeth with rocks and so broke them." It is probably best understood as a figure of extreme suffering or humiliation. In other words, the poet's suffering is like rocks breaking the teeth. FRCL says suitably "He made me chew rocks," or we may say "He made me suffer, and it was like breaking my teeth on rocks."

The Hebrew verb translated **cower** (to crouch down from fear) is changed by some scholars to mean "to feed someone," and so NEB has "fed on ashes." HOTTP gives the Hebrew text an "A" rating and translates "He laid me in the dust."

Both expressions in this verse may be taken to mean that the man was humiliated, degraded, rejected. In translation it may be necessary to make this point clear by saying, for example, "He made me bite rocks which broke my teeth, and put me down in the dust to show that I was worth nothing."

**3.17** In the next four verses the reader gets a glimpse of the poet's inner feelings. Verse 17 begins a transition that builds toward the hope the speaker still retains.

**My soul is bereft of peace** is literally "You cast off peace from my soul." The sense of "cast off" is "reject." However, the form of the verb can have as subject "you (singular)" or "she." Taken as "you" the reference would be to the LORD, as direct address. Understood as "she" the reference would be to **soul**, which is feminine in Hebrew. However, "My soul [meaning 'I'] rejects peace" does not give suitable sense. Some interpreters change the Hebrew slightly to get a passive construction, and so RSV has **my soul is bereft** (deprived) **of peace**. FRCL follows the Septuagint: "He has deprived me of a peaceful life." The HOTTP recommendations do not show how peace is related to the rest of the sentence. The Handbook recommends following RSV but in a reworded form; for example, "My soul has (that is, I have) been deprived of peace" or, as an active construction, "You have taken peace away from me."

**Peace** here translates the Hebrew *shalom*, which refers to more than just the end or the absence of fighting. It covers a wider range of meaning, such as security, peace, health, and prosperity. Note that TEV uses "health and peace" for the translation of *shalom*.

**I have forgotten what happiness is**: **forgotten** is used idiomatically here, because the poet does not mean that he literally has forgotten, but rather that he has gone so long without happiness, it is as though it has left his memory. In some languages the equivalent expression can be, for example, "Happiness left me so long ago, I cannot catch it" or "I have not known happiness for so long I forget what it is like."

**3.18** **So I say**: this verse is introduced by the Hebrew word meaning "I said," which often has the sense of "I thought" or "I said to myself." In a long Hebrew text this word often marks a transition in the outlook of the speaker, as in Jonah 2.4. It indicates that the situation is not really as bad as it seems. So here, when his despair is at its deepest, the sufferer is about to find grounds for hope.

What he says is literally "Gone is my enduring and my hope from the LORD." "Enduring" and "hope" are two connected nouns which have essentially one meaning. **Glory** (RSV) is one meaning of the first noun, but in this context the sense is the capacity to endure, survive, go on living. The poet is thinking here of the possibility of a long life. His hope for the future, which is based on the LORD, appears to be lost. TEV expresses the thought well: "I do not have much longer to live." **Expectation** is "hope," as used also in Psalm 39.7: "My hope is in thee." See also Proverbs 10.28; 11.7; 13.12.

The expression **gone is . . . my expectation from the LORD** suggests that there is no longer anything to look forward to; it may be rendered, for example, "I have decided that the LORD will not let me see another day" or "I feel that God will soon make me die."

| 3.19-21 | RSV | TEV |
|---|---|---|
| 19 | Remember my affliction and my bitterness,^k the wormwood and the gall! | 19 The thought of my pain, my homelessness, is bitter poison. |
| 20 | My soul continually thinks of it and is bowed down within me. | 20 I think of it constantly, and my spirit is depressed. |
| 21 | But this I call to mind, and therefore I have hope: | 21 Yet hope returns when I remember this one thing: |

^k Cn: Heb *wandering*

**3.19** The development in the poet's thought progresses as he now pleads with God to **remember my affliction**. **Remember**, taken by RSV as an imperative, is thought by others to be out of place here, and so some change it to "I remember" as in the Septuagint. Accordingly NIV translates "I remember my affliction." NJV prefers an infinitive, "To recall my distress," while TEV takes it to require a verbal noun, "The thought of," and NEB "the memory of." Since the form of the verb **Remember** can be interpreted into so many different forms, the translator is free to decide. However, the context is still that of despair, which suggests that TEV's expression may be the most satisfactory. If taken as an imperative, the poet asks God to **remember**, that is, to think about his situation: "Think how much I have suffered." **Remember my affliction** may sometimes be rendered as a time clause; for example, "When I remember . . ." or "When I think of . . . ." RSV's footnote shows that **bitterness**, as in 1.7, translates the Hebrew for "wandering." Only one consonant is changed to yield the word for **bitterness** that was used in verse 15. See 1.7 for comments. In this context the original Hebrew, translated in TEV as "homelessness" and in NEB as "wanderings," makes good sense, and there is no need for any change.

**Wormwood** is the same word used in verse 15. The two Hebrew words which RSV translates as **wormwood** and **gall** often occur together as a more emphatic substitute for the one word used alone in verse 15; for example, Deuteronomy 29.18 "a bitter and poisonous plant" (TEV). If the translator uses a term or terms equivalent to **wormwood** and **gall**, it should be made clear that these are used in a figurative sense. Therefore it is often better to shift to a simile; for example, "When I think of my suffering and living away from home, it is like the taste of bitter liquid."

<table>
<tr><td>3.20</td><td></td></tr>
</table>

This verse has two related textual problems. The first is the word **soul** in **My soul continually thinks of it**. This is said to be one of the so-called "scribal corrections." According to Jewish tradition, some words in the Old Testament were intentionally altered so as to avoid saying something unsuitable about God. NEB restores what is thought to be the original form, "your soul," and so translates verse 20 as "Remember, O remember, and stoop down to me," with a footnote saying that "stoop down to me" is probably the original wording but has been altered in the Hebrew to mean "I sink down." TEV translates the text as it now stands, "my spirit is depressed." Most translators agree with this interpretation, which is supported also by HOTTP. **My soul**, meaning "I," may be taken as the subject of both Hebrew verbs.

The other textual problem in this verse relates to the interpretation of the verb translated **is bowed down**. According to one form of the Hebrew text, it means "think, meditate," which evidently lies behind the Septuagint translation. But the great majority of modern translators accept the other form of the verb, meaning "to stoop or to bow down." The two verbs can in fact be understood to have much the same meaning in this context, so that TEV's wording "my spirit is depressed" safely represents the intended meaning. **My soul . . . is bowed down within me** expresses a depressed emotional state which may sometimes be translated idiomatically; for example, "My eyes look down," "My heart fades away," "I am like a shadow," or "I sit apart from my people."

<table>
<tr><td>3.21</td><td></td></tr>
</table>

**But this I call to mind** is treated by some translations as pointing back to what has already been said. But it is more convincing for **this** to point forward to the thoughts of verses 22-25. TEV and others make clear that **this** points forward, by saying "When I remember this one thing: . . . ." Most translations use a colon to show that the thought of 21 is carried forward into verse 22; however, punctuation is not always sufficient for hearers, and so a clear forward linking should be made. A good example is found in Mft, who begins verse 22 with "that": "But I will call to mind, to give me hope, (22) that the Eternal's love is lasting . . . ." We may also translate, for example, "I have hope when I remember (22) that the steadfast love of the LORD never ceases . . . ."

In many languages **hope** is more related to wishing than to confidence. Here the poet is stating his confidence in God's love and mercy, not merely wishing that it might be so. "Hope returns" in TEV must be expressed differently in many languages so that a subject expresses the feeling of hope; for example, "I have confidence when I remember this: . . ." or "I put my trust in it when I remember this: . . . ."

| 3.22-24 | RSV | TEV |
|---|---|---|
| 22 | The steadfast love of the LORD never ceases,[1] | 22 The LORD's unfailing love and mercy still continue, |

|  |  |
|---|---|
| his mercies never come to an end; | 23 Fresh as the morning, as sure as the sunrise. |
| 23 they are new every morning; great is thy faithfulness. | 24 The LORD is all I have, and so in him I put my hope. |
| 24 "The LORD is my portion," says my soul, "therefore I will hope in him." |  |

*l* Syr Tg: Heb *we are not cut off*

---

**3.22**   **Steadfast love** translates the Hebrew *chesed*, which is in TEV "unfailing love," and in NEB "true love." This important Old Testament word refers to the faithful, loyal, constant goodness and love that God shows to his people. **Love of the LORD** is God's act of loving his people. The RSV footnote shows that RSV follows the ancient versions with **ceases** by making a slight alteration in the Hebrew. The Hebrew text says "we are not cut off." Some scholars feel that the isolated use of "we" in a discourse where only the first person singular is used is not likely to be correct. HOTTP, on the other hand, keeps the Hebrew and says something like "We have not come to the end of the LORD's steadfast love." If "we" is to be avoided, the clause may be rendered, for example, "The faithful love of the LORD has not come to an end" or "The LORD's unfailing love has not finished." Stating it positively we may say "The LORD still shows his loyal love to his people."

The second half-line of this verse is fully parallel in meaning with the first. **Mercies**, meaning kindness, goodness, compassion, love, is in the plural form in the Hebrew. If the first half-line has been translated positively, it may be best to do the same with the second; for example, "His kindness lasts forever." It will be noticed that TEV has restructured the parallel half-lines so that the one verb phrase "still continue" serves for both topics: "unfailing love and mercy."

The translation of **steadfast love of the LORD** requires restructuring into a verb phrase in many languages and naming the object of the act of love. For example, "The LORD has loved his people faithfully," or idiomatically, "The LORD has loved his people with one heart." This entire verse may sometimes be translated, for example, "The LORD has shown kindness and has loved his people faithfully, and he still does" or ". . . and he has never stopped loving them."

**3.23**   **They are new every morning: they**, referring to "steadfast love" and "mercies" of verse 22, are said to be **new every morning. New** does not refer here to something that never existed before, but rather to a fresh renewal of what has been experienced before. Accordingly it may be better to say in some languages "every morning they are renewed," or "they are fresh every morning," or "each new day God makes his people see them as if for the first time."

The whole of verse 23 in TEV is a further description of "the LORD's unfailing love and mercy," and so it does not begin with a pronoun, as it does in RSV. TEV has also restructured the final phrase of verse 23 so that **great is thy faithfulness** is expressed as being dependable and regular: "sure as the sunrise." In this case TEV has shifted from nonmetaphor to metaphor and has done so in a manner which is particularly suitable in this context. The translator may follow this model, or may prefer to keep the nonfigurative **great is thy faithfulness**. God's **faithfulness** is translated idiomatically in some languages; for example, "You are a one-hearted God," "You are a God I can always count on," or "You are a God on whom people can lean."

| **3.24** | Verse 24 brings to a close this section containing the first person singular pronouns. |

**The LORD is my portion** picks up a thought from Numbers 18.20, in which Aaron, as representative of Israel's priests, is told by the LORD, "You shall have no inheritance in their land, neither shall you have any portion among them; I am your portion and your inheritance . . . ." So here the poet says the LORD is his **portion** or inheritance. In many languages it is not possible to say that one possesses God as does TEV, "The LORD is all I have." The sense of **The LORD is my portion** may often be rendered, for example, "I trust God and I need nothing more," "God is everything; I need nothing else," or "I need nothing because God is with me."

**Says my soul** is not translated by TEV. However, translators may retain this expression as revealing the poet's innermost thoughts and introducing a direct quote: "I say this: 'The LORD is all I need' "; or "I say it like this: 'The LORD is what I have inherited.' "

The consequence of everything from verse 22 up to this point is expressed as **therefore I will hope in him**. For **hope** see verse 21. **Hope** as an action may be translated, for example, "I put my trust in him," "I look to him with confidence," or "I wait for him because I trust him."

| 3.25-27 | RSV | TEV |
|---|---|---|

| | RSV | TEV |
|---|---|---|
| 25 | The LORD is good to those who wait for him, to the soul that seeks him. | 25 The LORD is good to everyone who trusts in him, |
| 26 | It is good that one should wait quietly for the salvation of the LORD. | 26 So it is best for us to wait in patience—to wait for him to save us— |
| 27 | It is good for a man that he bear the yoke in his youth. | 27 And it is best to learn this patience in our youth. |

In the outline given at the beginning of the chapter, the display of pronoun changes shows that the theme of this section (verses 25-39) is "God is good even if he punishes." Also in this section the pronouns in the Hebrew text shift from first person singular ("I," "me," "my") to an indefinite third person ("one," "he," "him," "a man"). TEV, however, begins at verse 26 to use the first person plural ("we," "us," "our"). This change is made in TEV for two reasons: (1) The third person pronouns are indefinite, whereas the first person pronouns from verse 1 to 24 were clearly definite references to the speaker; by shifting to the first person plural TEV retains this directness of reference. (2) Since the Hebrew text will again shift to "we," "us," "our" in verse 40, TEV anticipates this change and thus keeps the same pronouns from verse 26 to verse 47. The pronouns "we," "us," "our" are inclusive, meaning that they refer to the speaker and those around him, that is, the people of Jerusalem. Translators may find it more satisfactory to follow this pattern of TEV.

**3.25** Verses 25, 26, and 27 each begin with the Hebrew *tob* "good." **The LORD is good to those who wait for him**: good applies to the quality of the relationship the LORD has with **those who wait for him**. See also Psalm 34.8; 86.5. The expression **The LORD is good to those** must sometimes be expressed in such a form as "The LORD does good things to those . . ." or "The LORD gives good things to those . . . ." **Wait for** translates a verb whose meaning is most probably "trust in, have confidence in, depend on." GECL and FRCL say "who count on him" as an expression of trust. In some languages "trust in him" may be translated idiomatically; for example, "who put their heart on God" or "who have a quiet innermost toward God."

**The soul that seeks him** is parallel in meaning to **those who wait for him** in the previous half-line. **Soul** is the Hebrew *nefesh*, meaning here "the person, anyone, everyone, all." **Seeks** literally means to search, look for. The same verb is used in this way in many passages in the Psalms; for example, Psalm 9.10 ". . . for thou, O LORD, hast not forsaken those who seek thee." See also Psalm 22.26; 34.4,10; 69.32. With God as object the word may mean "to pray to, worship, or serve." It is sometimes translated "turn to," as in FRCL, which says in verse 25 "for those who turn to him." It is necessary in translating this term to avoid giving the impression that God is a lost object to be found. Accordingly we may sometimes translate "to everyone who comes to you," "to all who worship you," or "to everyone who wants to serve you."

**3.26** The first word of this verse has an impersonal subject: **It is good**. The verse goes on to describe the kind of attitude that is good, that is, patiently and silently waiting for the LORD to intervene and save. In verse 26 TEV has shifted from the indefinite **that one should** to the definite "for us" and has expressed the phrase **salvation of the LORD** as a verb phrase, "wait for him to save us." TEV switches to "we" and "us" from verse 26 through the rest of this section to verse 39.

In some languages it will be necessary to go even further than TEV and make clear what we are to be saved from. Here the reference is to salvation from the enemies of Israel, not from the sufferings inflicted by God. We may also say, for example, "we wait quietly for God to help us."

**3.27** The third verse beginning with the Hebrew word for "good" starts in the same way as verse 26. **Man** does not single out a male in contrast to a female, and so it may be rendered "a person, anyone," that is, "It is good for anyone . . ." or simply "It is good to learn to be patient . . . ."

**Bear the yoke** is a metaphor referring to the yoke placed on the necks of working animals to enable them to pull together. For comments see 1.14. The sense of the expression is, as in TEV, "to learn patience." FRCL says "submit himself to restraint," SPCL "humble himself." Interpreters differ in regard to **in his youth** (RSV) and "from his youth," which is found in some Hebrew and Greek manuscripts and in the Vulgate. HOTTP supports RSV. This verse may be translated, for example, "It is good for a person to learn to be patient while he is still young."

| 3.28-30 | RSV | TEV |
|---|---|---|

| | RSV | TEV |
|---|---|---|
| 28 | Let him sit alone in silence when he has laid it on him; | 28 When we suffer, we should sit alone in silent patience; |
| 29 | let him put his mouth in the dust— there may yet be hope; | 29 We should bow in submission, for there may still be hope. |
| 30 | let him give his cheek to the smiter, and be filled with insults. | 30 Though beaten and insulted, we should accept it all. |

**3.28** The Hebrew verbs in verses 28-30 are translated by RSV as third person commands in which **let** is followed by **him** plus the verb. TEV has shifted to "we should" in each case. The verbs in Hebrew are in the third person, and so the identity of the person commanded must be taken as "anyone, everyone"; but since "everyone" includes both the poet and his readers or hearers, the inclusive first person plural used by TEV must be seen as very appropriate.

**Sit alone in silence** may need to be translated "sit by himself and keep silent."

**When he has laid it on him**: **he** presumably refers to the LORD, last mentioned in verse 26. **It** refers to the yoke in verse 27, and **him** is the person, the "man" of verse 27, that is, anyone who has been told to sit in silence. However, another interpretation of the verb translated **he has laid** may be "it is heavy" (AB, NEB). In this case the sense is "Let him sit in silence when it (the yoke) is heavy on him." It seems a reflexive meaning is less likely here, and so the Handbook supports RSV. The meaning in RSV is not clear, but it can be made clearer by saying, for example, "When the LORD makes someone suffer, that person should sit alone and be silent." FRCL gives another model: "Let him isolate himself in silence when the LORD tests him."

**3.29** The second command is **put his mouth in the dust**, an expression found nowhere else in the Old Testament. TEV understands this expression to refer to submission, which agrees with many others. Expressions like "grovel" and "kiss the dirt" are found in this same sense in many languages; but in other languages the metaphor alone may not convey the idea without making clear its nonfigurative sense. For example, SPCL says "In humiliation he should kiss the ground . . . ." FRCL has "Let him bow down with his mouth in the dust." In some languages "bow in submission" is translated, for example, "to make yourself low," "to place the heart at the feet of," or "to open one's insides to another."

**There may yet be hope** is similar to Job 11.18. Although many translate like RSV, **hope** may refer to God's helping his people, or to something similar to the "salvation of the LORD" in verse 26. Translators may make this general, as in RSV, or as in FRCL, express what it is that he hopes for: "in the hope that the LORD will intervene."

**3.30** The third command, **give his cheek to the smiter**, recalls Isaiah 50.6: "I gave my back to the smiters, and my cheeks to those who pulled out the beard." See also Job 16.10. This expression is an idiom and will require adjustment in many languages. The sense is to submit, to accept without striking back. (Note also "turn . . . the other cheek," Matt 5.39.) The translator must decide if offering the cheek to the enemy carries the intended meaning, namely, accepting mistreatment and insults. If it does not, and no equivalent saying is available, it is often necessary to say, for example, "He should accept bad treatment and insults."

**3.31-33**         RSV                                    TEV

| | RSV | | TEV |
|---|---|---|---|
| 31 | For the Lord will not cast off forever, | 31 | The Lord is merciful and will not reject us forever. |
| 32 | but, though he cause grief, he will have compassion according to the abundance of his steadfast love; | 32 | He may bring us sorrow, but his love for us is sure and strong. |
| 33 | for he does not willingly afflict or grieve the sons of men. | 33 | He takes no pleasure in causing us grief or pain. |

**3.31** Verse 31 is exceptionally short in Hebrew, and so NEB alters the Hebrew by providing an object for the verb, "his servants." TEV, in line with the verses before this, has a first person plural object. **Cast off forever** requires an object in order to be meaningful. Here we may say, for example, "cast off anyone," or better, "reject anyone." TEV "reject us" in some languages may be rendered "abandon us," "turn his back to us," or "say 'No' to us."

The words "is merciful" are transferred by TEV from verse 32, **will have compassion**, to verse 31.

**3.32** **Though he cause grief**: that is, "He may cause someone to suffer" or ". . . bring people sorrow." The positive side of his character is **he will have compassion**, that is, "He will be merciful." (This is the expression TEV has transferred to verse 31.)

**According to the abundance** must often be expressed as a clause of reason; for example, "because his steadfast love is so great . . ." or "because he loves people so much . . . ." For **steadfast love** see the discussion in verse 22.

**3.33** **He does not willingly afflict** is literally "does not inflict from his heart." FRCL says "It is not from a good heart . . . ." The sense is that God does not wilfully inflict suffering. GECL translates "It gives him no happiness . . . ," and this is similar to TEV "He takes no pleasure in . . . ." We may also translate, for example, "The Lord takes no delight in causing people to suffer."

**Sons of men** refers to people or mankind in general and is rendered by the pronoun "us" in TEV.

| 3.34-36 RSV | TEV |
|---|---|
| 34 To crush under foot<br>all the prisoners of the<br>earth,<br>35 to turn aside the right of a<br>man<br>in the presence of the Most<br>High,<br>36 to subvert a man in his cause,<br>the Lord does not approve. | 34 The Lord knows when our<br>spirits are crushed in<br>prison;<br>35 He knows when we are de-<br>nied the rights he gave us;<br>36 When justice is perverted in<br>court, he knows. |

Verses 34, 35, and 36 each begin with a Hebrew particle prefixed to the verb and translated by RSV as an infinitive form of the verb: **To crush . . . to turn . . . to subvert**. The use of the infinitive form of these verbs as subjects makes an awkward, long sentence in RSV, and the main clause comes only in the second half of verse 36. TEV has modified this structure with finite verbs in 34 and 35: "The Lord knows when . . . He knows when . . . ." Perhaps a better way for many languages is to begin with the main clause and say, for example, "The Lord does not approve when someone crushes . . . turns aside . . . subverts . . . ." If this type of restructuring is followed, the verses should be numbered together as 34-36.

**Approve** in the main clause (verse 36b) translates the Hebrew for "see." Many Old Testament passages speak of the Lord not seeing evil; for example, Psalm 64.5; 94.2-7; Ezekiel 9.9. This expression is literally "the Lord does not see," but this does not agree with the context of a demand for justice. It is also possible and far more likely for this to be taken as a rhetorical question: "Doesn't the Lord see it?" which is to be answered affirmatively. In other words we may say "And the Lord sees it all!" or, employing the negative, "The Lord does not look at it with approval."

The thought being expressed in verses 34-36 concerns God's justice. It is closely related to the idea of God causing grief in verses 32-33. God may bring pain and suffering, but that is not his final purpose. Therefore when prisoners are crushed, God does not approve.

**3.34**    **To crush under foot** in RSV is the first of the three things in these verses of which God does not approve. In some languages it will be more natural to restructure this as a passive; for example, "When all the prisoners of a country are crushed under foot (trampled on) . . . ." In languages in which a passive cannot be used, it may be necessary to use an impersonal subject; for example, "If anyone tramples on all the prisoners . . ." or "If someone mistreats the prisoners . . . ."

**All the prisoners** may also be taken as a collective or as an individual representing prisoners as a group: "any prisoner" (NEB). There are two possible interpretations of these verses: (1) that the reference is to people in general, and that we have here a demand for universal justice; or (2) that the poet is speaking in general terms, but with particular reference to the people of Jerusalem and Judah. The Handbook prefers to believe that the writer's concern is with Jerusalem and Judah, since this is the theme of the entire book.

**Of the earth** is taken by those who interpret the poet as speaking universally to mean in any country, or as NJB has it, "in a country." However, the meaning is more likely to apply to prisoners in Judah. TOB translates "of a country" and defines that in a footnote as Judah. GECL says "in our country."

---

**3.35**    **To turn aside the right of a man: turn aside** translates a verb which, when used with **right** or "justice," means "to violate, deny," that is, "to fail to do justly." NEB has "to deprive a man of his rights," and SPCL "to violate the rights of a man."

**In the presence of the Most High: Most High** is Hebrew *'elyon*, an honorific title for God used many times in the Old Testament, particularly in the Psalms. It describes God as the greatest and most powerful of the gods. See the section entitled "God in Lamentations" in "Translating Lamentations," beginning on page 9 of this Handbook. The translation of this title may be expressed, for example, "God who is above all gods," or "God who is greatest of all."

Verse 35 is translated by FRCL "When someone defies God the Most High by violating the rights of man . . . ," and by NEB "to deprive a man of his rights in defiance of the Most High." We may also say, for example, "When someone takes away the rights people have, and does so right in front of the God who is above all others . . . ."

---

**3.36**    The first half-line of verse 36 is parallel in meaning to the first half-line of verse 35. **Subvert** means to corrupt, pervert, twist. **Man** in the Hebrew is *'adam* and refers to people in general, not just to an adult male, singular or plural. **In his cause: cause** in this context refers to his legal case, or more particularly his court case, lawsuit. Therefore we may translate as in TEV, or say, for example, "When someone prevents justice from being carried out in the court . . ." or "If someone is prevented from getting what is right in his lawsuit . . . ."

For discussion of the second half-line, see the comments on the whole section of verses 34-36 above.

---

**3.37-39**     RSV

37   Who has commanded and it
      came to pass,
     **unless the Lord has ordained
      it?**
38   Is it not from the mouth of the
      Most High
     **that good and evil come?**
39   Why should a living man com-
      plain,
     **a man, about the punish-
      ment of his sins?**

TEV

37   The will of the Lord alone is
      always carried out.[f]
38   Good and evil alike take
      place at his command.
39   Why should we ever com-
      plain when we are pun-
      ished for our sin?[g]

[f] The will . . . out; *or* No one can make anything happen unless the Lord is willing.
[g] Why should . . . sin; *or* Why should we complain about being punished for sin, as long as we are still alive?

**3.37** Verses 37, 38, and 39 are all rhetorical questions in the Hebrew. That is to say, they are questions which do not require an answer in English, and which can be expressed as statements, as in TEV's translation of verses 37 and 38. Because RSV follows the order of the words in Hebrew, verse 37 is awkward English.

As a question we may reformulate verse 37 to say, for example, "Who has said something and made it happen without first the Lord ordering it to happen?" If a reply is required, as in some languages, the answer will be "Nobody!" Many languages find it more natural to translate as a limiting statement; for example, "Only if the Lord is willing can anyone cause something to happen" or "Only if the Lord wants something to happen can anyone make it happen."

TEV gives an alternative translation for verse 37. In the text of TEV the emphasis is upon the positive fulfillment of the "the will of the Lord," and in the footnote it is on the negative aspect of man's ability to achieve anything except with God's help. Most translations agree with the meaning given in the footnote of TEV. Verse 37 is a reference to Psalm 33.9; but the wording of the two verses is more alike in Hebrew than in most modern translations. AB is an exception: "Who was it who 'spoke and it was done'? It was the Lord who gave the command." This fits in with the emphasis in verses 34-36 on God's activity today; but here the reference is to God's activity in creation.

**3.38** **From the mouth of the Most High** means "when God speaks, orders, commands."

**Evil** is to be understood here as in Amos 3.6, "Does evil befall a city . . . ?" in which **evil** is not moral evil but rather "disaster, misfortune, trouble." The wording of both RSV and TEV may seem to say that God is responsible for moral evil. Perhaps a better rendering is NIV, "Is it not from the mouth of the Most High that both calamities and good things come?" The same emphasis is to be found in Isaiah 45.7: "I bring both blessing and disaster. I, the LORD, do all these things" (TEV).

**3.39** This verse marks an important point in the development of the thought of the poet, who began the chapter by describing his suffering in verses 1-20. Verses 21-38 have described God as being good, and now in verse 39 the poet concludes that a person should not complain when he is punished for his sins.

**A living man** is a person who is alive, not dead. In Deuteronomy 30.15 good is associated with life, and evil with death: "I have set before you this day life and good, death and evil." The continued possession of life, being alive, is to be seen as a sign of God's blessing. Therefore the poet asks the question **Why should a living man complain . . . ?** which may also be expressed as "Why should anyone who is alive have reason to complain?" Since death comes to all, those who are still living should not complain but should give thanks.

Hebrew has two words here that are rendered **man** by RSV; however, there is no reason to seek a difference in their meaning. In fact the second may sometimes be translated as a pronoun; for example, FRCL says, "Why should a man complain, if he is still alive . . . ?"

**About the punishment of his sins** is literally "because of his sins." A literal translation is "Why should a man complain about his sins?" But this translation does not suit the context. In Hebrew the action (sin) and its consequence are expressed by the same term. The noun "labor" in such passages as Isaiah 55.2; Job 10.3;

39.11,16 is to be understood not as labor, but rather as "wages, reward received for labor"; in the same way here **sins** is to be understood as the consequences of sin, that is **punishment of his sins**.

TEV, which agrees with RSV, gives an alternative translation in the footnote. In its text TEV implies **living**, although it does not mention it: "Why should we [the living people] ever complain . . . ?" A model translation for verse 39 may be "Why should anyone complain to God because he is punished for the wrong he has done?" or as a statement, "No one should complain when God punishes him for his sins."

| **3.40-41** | RSV | TEV |
|---|---|---|

| | RSV | TEV |
|---|---|---|
| 40 | Let us test and examine our ways, and return to the LORD! | 40 Let us examine our ways and turn back to the LORD. |
| 41 | Let us lift up our hearts and hands to God in heaven: | 41 Let us open our hearts to God in heaven and pray, |

With verse 40 (and continuing to verse 47) begins the first use of the Hebrew first person plural pronouns, and RSV reflects this use. The reference is to the writer and the people of Jerusalem. The general theme in these verses is confession and lament. Verses 40 and 41 are a call to repentance, and verses 42-47 the content of the prayer of confession which the poet and his readers are to pray to God. Translators should note that neither RSV nor TEV show by their punctuation that verse 47 closes the poet's prayer of confession. This is done, however, in NIV by placing closing quotation marks after verse 47. Mft employs both closing quotation marks and white space.

**3.40** **Let us test and examine our ways: Let us** translates a command in the first person plural, which may also be expressed, for example, "We should test . . . ." **Us** refers to the speaker and those he addresses his words to, and so some languages will require the inclusive pronoun. **Test and examine** are words of very similar meaning which TEV and others reduce to a single verb, "Let us examine . . . ." **Our ways** refers to "our way of life," "the way we live," "our conduct." The thought is that by looking closely at our wrong manner of living, that is, our sinful lives, we will see that we should **return to the LORD**. This expression is used many times by the prophets in the sense of repenting of sins. For examples see Hosea 6.1; 7.10; 14.1; Amos 4.6,8-11.

Verse 40 may sometimes be translated "We should examine carefully the way we are living, and we should then repent of our sins to the LORD" or, more idiomatically, "Let us look carefully at the wrong path we have taken, and let us say to the LORD, 'Forgive us the wrong way we have walked.'"

**3.41** In verse 41 the theme of confession is carried forward. **Let us lift up our hearts and hands**: translators do not agree on the meaning of the Hebrew preposition found before the word **hands**. It usually means "to," but it can also mean "along with, together with, in addition to." Accordingly we may translate

94

as in AB: "Let us lift our heart(s) along with our hands." However, Gordis finds a parallel in Joel 2.13, "rend your hearts and not your garments," which suggests we translate "Let us lift up our hearts, and not our hands . . . ." The point is that confession of sin requires sincerity, here symbolized by the inclusion of the heart.

In some languages it is unnatural to say "lift our hearts," as this would be taken only in a literal sense. Therefore it may be necessary to say, for example, as does FRCL, "Let us pray with all our heart, lifting our hands." Even this model may require adjustment; for example, ". . . praying with all sincerity" or ". . . praying with a warm heart." TEV avoids referring to the lifting of either hearts or hands, with "Let us open our hearts to God . . . ."

For **God**, which translates the Hebrew *'el*, see the section entitled "God in Lamentations" in "Translating Lamentations" at the beginning of this Handbook, page 9.

| | | | |
|---|---|---|---|
| **3.42-45** | RSV | | TEV |

| | RSV | | | TEV |
|---|---|---|---|---|
| 42 | "We have transgressed and rebelled<br>and thou hast not forgiven. | | 42 | "We have sinned and re-<br>belled, and you, O LORD,<br>have not forgiven us. |
| 43 | "Thou hast wrapped thyself<br>with anger and pursued<br>us,<br>slaying without pity; | | 43 | "You pursued us and killed us;<br>your mercy was hidden by<br>your anger, |
| 44 | thou hast wrapped thyself with<br>a cloud<br>so that no prayer can pass<br>through. | | 44 | By a cloud of fury too thick<br>for our prayers to get<br>through. |
| 45 | Thou hast made us offscouring<br>and refuse<br>among the peoples. | | 45 | You have made us the gar-<br>bage dump of the world. |

**3.42** The call to repentance in verses 40-41 now becomes a prayer of confession addressed to God. Verse 42 shows the comparison between what Israel has done and what God has done or failed to do in response to his people's deeds.

**We have transgressed and rebelled**: for **transgressed** see the discussion of "transgressions" in 1.5. For **rebelled** see the discussion at 1.18.

**Forgiven** translates a Hebrew word for which God is always the actor, the one who forgives his people. The central element in the meaning is the removal of the wrong behavior (disobedience) and the subsequent establishment of a right relationship between God and the people.

**Transgressed and rebelled** may be rendered in some languages, for example, as "We have sinned and made our hearts hard toward God" or "We have done evil things and said 'No' to God." **Forgiven** is expressed in idiomatic forms in some languages; for example, "healed the neck," "caused the heart to soften," "handed back someone's sins to him," or "thrown away someone's evil."

**3.43**    **Wrapped thyself with anger** is a picturable metaphor. In similar terms the mountain is "wrapped in darkness" in Deuteronomy 4.11, while Ezekiel 7.27 has "wrapped in despair," and Psalm 109.29 says "wrapped in . . . shame." **Wrapped** in the sense of "cover" is taken by Mft to refer to a veil: "thou hast veiled thy face in anger." This is ambiguous, meaning either "because of anger" or "with a covering of anger." A better sense is expressed in SPCL, "You surround us with your anger." In languages which cannot follow the figure of being wrapped in an abstract expression such as anger, it may be possible to follow SPCL, or to say, for example, "All around us we see that you are angry" or "Everywhere we turn we find that you are angry." In some languages it may be necessary to translate verse 43, for example, as "You have been angry, and so you chased us and killed us, and you have had no pity on us."

     **Slaying without pity: slaying** translates a different Hebrew verb than that used in the similar expression in 2.21; however, the two verbs mean the same. **Without pity** is the same in Hebrew as "without mercy" in 2.2 and 2.21. See there for comments.

**3.44**    In **wrapped thyself with a cloud, wrapped** translates the same verb used in the previous verse. The poet uses the expression "wrapped thyself with a cloud" as a description of God as the one who is present but hidden. TEV takes **cloud** to mean "cloud of fury," so that it becomes parallel to "hidden by your anger" in verse 43. However, the poet may well have been thinking in terms of the cloud in which God accompanied Israel in the wilderness, but which has now become an obstacle between him and his people's prayers rather than a sign of his presence. It is characteristic of Lamentations that prayer is only mentioned in order to refer to its ineffectiveness.

     We may take **wrapped . . . with anger** and **wrapped . . . with a cloud** to refer to God's remoteness. In that case this may be expressed in nonfigurative terms; for example, "Because you were angry you hid yourself" and ". . . you kept yourself far from us." Because the interpretation of these figures differs so much in translations, translators may wish to follow the model of a major language in their own area.

     **So that no prayer can pass through** may also be rendered, for example, "so that you will not hear our prayers," "so that you will not hear us when we pray to you," or ". . . when we call on you to help us."

**3.45**    **Offscouring and refuse**: these two words in their Hebrew forms occur nowhere else in the Old Testament. The first seems to mean "what is scraped off," and the second "what is rejected." So the two together suggest something dirty and useless that is scraped off and thrown away. The writer of 1 Corinthians 4.13 does not use the wording used in verse 45 by the Septuagint, but his description of the apostles as "the refuse of the world, the offscouring of all things" clearly echoes this description of the people of Jerusalem.

     **Among the peoples** refers to the other nations, probably those surrounding Israel. In most areas where there are large cities and smoldering refuse dumps, the translation of **offscouring and refuse** may not be difficult. In remote areas unfamiliar with such things, the idea may be less well known. However, we may sometimes say, for example, "You have made us like dirt scraped from our feet" or

"You have made us like a pile of dung." In nonfigurative language we may say "Everyone has seen how much you have humiliated us."

| 3.46-47 | RSV | | TEV |
|---|---|---|---|
| 46 | "All our enemies rail against us; | 46 | "We are insulted and mocked by all our enemies. |
| 47 | panic and pitfall have come upon us, devastation and destruction; | 47 | We have been through disaster and ruin; we live in danger and fear. |

**3.46** Verses 46 and 47 bring the prayer of confession to a close. The wording of verse 46 is essentially the same as that of 2.16. See there for discussion.

**3.47** **Panic and pitfall** begin with the same initial consonants in Hebrew, just as they do in English. The words mean "fear and the pit." **Pitfall** refers to a hole dug in the ground as a trap to catch something. Its opening is lightly covered over so that the hole will not be seen, and any person or animal stepping on it will fall through and be caught. For similar combinations as here see Job 22.10; Isaiah 24.17-18; Jeremiah 48.43. **Have come upon us** is literally "is to us," and the full sense is well expressed by TEV "We have been through disaster and ruin." We may also translate, for example, "We have suffered from fear and terror."

The second pair of words, which also begin with the same letter and sound somewhat alike in Hebrew, are translated **devastation and destruction**. Translators may be able to retain something of the poetic effect through the use of words beginning or ending with similar letters or tones, or through the use of other poetic devices in their own languages. It will often be necessary to express the nouns used in RSV and TEV as verb phrases; for example, "Our enemies have devastated and ruined us, and have killed us and destroyed all the things we had."

| 3.48-51 | RSV | | TEV |
|---|---|---|---|
| 48 | my eyes flow with rivers of tears because of the destruction of the daughter of my people. | 48 | My eyes flow with rivers of tears at the destruction of my people. |
| 49 | "My eyes will flow without ceasing, without respite, | 49 | "My tears will pour out in a ceaseless stream |
| 50 | until the LORD from heaven looks down and sees; | 50 | Until the LORD looks down from heaven and sees us. |
| 51 | my eyes cause me grief at the fate of all the maidens of my city. | 51 | My heart is grieved when I see what has happened to the women of the city. |

In verses 48-51 the poet's point of view changes as he draws attention to his own grief and pain at the destruction of his people. From verse 48 to 63 the pronouns will be "I" and "me," as they were in verses 1-24. See outline at the beginning of chapter 3, page 72. Translators may wish to insert blank space before verse 48 to show that a new division in the text is beginning.

**3.48** **My eyes flow with rivers of tears** is similar to part of the first unit of 1.16. See there for comments. In translation it may be helpful to shift to the use of a simile in this verse and say, for example, "I cry and tears flow from my eyes as a river flows with water."

The reason for the poet's weeping is the **destruction of the daughter of my people**; this expression occurs also in 2.11. In some languages it will be necessary to place the cause for the weeping at the beginning; for example, "My people have been killed, and this makes tears flow like a river from my eyes."

**3.49** In this stanza verses 49 and 51 have **my eyes**, and verse 50 has **the LORD . . . sees**.

The thought of verse 49 is parallel in meaning and partly parallel in form to the first half of verse 48. **My eyes** is singular in the Hebrew, "my eye," but this need not be followed literally. TEV switches to "my tears."

The word which RSV translates **without** in the second half of verse 49 usually means "for lack of," so NEB alters it to a verb meaning "refuse": "and refuse all comfort." But here the word is better taken as an emphatic form of the negative, "without stopping," and no change in the text is necessary.

TEV "ceaseless stream" is equivalent to the double expression in RSV **without ceasing, without respite**, which follows the Hebrew formally. The Hebrew for **respite** not only means rest from distress but includes the idea of numbness as part of the relief from feeling pain or distress.

**3.50** **Until the LORD from heaven looks down and sees** gives the conditions for the poet to cease weeping. As in Psalm 2.4, **heaven** is said to be the dwelling place of the LORD. **Looks down and sees** is the literal form which will require in some languages to say what the LORD sees, that is, "sees us," or "sees his people," or "sees how his people are suffering."

**3.51** **My eyes** is, as in verse 48, literally "my eye," but most translate as a plural. NEB and others change the Hebrew slightly to get "my affliction," which is placed in verse 50 as the thing God sees.

The Hebrew for **my eyes cause me grief** is literally "my eye torments my soul," where "my soul" equals "me." However, NEB and others alter the Hebrew to get "the LORD torments me." HOTTP supports the unaltered text, which RSV follows. TEV has switched to another organ of the body, "My heart is grieved," which is more natural for English.

There is no verb in the Hebrew of verse 51 which means "see." The form of the Hebrew text may not seem to be a very natural way of expressing the intended meaning, but it must be remembered that the poet was restricted not only by the number of words he could use in a verse, but also by the need to begin each verse with a particular letter of the Hebrew alphabet.

**At the fate** is supplied by RSV, as the literal expression is "My eye torments my soul from all the daughters of my city," and this does not make very clear sense. TEV, however, is clearer with "When I see what has happened to . . . ." **Maidens of my city** translates the Hebrew for "daughters of my city." This expression is unusual. It could well have been used here based on the analogy of the expression "daughter of Jerusalem," though that is more often in the singular, referring either to the city itself or to all its people. If the reference is to women only, the text does not make clear what may have happened to them. But it is just as possible that it refers to the general destruction of the city and its people, as mentioned in verse 48. We may translate, for example, ". . . when I see what the enemies have done to the people of Jerusalem" or ". . . when I see how the enemies of Jerusalem have destroyed the city."

| 3.52-54 | RSV | TEV |
|---|---|---|
| 52 | "I have been hunted like a bird by those who were my enemies without cause; | 52 "I was trapped like a bird by enemies who had no cause to hate me. |
| 53 | they flung me alive into the pit and cast stones on me; | 53 They threw me alive into a pit and closed the opening with a stone. |
| 54 | water closed over my head; I said, 'I am lost.' | 54 Water began to close over me, and I thought death was near. |

**3.52** With verse 52 the lament begins again; however, in contrast to verses 46-47, the poet now speaks in the singular.

**Hunted like a bird** is a common image for a lament found, for example, in Psalm 11.1; 124.7; 140.5c; Jeremiah 16.16. Here, as in Psalm 35.19 and 69.4, the poet complains that his enemies had no reason for hating him. In some languages it will be necessary to shift **I have been hunted like a bird** from the passive to an active construction; for example, "My enemies have trapped me like a bird."

In some languages it will be necessary to make a separate sentence of "who had no cause to hate me" (TEV). For example, "My enemies trapped me like a bird; they had no reason to hate me." It may also be possible to begin with a limiting phrase; for example, "Without any reason my enemies captured me as they capture a bird."

**3.53** From the picture of the hunted bird in verse 52, the poet now turns to the image of an animal that falls into a pit. He is probably not so much emphasizing the idea that he was **alive** when he fell into the pit, as that the intention of his enemies was to bring his life to an end. SPCL expresses this well with "They buried me alive in a well."

**They cast stones on me** depicts the enemies throwing down stones on the trapped victim. However, since the word **stones** is singular in Hebrew, many understand the expression to refer to covering the opening of the pit or well with a large stone to prevent his escape. For example, NEB says "They closed it over me with a stone." Since either translation is acceptable, translators may wish to give the alternate rendering in a footnote, as FRCL does.

**3.54** This verse gives a picture of a drowning man and closely resembles the prayer in Jonah 2.3-5. **Water closed over my head** means that the water rose above the trapped person's head.

**I said** indicates that what follows is what the person thought or how he felt. Accordingly TEV has "I thought death was near." We may also say, for example, "I thought to myself, 'I am about to die.'" **I am lost** translates the verb "to cut" and means the person is now cut off from air to breathe, and so from life. This may also be expressed "I am drowning."

**3.55-57**

| RSV | TEV |
|---|---|
| 55 "I called on thy name, O LORD, from the depths of the pit; | 55 "From the bottom of the pit, O LORD, I cried out to you, |
| 56 thou didst hear my plea, 'Do not close thine ear to my cry for help!'*m* | 56 And when I begged you to listen to my cry, you heard. |
| 57 Thou didst come near when I called on thee; thou didst say, 'Do not fear!' | 57 You answered me and told me not to be afraid. |

*m* Heb uncertain

**3.55** The language of the sufferer continues along the same lines as in Psalm 130.1-2, where the psalmist appeals to God from "out of the depths" of his despair. **Called on thy name** is a common Old Testament expression meaning "cried out, implored, asked for help." **Thy name** is the equivalent of "to you," and so TEV has "I cried out to you"; alternatively we may say "I cried out to you for help" or "I cried out, 'LORD, help me.'" See also Genesis 4.26; 12.8; 26.25; Isaiah 12.4; 65.1.

**Depths of the pit: pit** translates the same word used in verse 53. However, here the word refers not to a trap for animals but rather to the place of the dead, as in Psalm 88.6, and this is sometimes translated "the grave" or "burial place." Verse 55 may be expressed, for example, "From the bottom of the grave I called to you, LORD," "From the deepest hole, LORD, I called out to you for help," or "From the bottom of the pit I cried out 'LORD, help me.'"

**3.56** Translators will notice some differences between versions in the translation of verse 56. For example RSV, **thou didst hear my plea**, along with NEB, TEV, NJB, translates the verb as a past event. On the other hand NJV, SPCL, GECL, and others translate as an imperative, "Hear my plea." As an imperative a closer formal parallel is made with the second clause. **Hear** in the first clause is not an imperative in Hebrew but a perfect, "You heard," and so RSV is preferred.

Most translations, including RSV and NIV, translate the second part of the verse as direct speech, quoting the words of the sufferer's prayer. The Hebrew does not use quotation marks to distinguish direct speech from indirect, so the second part of the verse can also be translated in indirect speech as in TEV, or as "You heard me when I asked you not to turn a deaf ear to my appeal."

In regard to the second half of the verse, the RSV footnote shows the Hebrew to be uncertain. This part seems to say "Do not hide your ear to my relief, to my cry for help." RSV, following the Septuagint, has dropped "to my relief." NJV retains both expressions in the form of "to my groan, to my cry." The second of these two words is used several times in the Book of Psalms, but the first word only occurs here and in Exodus 8.15, where it means "relief, breathing space." Such a meaning is unsuitable here, as can be seen by the difference between NEB's translation, "Do not turn a deaf ear when I cry, 'Come to my relief,'" and the literal meaning given in an NEB footnote, "Do not turn a deaf ear to my relief, to my cry." (This footnote no longer appears in recent printings of NEB.) According to HOTTP, "to my relief" may also mean "to my breathing." Accordingly HOTTP proposes translating "Do not close your ear to my breathing." If "breathing" is to be taken in the sense of sighing, groaning (Vulgate translates "from my groaning"), we may say with FRCL "You have heard me cry out to you: 'Do not close your ears to my sighs and to my cries.'" This seems to be a satisfactory model for translation.

**3.57** By the time verse 57 is spoken, the poet has regained his confidence that God has heard him, and he is no longer conscious of a barrier blocking his prayers, as he was in verse 44.

**Thou didst come near: come near** translates a verb meaning approach, advance, and so suggests coming close in distance or space from the speaker's point of view. A parallel usage is found in Psalm 145.18: "The LORD is near to all who call upon him." TEV translates "You answered me," which gives the meaning. **When** translates what is literally "in the day."

Most translations accept **Do not fear** as direct address. In verses 56 and 57, as at many other places where direct discourse may be used, the translator must decide if direct or indirect speech is the more natural. Some languages, particularly with verbs of communication, show a preference for direct speech. Where the language accepts both, the translator must decide which form is better, on the basis of style and impact on the reader.

| **3.58-60** RSV | TEV |
|---|---|
| 58 "Thou hast taken up my cause, O Lord, thou hast redeemed my life. | 58 "You came to my rescue, Lord, and saved my life. |
| 59 Thou hast seen the wrong done to me, O LORD; judge thou my cause. | 59 Judge in my favor; you know the wrongs done against me. |
| 60 Thou hast seen all their vengeance, all their devices against me. | 60 You know how my enemies hate me and how they plot against me. |

**3.58** **Taken up my cause** is literally "the cause (case) of my soul." The legal language in this verse is well represented in translations such as FRCL "Lord, you have pleaded in my favor," and TOB "Lord, you plead my defense in a trial." In other words, the sufferer thanks the Lord for being his advocate in a legal dispute in which his life was in danger. In some languages it is possible to retain the law-court image suggested in the original. It appears here that the poet is appealing to God to serve as his defense as well as his judge. This is because he is sure he has done no wrong. If legal language is not used to translate this passage, the translator may use more general terms and say, for example, "You have defended me in my fight, Lord," or as a command, "Defend me in my struggle, Lord."

**Redeemed my life** or "saved my life" may sometimes require some modification, since in some languages it is not the life but the person bearing the life that is saved; for example, "you saved me," "you rescued me," or idiomatically, "you handed me back my breath."

**3.59** The language of the law-court continues into verse 59, which TEV opens with "Judge in my favor." The Hebrew verb here is an imperative, but NEB follows the Septuagint in making the wording of this verse parallel to the wording of verse 58: "and gavest judgment in my favour." However, parallelism with the previous verse is not a strong enough argument for altering the Hebrew text, which leads on appropriately to the remaining verses of the chapter with their appeal to God for justice.

**The wrong done to me** is passive and may need to be expressed in an active form; for example, "LORD, you have seen the wrongs my enemies have done to me" or ". . . you have seen how my enemies have wronged me."

**Judge thou my cause**: **judge** is a command, although, for the sake of parallelism with verse 58, NEB translates "and gavest judgment in my favour." It is best, however, to follow the Hebrew text along with RSV and TEV "Judge in my favor"; this may also be rendered "Give me justice" or "Do what is right for me."

In some cases it is necessary to make clear the reason the poet is asking God to be his judge; that is, because God knows how he has been injured unjustly by his enemies. This may be expressed as, for example, "My enemies have done many evil things to me. So now, LORD, decide my case and show that I am right."

**3.60** **Seen all their vengeance**: **their** refers to the poet's enemies, who are also the unnamed opponents in verses 58 and 59. **Vengeance** refers to repaying harm to someone who has supposedly committed an injustice. In this case **their vengeance** refers to the vengeful acts committed by the poet's enemies to get even with him, to repay him for his evil. This explanation no doubt says more than the writer intends to say, since he believes that he has not committed evil against them; accordingly NJB and the New American Bible (NAB) translate "their vindictiveness," which means "their desire to get revenge." SPCL says the same with "their desires for vengeance." NJV says still more generally "their malice."

**Their devices against me**: **devices** translates a word meaning "plans, schemes, plots." Such **devices** are secretive and have harmful consequences. The same word is used in Job 5.12; Isaiah 65.2; Jeremiah 6.19. In some cases this expression may be rendered, for example, "You know all their secret plans to harm me" or "You know all their secret plans to get revenge and to harm me."

RSV                                    TEV

61    "Thou hast heard their taunts,          61    "You have heard them insult
          O LORD,                                       me, O LORD; you know all
      all their devices against me.                  their plots.
62    The lips and thoughts of my             62    All day long they talk about
          assailants                                   me and make their plans.
      are against me all the day             63    From morning till night they
          long.                                        make fun of me.
63    Behold their sitting and their
          rising;
      I am the burden of their
          songs.

**3.61**    Verse 61 is closely parallel in meaning to verse 60. In verse 60 God has
            seen what the enemies of the sufferer have done, and in verse 61 he has
heard their insults. The second half of each verse is almost identical in its reference
to the plots which they are making against him.

What the LORD has heard are the **taunts** of the poet's enemies. **Taunts**
translates a word meaning "insults, mockery, ridicule." These are words or
expressions shouted out to insult the poet.

**All their devices** repeats the second half of verse 60. Here the LORD has
heard these harmful schemes that are planned in secret.

**3.62**    This verse summarizes the content of verses 59-61.
            **The lips** is a poetic way of referring to what comes out of the enemies'
mouth. This refers to their harmful talk, which SPCL calls "gossip" or "empty talk."
NJB has "the whispering and murmuring," NIV "what my enemies whisper and mutter
against me."

**Against me all day long** represents the literal Hebrew wording; this is
expressed in the same manner by TEV but is placed before the main clause.

**3.63**    **Behold** (as in 1.18) is a plea addressed to the LORD, meaning "Look and
            see." **Their sitting and their rising** is a figure of speech, which emphasiz-
es the totality of their activities. The thought is similarly expressed in Deuteronomy
6.7 ". . . when you sit . . . and when you walk . . . when you lie down and when you
rise." The sense is "all the time, no matter what you are doing, anytime, day or
night." TEV "From morning to night" means "all the time."

For **burden of their songs** see 3.14.

3.64-66    RSV                                    TEV

64    "Thou wilt requite them, O              64    "Punish them for what they
          LORD,                                         have done, O LORD;
      according to the work of               65    Curse them and fill them
          their hands.                                 with despair!
65    Thou wilt give them dullness of        66    Hunt them down and wipe

heart;
thy curse will be on them.

66   Thou wilt pursue them in anger and destroy them
from under thy heavens, O
LORD."[n]

them off the earth!"

[n] Syr Compare Gk Vg: Heb *the heavens of the LORD*

Verses 64-66 form the conclusion of chapter 3, in which the poet expresses his assurance that God will destroy his enemies (**Thou wilt . . .**). These concluding verses are more outspoken in their desire for vengeance than anything that has gone before.

Translators will notice that the verbs in verses 64-66 are translated in various ways. In the Hebrew these verbs are in the imperfect, which is normally translated in English as the present or future tense. However, when used in the context of a prayer or supplication, they can express a plea or request and so are frequently translated as imperatives. Therefore TEV, NJB, NEB, NIV, NJV, GECL, and SPCL translate them as imperatives, while RSV, FRCL, Mft, and TOB translate as future tense. Unless a future tense carries the sense of prayer or plea in the translators' language, the Handbook recommends following TEV.

| **3.64** |

In verse 64 the poet asks God to pay back his enemies in proportion to what they have done to him. **Requite** means repay, give back harm for harm received, take vengeance. The idea is also expressed in Psalm 28.4, "Requite them according to their work, and according to the evil of their deeds; requite them according to the work of their hands . . . ." TEV "punish" fails to express the revenge motive which is in the poet's words.

**According to the work of their hands** means "as they deserve, in proportion to what they have done," and in this case this means what they have done to the poet. We may also translate, for example, "Make them suffer in the way they made me suffer."

| **3.65** |

**Dullness of heart**: **dullness** translates a word that occurs only here in the Old Testament; its meaning is therefore uncertain. Scholars have attempted to find a word in Hebrew or some other language, such as Arabic, that it may be related to, but there has been little success. Translators for their part have tried to come up with something that fits the context: TEV has "fill them with despair," which is a reasonable attempt. NIV, appealing to a verb meaning "cover," which has the same consonants, translates "Put a veil over their hearts," but this can mean almost anything. NJB has "Lay hardness of heart," and NEB "Show them how hard thy heart can be." Since nothing really better is available, translators are advised to follow TEV or RSV.

In the entire Old Testament RSV uses the word **curse** to translate ten different Hebrew words. The one used here, like **dullness** above, is found nowhere else in the Old Testament. However, translators are generally agreed on the use of the word **curse** in this case, except for NEB, which has "Show . . . how little concern thou hast for them." No explanation is given for this rendering. Translators are again advised to follow RSV and TEV.

A curse normally involves calling on a supernatural being or force to bring about the effects of the spoken curse. From the content of verse 66 there can be no doubt what the object of the curse is. If a verb form for **curse** is not available, we may sometimes say, for example, "Cause evil to happen to them" or "Speak harmful words to them and punish them."

**3.66** The poet now reaches a climax in vengeful desire in his plea to God to destroy his enemies.

**Pursue them in anger** echoes the thought of verse 43. See there for comments. **Pursue** means to chase or follow with the purpose of capturing or killing. God is to do this **in anger**. So the sense is "Chase them with anger," "In your anger go after them," "Angrily chase them," ". . . hunt them down." Hebrew is exceedingly rich in words related to the idea of destruction, and here RSV translates one of them. They are to be killed, eliminated, done away with, or in the words of TEV, "wipe them off the earth!"

In some languages it will be clearer to translate **pursue them . . . and destroy them** as, for example, "Hunt them like animals and kill them" or "Chase them like a hunter chases an animal and then kill them."

**From under thy heavens, O LORD** is literally "from under the heavens of the LORD." RSV, as its footnote shows, has followed the ancient Syriac version. This expression has three variants in Hebrew manuscripts. The one recommended by HOTTP is the literal form cited above, to which it gives a "B" rating. RSV translates a second alternative, and a third is "from under your heavens." As a prayer addressed to the LORD, the literal form sounds strange, whereas the wording of RSV, and NEB "from beneath thy heavens, O LORD," is more suitable in the context. TEV and others take the expression to refer to the whole world; so SPCL has "Make them disappear from the world," and FRCL "You will eliminate them from the earth." All of these are suitable models for translating.

# Chapter 4

In the Hebrew Bible the line arrangement in chapter 4 is different from that in the previous chapters. Here each verse has only two lines or units, and each line has two parts or half-lines. In some verses each set of half-lines displays parallelism, so that the first half of the verse has its own parallelism and the second half another.

There are again twenty-two verses, and the first word of each verse begins with the successive letter of the Hebrew alphabet.

The themes of chapter 4 do not serve to structure the chapter in any balanced way. The first two verses speak of Jerusalem's former wealth and compare its people to gold, but describe them now as only clay pots. Verses 3-10 describe the starvation of the people and conclude this unit with the picture of women boiling their own children for food. In verses 11-16 the poet turns his attention to the cause of Jerusalem's collapse. Like a mark of parenthesis, verse 11 opens by saying it is the Lord's anger which has brought Jerusalem to her knees, and verse 16, like a second mark of parenthesis, closes this section by repeating the same thing. That such a calamity could ever happen was beyond belief, and verse 13 states that the prophets and priests are at fault.

Verse 17 is a reminder that Jerusalem sought in vain for allies to help her. Verses 18-20 speak of the pursuit of the people of Jerusalem by their enemies, and verse 20 bemoans the loss of the king as a leader of the people—most likely a reference to King Zedekiah. The closing two verses stand as a warning to Edom and Uz that their punishment is still to come.

## 4.1-22

| RSV | TEV |
|---|---|
| | *Jerusalem after Its Fall* |

| | RSV | | TEV |
|---|---|---|---|
| 1 | How the gold has grown dim, how the pure gold is changed! The holy stones lie scattered at the head of every street. | 1 | Our glittering gold has grown dull; the stones of the Temple lie scattered in the streets. |
| 2 | The precious sons of Zion, worth their weight in fine gold, how they are reckoned as earthen pots, the work of a potter's hands! | 2 | Zion's young men were as precious to us as gold, but now they are treated like common clay pots. |
| 3 | Even the jackals give the breast and suckle their young, but the daughter of my people has become cruel, like the ostriches in the wilderness. | 3 | Even a mother wolf will nurse her cubs, but my people are like ostriches, cruel to their young. |
| | | 4 | They let their babies die of hunger and thirst; |

106

4 The tongue of the nursling cleaves
   to the roof of its mouth for thirst;
the children beg for food,
   but no one gives to them.

5 Those who feasted on dainties
   perish in the streets;
those who were brought up in purple
   lie on ash heaps.

6 For the chastisement of the daughter of
   my people has been greater
   than the punishment of Sodom,
which was overthrown in a moment,
   no hand being laid on it.

7 Her princes were purer than snow,
   whiter than milk;
their bodies were more ruddy than coral,
   the beauty of their form was like sapphire.

8 Now their visage is blacker than soot,
   they are not recognized in the streets;
their skin has shriveled upon their bones,
   it has become as dry as wood.

9 Happier were the victims of the sword
   than the victims of hunger,
who pined away, stricken
   by want of the fruits of the field.

10 The hands of compassionate women
   have boiled their own children;
they became their food
   in the destruction of the daughter of
   my people.

11 The LORD gave full vent to his wrath,
   he poured out his hot anger;
and he kindled a fire in Zion,
   which consumed its foundations.

12 The kings of the earth did not believe,
   or any of the inhabitants of the world,
that foe or enemy could enter
   the gates of Jerusalem.

13 This was for the sins of her prophets
   and the iniquities of her priests,
who shed in the midst of her
   the blood of the righteous.

14 They wandered, blind, through the
   streets,
   so defiled with blood
that none could touch
   their garments.

children are begging for food that no
   one will give them.

5 People who once ate the finest foods die
   starving in the streets;
those raised in luxury are pawing
   through garbage for food.

6 My people have been punished even more
   than the inhabitants of Sodom,
which met a sudden downfall at the
   hands of God.

7 Our princes were undefiled and pure as
   snow,
vigorous and strong, glowing with
   health.

8 Now they lie unknown in the streets. their
   faces blackened in death;
their skin, dry as wood, has shriveled
   on their bones.

9 Those who died in the war
   were better off than those who died
   later,
who starved slowly to death, with no
   food to keep them alive.

10 The disaster that came to my people
   brought horror;
loving mothers boiled their own children for food.

11 The LORD turned loose the full force of
   his fury;
he lit a fire in Zion that burned it to
   the ground.

12 No one anywhere, not even rulers of
   foreign nations,
believed that any invader could enter
   Jerusalem's gates.

13 But it happened, because her prophets
   sinned and her priests were causing
   the death of innocent people.

14 Her leaders wandered through the streets
   like blind men,
so stained with blood that no one
   would touch them.

15 "Get away!" people shouted. "You're
   defiled! Don't touch me!"
So they wandered from nation to nation, welcomed by no one.

15 "Away! Unclean!" men cried at them;
      "Away! Away! Touch not!"
   So they became fugitives and wanderers;
      men said among the nations,
   "They shall stay with us no longer."

16 The LORD himself has scattered them,
      he will regard them no more;
   no honor was shown to the priests,
      no favor to the elders.

17 Our eyes failed, ever watching
      vainly for help;
   in our watching we watched
      for a nation which could not save.

18 Men dogged our steps
      so that we could not walk in our
         streets;
   our end drew near; our days were num-
         bered;
      for our end had come.

19 Our pursuers were swifter
      than the vultures in the heavens;
   they chased us on the mountains,
      they lay in wait for us in the wilder-
         ness.

20 The breath of our nostrils, the LORD's
         anointed,
      was taken in their pits,
   he of whom we said, "Under his shadow
      we shall live among the nations."

21 Rejoice and be glad, O daughter of
         Edom,
      dweller in the land of Uz;
   but to you also the cup shall pass;
      you shall become drunk and strip your-
         self bare.

22 The punishment of your iniquity,
      O daughter of Zion, is accomplished,
      he will keep you in exile no longer;
   but your iniquity, O daughter of Edom,
      he will punish,
   he will uncover your sins.

16 The LORD had no more concern for
      them; he scattered them himself.
   He showed no regard for our priests
      and leaders.

17 For help that never came we looked until
      we could look no longer.
   We kept waiting for help from a na-
      tion that had none to give.

18 The enemy was watching for us; we could
      not even walk in the streets.
   Our days were over; the end had
      come.

19 Swifter than eagles swooping from the
      sky, they chased us down.
   They tracked us down in the hills; they
      took us by surprise in the desert.

20 They captured the source of our life, the
      king the LORD had chosen,
   the one we had trusted to protect us
      from every invader.

21 Laugh on, people of Edom and Uz; be
      glad while you can.
   Your disaster is coming too; you too
      will stagger naked in shame.

22 Zion has paid for her sin; the LORD will
      not keep us in exile any longer.
   But Edom, the LORD will punish you;
      he will expose your guilty acts.

## Section Heading

TEV's heading "Jerusalem after Its Fall" may need to be expressed differently in other languages to say, for example, "How Jerusalem was after the enemy conquered it," "The suffering of the people of Jerusalem after it was captured," "The final days of Jerusalem," or "How the people suffered in the last days of Jerusalem." Some other headings are: "The fourth lamentation" (NJB), "The horrors of the siege of Jerusalem" (FRCL), "Fourth lament" (SPCL), "The terror of the siege" (GECL).

**4.1**     RSV                              TEV

How the gold has grown dim,          Our glittering gold has grown
  how the pure gold is changed!        dull;
The holy stones lie scattered          the stones of the Temple lie
  at the head of every street.          scattered in the streets.

The first word of this chapter, as in chapters 1 and 2, is the Hebrew exclamatory word meaning "How . . . !" It introduces a contrast between the past and the present. The contrast is between the dullness of the **gold** in the present (after the fall of the city) and the way the gold appeared before. **Gold**, as verse 2 shows, is a poetic image standing for the people of Jerusalem.

**The gold has grown dim** is a problematic statement, if taken literally. **Gold** does not tarnish or darken, and is normally used in the Old Testament as a picture of the value of something. Therefore some scholars alter the word translated **has grown dim** to get "is despised." In the second line of RSV the word translated **is changed** is modified by changing one letter to get "is hated." However, poetry is not always guided by concern for factual statements, and nothing much is gained by changing the text to get a statement that may be more factual. The poet is using gold as a comparison to the very great worth of the young men of Jerusalem, as will become evident in verse 2. FRCL attempts to avoid the statement that gold tarnishes, by shifting to a question: "How can gold that is so brilliant, the metal that is so lovely, become tarnished?" TOB is similar. The Hebrew syntax does not support a question in verse 1, and so it is best to follow RSV. The first two half-lines are very closely parallel in meaning.

There are two Hebrew words translated **gold**. The second is a literary form meaning the same as the first, and is often translated "pure or fine gold." In Hebrew the adjective translated **pure** is "good." See also Job 31.24. The use of **pure gold** in the second half-line raises the poetic impact through the use of a literary-level word. Rather than mentioning two qualities of gold, TEV has "our glittering gold," which is an attempt to relate the image **gold** to "Zion's young men" in verse 2.

For translation **gold** is so widely known that translators have little trouble with the word. However, in some areas a borrowed word must be used. **Grown dim** may be translated "lost its brightness" or "is no longer bright to look at." In some cases one verb will be sufficient. If, however, the translator keeps the two parallel structures, we may say, for example, "dulled" in the first half-line and "tarnished" or "darkened" in the second. GECL says "Oh, how the gold has become dark, and the pure gold has lost its glitter."

These translations, however, do not make it clear that the poet is using **gold** as a reference to the value or worth of the people of Jerusalem, and the comparison may be lost unless some adaptation is made. One way to do this is to use a simile and say, for example, "Our young men are now as gold that has little value, as pure gold that has become worthless."

**Holy stones** is a literal translation, but it does not indicate what the poet has in mind. TEV "stones of the Temple" presumably means the stones from which the Temple was built; but if this is the meaning, we would expect to find a definite article before the Hebrew word for **holy**, making it refer to the Temple. NEB's translation agrees with that of TEV, but an alternative is offered in the footnote, "Bright gems." The verb which TEV translates "lie scattered" is more suited to the second of these meanings, or to the translation of this unit in NJV, "The sacred gems are spilled at every street corner." The poet may be thinking of the jewels forming part of the priestly garments, such as are listed in Exodus 28.17-20. On the other hand, the translation in the footnote of NEB is based on the view that the Hebrew expression used here is a general term for jewelry, unconnected with the Temple. This would continue the thought of the first unit, which speaks of **gold** but does not connect it with the Temple.

**Holy stones**, if rendered literally, will have little meaning in many languages, and so some adjustment is required. If the translator follows TEV, "stones of the Temple" could imply that these are merely stones associated with the Temple, but not necessarily the stones with which it was built. In order to make it clear that these are the stones from the destroyed Temple, it may be necessary to say, for example, "the stones remaining after the Temple was torn down" or "the stones from the walls of the Temple."

The **holy stones**, like **gold** in the first half of this verse, reinforce the comparison of the worth and even the sacredness of the people they represent poetically. Just as the stones of the Temple have been scattered, so have the young men of Jerusalem. In translation we may make this clear by translating the second half of the verse, for example, "They (the young men in the simile in the first half) are like the sacred stones of the Temple that now lie scattered in the streets."

For a discussion of **at the head of every street**, see 2.19.

<br>

**4.2**

| RSV | TEV |
|---|---|
| The precious sons of Zion,<br>    worth their weight in fine gold,<br>how they are reckoned as<br>    earthen pots,<br>    the work of a potter's hands! | Zion's young men were as precious to us as gold,<br>but now they are treated like common clay pots. |

This verse explains the underlying meaning of verse 1. In verse 1 there is a double contrast between bright and dull gold and between stones that were once precious but are now treated as worthless. The contrast in verse 2 is between the precious young men who once lived in Jerusalem and the common clay pots they now resemble. And so verse 2 makes clear the way "gold" and "stones" are used in verse 1.

**Precious sons of Zion: precious** refers to that which is costly, luxurious, but has here the extended sense of that which is esteemed and honored in reference to people. Compare Esther 6.6. The translation of **Zion** should follow the practice established in chapters 1 and 2. In chapter 4 **Zion** is mentioned three times and Jerusalem once. If the translator has used only Jerusalem in the previous chapters, it will be advisable to translate **Zion** in that way here also, as well as in verses 11 and 22. **Sons of Zion** may mean the young men of Jerusalem, but it need not be limited in sense to the young men; it can also refer to Jerusalem's men of all ages.

**Worth their weight** translates "weighed against." The picture is of a scale with gold on one pan and the men of Jerusalem on the other. The point is that these men were as valuable as enormous amounts of gold. **Gold** here translates still another term for the precious metal, but the meaning is the same as before. The language used here is similar to the description of Wisdom in Job 28.15-19. Just as "common clay pots" (TEV) are of limited value, so also those who were once highly respected now count for nothing.

**How** translates the same word as the opening word of the chapter. It means "How different it is now!" TEV's rendering for English is adequate: "but now." **They are reckoned** means "they are counted, valued." This reckoning or valuing is the opinion of the enemy and of those who delight in the fall of Jerusalem.

The comparison with **earthen pots** may sometimes be translated, for example, "But now they are no more valuable than a clay pot." **The work of a potter's hands** emphasizes the ordinariness of pots, in contrast to gold, which would be more the creative work of God. TEV does not translate the expression but says "common clay pots." If the full expression is kept in translation, we may say, for example, "They are treated like the clay pots a potter makes." In languages in which clay pots are not known, it may be possible to substitute something like wooden bowls or other containers of local manufacture that are easily thrown away when broken; for example, "but now they are discarded like common wooden bowls."

| 4.3 | RSV | TEV |
|---|---|---|

<table>
<tr><td>

Even the jackals give the breast
  and suckle their young,
but the daughter of my people
  has become cruel,
like the ostriches in the wilder-
  ness.
</td><td>

Even a mother wolf will nurse
  her cubs,
but my people are like ostrich-
  es, cruel to their young.
</td></tr>
</table>

In this verse the poet expresses another contrast, this time between the kindness of wild animals and the cruelty of the inhabitants of Jerusalem.

**Even the jackals: Even** serves here to introduce an unexpected comparison. There are two similar words found in Hebrew texts, one meaning **jackals** and the other "sea monster." In the opinion of HOTTP either word is admissible. However, in the context of ostriches and the wilderness, the Handbook takes the position that **jackals** is more likely to be correct. A jackal is a dog-like animal about the size of a fox. It is a scavenger and is hated by farmers for the destruction it causes to vineyards and gardens in the Middle East. The translator should consider these characteristics when selecting an equivalent animal. For example, translators may find similarities with such rodents as moles, squirrels, rats, and rabbits. For further information see *Fauna and Flora of the Bible*, pages 31-32. TEV translates **jackals** as "mother wolf," which is probably an attempt to find a widely known and somewhat similar animal.

**Gives the breast** is literally "draw out the breast" and seems to suggest the act of a human mother taking out her breast from her dress or robe. If this is so, there is a process in the two half-lines rather than a parallelism. "Give its teat" or "offer its teat" may be more suitable in some languages. FRCL says "Even jackals have a motherly instinct and suckle their young." SPCL says "Even the female jackal gives its teat and feeds its pup."

The second pair of half-lines calls attention to the cruelty of the people who are contrasted to the nurturing jackals. In Hebrew there is no **but** to mark the contrast; however, most modern translations supply a contrast word. For **daughter of my people** see 2.11. Some interpreters alter **daughter** to make it plural, assuming it refers only to women. For example, NEB says "but the daughters of my people are cruel." Some take **daughter of my people** to refer to all the inhabitants of Jerusalem, while others see in this context a reference to mothers only, which is preferable in this context.

**Cruel, like the ostriches in the wilderness** is a proverbial understanding of the ostrich as used in Job 39.14-18. It was assumed that the ostrich laid her eggs and abandoned them to be stepped on. Although the contrast of the jackal to the ostrich can be made clear (usually by supplying a footnote explaining the ostrich's proverbial behavior), it is not clear in what way the mothers in Jerusalem (or the people) are cruel to their children, unless, of course, reference is made to verse 10, in which there is the picture of women cooking their babies. See also 2.20. By making the unfavorable comparison the poet appears to be saying that the mothers, or the people, neglect their babies.

The translation of **like the ostriches** will in many languages have to be shifted to a general term by saying something like "big birds" or "big birds called ostriches," unless there is some local bird popularly looked upon as cruel for abandoning its eggs or young birds. The fact that ostriches do not normally abandon their eggs is not important. The poet is expressing a sense of cruelty that in traditional thinking was apparently associated with the ostrich. The whole verse may be translated, for example, "A mother jackal is kind enough to suckle her young, but the mothers of Jerusalem are cruel to their babies; they are like a big bird in the desert that abandons its eggs."

Translators may find it helpful to supply a footnote, such as in FRCL, which says "*The ostrich* had the reputation of being a bad mother, because she left her eggs to incubate in the sun; compare Job 39.14-16."

**Wilderness** refers to the desert or to uninhabited areas with very little vegetation. It may sometimes be translated "place where people do not live" or "place where nothing will grow."

**4.4**

| RSV | TEV |
|---|---|
| The tongue of the nursling cleaves<br>   to the roof of its mouth for thirst;<br>the children beg for food,<br>   but no one gives to them. | They let their babies die of hunger and thirst;<br>   children are begging for food that no one will give them. |

This verse describes the consequences of the situation mentioned in verse 3. Attention is drawn to the thirsting and starving babies and children.

**The tongue of the nursling cleaves to the roof of its mouth for thirst**: in other words "The nursing babies have such thirst that their tongues stick to the roofs of their mouths." TEV "They let their babies die" gives the impression that the mothers do so willingly. This may agree with the cruelty suggested in verse 3, but the subject here is not the mothers but the tongues of the babies. **Roof of its mouth** translates the Hebrew for "palate."

The second unit speaks of those **children** who are old enough to **beg for food** (for translation comments on **children** see 1.5). **Food** is the Hebrew for "bread," as in 1.11. See there for comments. In 2.12 the children were said to be asking their mothers for food, but here they **beg** from anyone and get nothing. Once again it is implied that the mothers or the inhabitants of Jerusalem are cruel, not because it is their nature to be cruel to their children, but because anyone who has a scrap of food to eat uses it to keep himself alive.

| 4.5 | RSV | TEV |
|---|---|---|
| | Those who feasted on dainties perish in the streets; those who were brought up in purple lie on ash heaps. | People who once ate the finest foods die starving in the streets; those raised in luxury are pawing through garbage for food. |

Once again the scene is the contrast between past and present. After describing starving children the poet proceeds now to describe the fate of starving adults. It is not only the common people who suffer but also those accustomed to luxury. The two halves of this verse are closely parallel in meaning.

**Those who feasted on dainties** refers to the wealthy, who had the choicest food to eat. **Dainties** translates a word used in Genesis 49.20, where it is used in parallel with "rich food" and is translated by TEV "food fit for a king." In some language areas there is little distinction made between different qualities of food. Rather the distinction may be made between those who have ample food and those who have little. In the present context it may be clearer in some cases to speak of the abundance of food; for example, "Those who had all they could eat" or "The people who had more food than they could eat."

**Perish in the streets** is literally "are desolate in the streets," meaning they are wasted away, and so TEV "die starving." For translation comments on **streets** see 2.11.

**Brought up in purple**: **purple** was the color of the robes worn by kings. See Judges 8.26; Song of Songs 7.5. The sense of this is that **brought up in purple** (clothing) means those who were raised in the king's palace, or, more generally, the rich, those raised in luxury. And so this line in RSV is parallel in meaning to the opening line of verse 5. **Brought up in purple** must be adjusted in many languages to say, for example, "people who had all they wanted as they grew up," "people who had wealth and possessions," "people who grew up wearing fine clothing."

**Lie on ash heaps** is literally "embrace rubbish heaps." The idea is that they take hold of the rubbish with both hands, trying to find something to eat. TEV is picturable: "pawing through garbage for food."

**4.6**        RSV                                     TEV

| RSV | TEV |
|---|---|
| For the chastisement[o] of the daughter of my people has been greater than the punishment[p] of Sodom, which was overthrown in a moment, no hand being laid on it.[q] | My people have been punished even more than the inhabitants of Sodom, which met a sudden downfall at the hands of God. |

[o] Or *iniquity*
[p] Or *sin*
[q] Heb uncertain

**Chastisement of the daughter of my people: chastisement**, according to the RSV footnote, may also be rendered "iniquity." Here, as in 3.39, the consequence of iniquity is in focus, and so the term may more aptly be rendered "punishment." **The daughter of my people** is again the people of Jerusalem or, from the poet's point of view, "My people" (TEV). Their punishment has, in the poet's view, been greater than the **punishment** (in Hebrew, "sin") of Sodom. For the account of the destruction of Sodom, see Genesis 19.24-25. Another comparison between the sin of Sodom and that of Jerusalem is found in Ezekiel 16.46-52. The destruction of Sodom is referred to several times in the Old Testament as a supreme example of the punishment of sin. Jeremiah 23.14 indicates that Sodom was regarded as a standard of comparison for sinfulness.

In translation it will sometimes be clearer to say that Sodom was a city punished for its sinfulness; for example, "Jerusalem and its people have been punished more than the people who lived in the sinful city of Sodom. It (Sodom) was also destroyed."

**Which was overthrown in a moment: overthrown** is used as a technical term referring to the fate of Sodom, as in Deuteronomy 29.23; Jeremiah 20.16. The tradition that Sodom's destruction was sudden is reflected in the account in Genesis 19, where the members of Lot's family are said to be the only ones who escaped its "downfall." The context here emphasizes the suddenness of Sodom's destruction, in contrast to the long siege endured by Jerusalem, which was destroyed by human enemies. This suggests that the poet stresses the swift and supernatural nature of Sodom's destruction, rather than the reaction of the people of his time to the condition of Sodom. If the translator follows TEV, "at the hands of God," it will be necessary in many languages to make God the agent of the destruction; for example, "Sodom is the city that God quickly destroyed" or "God suddenly destroyed the wicked city of Sodom."

**No hand**, meaning no human hand, **being laid on it**: since no human agency was responsible for the destruction of Sodom, it was clearly the work of God. This may not, however, be the meaning intended by the poet, since the Hebrew verb means "twist." NIV reflects this meaning: "without a hand turned to help her." But this is an English idiom and not Hebrew usage. NEB comes closer to the meaning of "twist" for this verb with "and no one wrung his hands (in sorrow)."

| **4.7** | RSV | TEV |
|---|---|---|

Her princes were purer than
   snow,
  whiter than milk;
their bodies were more ruddy
   than coral,
  the beauty of their form[r] was
   like sapphire.[s]

Our princes[h] were undefiled and
   pure as snow;
vigorous and strong, glowing
   with health.

[h] princes; *or* Nazirites.

[r] Heb uncertain
[s] Heb *lapis lazuli*

This verse and the next form another contrast. Verse 7 describes how strong and beautiful the men of Jerusalem were in the past, and verse 8 goes on to describe what they looked like when the poet wrote.

**Her princes were purer than snow**: **her** refers to Jerusalem, not to Sodom, and so TEV has "our princes." **Princes** is literally "Nazirites." However, some interpreters alter one letter in that word and get "youths," and so NJB has "young people." There is no good reason, however, to change the Hebrew. The word is used in Genesis 49.26 and Deuteronomy 33.16, in which Joseph is called the *nazir* of his brothers, and which TEV translates as "the one set apart" and "the leader." A Nazirite took a special vow not to drink wine, not to touch a dead body, and to let his hair grow long. TEV and others that translate "princes" in the text place "Nazirite" in the footnote. If this is done, a brief explanation of "Nazirite" should be given. In any case, **princes** should not be translated as "sons of a king" but as people set aside to serve as leaders or rulers.

**Purer than snow, whiter than milk**: these comparisons probably describe moral attributes as much as physical ones. The physical reference may be to the clear and unblemished condition of their skin rather than its color, which is referred to in the next unit. **Snow** and **milk** used here are contrasted with "blacker than soot" in verse 8. Most modern translations keep the images of snow and milk. However, TEV is probably right when it translates "undefiled and pure as snow." In languages where snow is unknown, or not in any way associated with purity, we may translate "very pure" or "very good," or idiomatically in some languages, "with very good hearts."

**Bodies more ruddy than coral**: **bodies** is literally "bones," which may be an example of a part of the body standing for the whole body. See also Proverbs 15.30; 16.24. Here, however, the comparison is clearly between the color of the skin on the body and the color of coral. **Coral** in the Mediterranean is a reddish-colored limestone produced by small sea creatures; it is in the form of small branches and is valued for making ornaments. NJV understands "bones" here to refer to the limbs (arms and legs) of these men and translates "Their limbs were ruddier than coral." Since **coral** will not be known in some languages, translators may find it necessary to use a very different object for the color comparison; for example, a certain wood or stone with a reddish hue.

Yet another precious and beautiful substance is mentioned in the final line of RSV, **the beauty of their form was like sapphire.** NEB says "their limbs were lapis lazuli." Both sapphires and lapis lazuli are blue, and this same material is also mentioned in Job 28.6 in the poem in praise of Wisdom. Lapis lazuli is an opaque blue stone, speckled with yellow, which was often used in jewelry in the Middle East, and is the more likely stone here. It is not clear why the princes should be described as being blue in color, although some interpreters think it is a reference to the blue color of their veins.

RSV remarks in its footnote that **the beauty of their form** is uncertain. AB translates this expression as "beards," in view of the use of lapis lazuli in ancient eastern art to represent the hair or the beard. It must be admitted that any translation of this expression can be no more than a guess. So TEV sums up the essential meaning of the half-line with its emphasis on the bright, healthy color of Jerusalem's nobles in former days as "vigorous and strong, glowing with health." Translators are well advised to attempt to do the same.

**4.8**  RSV  TEV

| RSV | TEV |
|---|---|
| Now their visage is blacker than soot, they are not recognized in the streets; their skin has shriveled upon their bones, it has become as dry as wood. | Now they lie unknown in the streets, their faces blackened in death; their skin, dry as wood, has shriveled on their bones. |

**Now their visage is blacker than soot**: RSV and most others make the contrast between the appearance of these men in verse 7 and their appearance in verse 8 with **Now** or "But now." **Visage** in English normally refers to the human face, but it can also refer to the more general appearance. Translators are divided between those who take the word in its more limited sense as "face" and those who give it the wider meaning of "they appear." **Soot** translates a word which also means "blackness." **Soot** is the black carbon formed by burning and is usually found on chimneys, stones used for fire places, and cooking pots that are exposed to flames. We may translate, for example, "But now their faces are black as soot," "Now, however, they are black as soot," "But now they appear black as soot." Mft translates "now they look more darksome than the night," and SPCL "But now they look darker than the darkness (of night)."

**Soot** is known everywhere, but it is not necessarily used in a figurative expression for comparing something with blackness. Translators should use the expression that is most natural and widely used in their own language.

TEV has reversed the first two printed lines of RSV, so that the reason for the princes being unrecognizable is placed in the second line. This tends to obscure the contrast with "whiter than milk" in verse 7.

TEV understands these people to be dead bodies with "faces blackened in death"; but most modern versions take them to be alive, because **they are not recognized in the streets** suggests that the people are still walking about. For **in the streets** see 2.11.

**Their skin has shriveled upon their bones**: the skin of the victims has no flesh between it and the bones, nor does it have any healthy moisture.

| **4.9** | RSV | TEV |
|---|---|---|
| | Happier were the victims of the sword<br>than the victims of hunger,<br>who pined away, stricken<br>by want of the fruits of the field. | Those who died in the war were better off than those who died later,<br>who starved slowly to death, with no food to keep them alive. |

In this verse the contrast is not between past and present but between two forms of death experienced by the inhabitants of Jerusalem.

**Happier** translates the Hebrew for "better," meaning that those who were killed by the enemy were more fortunate than those who starved to death. **Victims of the sword** translates a phrase meaning "pierced by the sword," as also used in Numbers 19.16, "slain by the sword." "Pierced" occurs as "slain" by itself in Deuteronomy 21.1. In a more general way of speaking we may say "killed by the enemy," "died fighting the enemy," "killed while fighting."

**Victims of hunger**: **victims** is the same word repeated, and so the poet creates a parallel poetic image in which hunger is the slayer, "killed by hunger." If this is possible in the translator's language, it may be poetically useful to attempt to retain the parallelism of expression.

In RSV and others the expression **who pined away** refers back to those who died of hunger in the previous unit of the verse. But the Hebrew is not clear. AB makes **who** refer to those who died of wounds, and so makes the second half of the verse parallel to the first half: "Those killed by the sword had it better than those killed by famine, Those who perished of wounds, than those who lacked the fruits of the field."

**Pined away** translates a word meaning to flow or melt, and in this context "wasted away" (NEB) is the equivalent of RSV. **Stricken** translates a word which appears to mean "pierced." See also the same word translated "wounded" in Jeremiah 37.10; 51.4. Here **want of the fruits of the field** serves the same purpose as the sword and hunger. **Fruits of the field** means food, produce, something to eat. It is the contrast between a quick death in battle and a slow death by starvation that is the main theme of the verse, whatever may be the details about the way in which this is expressed.

The contrast expressed in **Happier were the victims . . . than . . .** must be expressed in a different way in many languages, so that the comparison is seen to be in the degree of suffering; for example, "Those who were killed in battle suffered, but those who slowly starved to death suffered more," or "The suffering of those who died in battle was much, but the suffering of those who died from starvation was still more."

For the second half of the verse, translators may follow the model of AB above; or, if following RSV **who pined away, stricken by . . .** , they may need to express this, for example, as "They are the ones who slowly starved because there was no food to eat" or "They slowly died from lack of something to eat."

| **4.10** | RSV | TEV |
| --- | --- | --- |

| | |
| --- | --- |
| The hands of compassionate women | The disaster that came to my people brought horror; |
| have boiled their own children; | loving mothers boiled their |
| they became their food | own children for food. |
| in the destruction of the | |
| daughter of my people. | |

In verse 3 the women or people of Jerusalem were described as "cruel to their young," but this was not because they deprived their children of food willingly. Here the same women are described as **compassionate**, but their actions appear to be the opposite. Circumstances force them to act in a way contrary to their nature. In 2.20 they were accused of "eating the bodies of the children they loved." Now they are seen boiling them to eat. It is as though the poet is describing in detail the fulfillment of the threat made to Israel in Deuteronomy 28.53-57.

**The hands of compassionate women**: in some languages it will be more natural to say "Tender-hearted women . . . ." **Compassionate**, which means showing concern for someone in trouble, is a descriptive term whose Hebrew form refers to the intestines. This is often translated in figurative language; for example, "women who have warm hearts," "women who feel with their stomachs," or "women with good livers."

**Boiled** (see also 2 Kings 6.29) means cooked in water or oil. NIV and others prefer the more general "cooked." **They** (the boiled bodies of the children) **became their** (mothers') **food**. The word translated **food** is different in Hebrew from any of the previous references to food; it is found nowhere else in this form in the Old Testament, but is usually taken as a form derived from a verb meaning "to eat."

**In the destruction of the daughter of my people**: that is, "when my people were destroyed," "at the time Jerusalem and its people were destroyed," or "in the disaster which killed the people of Jerusalem." The whole of verse 10 may be translated, for example, "The hands of loving mothers cooked their own children in order to eat them, when the people of Jerusalem were dying from war and famine."

It will be noticed that TEV has placed the last half-line of the Hebrew text at the beginning of the verse, so that eating the children is a specific instance of the more general disaster, or a consequence of the conditions of the destruction. TEV supplies "brought horror" as introductory to the statement that "mothers boiled their own children for food." In languages which require that reference to the circumstances be placed before events taking place in those circumstances, TEV may be adapted to say, for example, "When my people were dying from starvation, compassionate women boiled and ate their own children."

**4.11**

| RSV | TEV |
|---|---|
| The LORD gave full vent to his wrath, <br>   he poured out his hot anger; <br> and he kindled a fire in Zion, <br>   which consumed its foundations. | The LORD turned loose the full force of his fury; <br> he lit a fire in Zion that burned it to the ground. |

**The LORD gave full vent to his wrath**: **gave full vent to** translates a verb meaning to use up or to consume, in the sense that he showed his full anger, or, as FRCL says, "The LORD went to the very end of his fury," and GECL "The LORD let loose his full anger."

The second half-line is parallel in meaning, in which **poured out his hot anger** seems to intensify the first half-line (for comments on **poured out**, see 2.4,19). TEV reduces the two parallel statements to one. These two expressions are sometimes translated idiomatically; for example, "The LORD made his stomach hot with anger, and his eyes glowed red."

In the second half of the verse the question is whether **a fire in Zion** is a further reference to the LORD's anger, or whether it refers to a literal fire. It is clear from 2 Kings 25.9 that Jerusalem was, in part at least, destroyed by fire when it fell to the Babylonians, so that in fact **a fire in Zion** did burn it down. So here the poet is saying that the fire was not so much the consequence of plans made by the Babylonian army as the direct result of the LORD's anger against the sin of Jerusalem. In this way he brings up to date the description of the punishment of Assyria in Isaiah 30.33, and applies it to Jerusalem instead of to her enemies.

**4.12**

| RSV | TEV |
|---|---|
| The kings of the earth did not believe, <br>   or any of the inhabitants of the world, <br> that foe or enemy could enter the gates of Jerusalem. | No one anywhere, not even rulers of foreign nations, <br> believed that any invader could enter Jerusalem's gates. |

According to Isaiah 37.35, God had promised to defend Jerusalem against attack; and the same confidence that it could not be conquered was expressed in Psalm 46.5: "God is in that city, and it will never be destroyed" (TEV). In this verse the poet suggests that the rulers and people of other nations shared that popular belief of the people of Israel.

The two Hebrew half-lines (the first two lines of RSV) express very much the same sense. The verb **believe** serves for both. TEV has placed the second half-line first, "No one anywhere," as a translation of **any of the inhabitants of the world**, followed by "not even rulers . . . ," representing **The kings of the earth**. The thought expresses an attempt to be fully inclusive; that is, "Everyone, from the kings to the ordinary people . . . ," or, as FRCL says, "Neither the kings of the earth nor anyone in the world . . . ."

**Foe or enemy** are two words for the same group, which TEV reduces to one, "invader." **Could enter the gates of Jerusalem: enter** in this context means to come in by force or break in for the purpose of conquering. For **gates** see comments on 1.4.

Verse 12 may also be translated, for example, "Neither the kings that ruled the nations nor the people believed it possible to invade Jerusalem and conquer it."

| 4.13 | RSV | TEV |
|---|---|---|

| RSV | TEV |
|---|---|
| This was for the sins of her prophets and the iniquities of her priests, who shed in the midst of her the blood of the righteous. | But it happened, because her prophets sinned and her priests were guilty of causing the death of innocent people. |

The Hebrew text does not have anything equivalent to **This**, which seems to link verse 13 back to verse 12; instead it has a prefix to **sins** which means "because of, on account of . . . ." Therefore it is not clear from the Hebrew whether verse 13 is connected primarily back to verse 12 or forward to verse 14. Translators will no doubt find it necessary to make the link clear by adjusting the opening words. Some use **This was** (RSV) or "It was" (NEB), or more clearly "But it happened" (TEV), referring to the conquest of Jerusalem in verse 12. Others translate so that verse 13 joins to verse 14; for example, AB "On account of the sins of her prophets . . ." is followed by "They wandered . . ." in verse 14, where "they" refers back to the prophets and priests in verse 13. However, in the light of 2.14, the Handbook recommends the position followed by TEV.

In 2.14 the priests were blamed for the disaster that happened to Jerusalem. Here, however, the **priests** are linked with the **prophets** in common guilt. This guilt goes beyond the mere silence of 2.14 to include "causing the death of innocent people" (TEV). In many languages it will be clearer to use verbs rather than nouns in the expressions **sins of her prophets** and **iniquities of her priests.** For example, "But Jerusalem was invaded, and that was because her prophets and her priests had sinned . . . ." For translation suggestions on **prophets** and **priests**, see 1.4 and 2.9.

**Who shed in the midst of her the blood** . . . means "who (the prophets and priests) caused people in Jerusalem to die." **The righteous** refers to people who lived good lives, people who were not guilty of wrongdoing, innocent people. The final two lines of RSV probably refer to particular acts rather than simply bringing disaster on the ordinary citizens of Jerusalem. The poet no doubt had in mind the persecution which "innocent people" (TEV) could expect if they opposed the views of the priests and prophets. That this was a reasonable expectation is clear from Jeremiah 26.7,8,20-23. See also Hosea 6.9.

| RSV | TEV |
|---|---|
| They wandered, blind, through the streets, so defiled with blood that none could touch their garments. | Her leaders wandered through the streets like blind men, so stained with blood that no one would touch them. |

**They wandered**: there is no way of telling from the Hebrew who **They** refers to; however, in the light of verse 13, it is best to assume that **They** refers back to the prophets and priests. In some languages **They** will have to be identified, otherwise the pronoun may refer to the innocent people in verse 13. TEV says "Her leaders." It may be even clearer to say "These prophets and priests." **Wandered blind** is probably to be taken as a simile, "They wandered like blind men through the streets."

These prophets and priests, who are said to have shed the blood of innocent people in verse 13, are now **defiled with blood**. The **blood** with which these religious men are defiled is not their own blood but that of their victims. So those whose religious duties involved keeping themselves undefiled by others were now so stained with the blood of their victims that others would not even touch their clothes. According to Leviticus 21.11 the priests were not allowed to have contact with dead bodies, in order to maintain their purity, but now they cannot avoid such contacts. **Defiled** means having become ritually unclean, or unacceptable. "Unclean" or "dirty" are in most cases not suitable translations of **defiled**, since they only suggest physical filth. A term is required that has to do with ritual taboo, or unacceptability. Many languages have such terms, particularly in the sense of "taboo." In some languages such terms as "made forbidden" or "carrying the badness" express the idea.

In the case of a tabooed object, a person does not possess the power to protect himself from the power of the tabooed thing if he should happen to touch it. In the present case the priests have become taboo through their contact with the blood of the dead; and because of this they are a threat to the safety of the people, so that "no one would touch them" (TEV).

**4.15**

| RSV | TEV |
|---|---|
| "Away! Unclean!" men cried at them; "Away! Away! Touch not!" So they became fugitives and wanderers; men said among the nations, "They shall stay with us no longer." | "Get away!" people shouted. "You're defiled! Don't touch me!" So they wandered from nation to nation, welcomed by no one. |

In Leviticus 13.45 a person with leprosy (or person with a dreaded skin disease) is instructed to cry out "Unclean, unclean!" This is to announce to others that an infected person is approaching, so that people will be warned to stay away, and no physical contact will be made. However, in verse 15 it is probably not the defiled prophets and priests who call out but rather those who are not defiled. (See the discussion in the next paragraph.) Two exclamations are used: the first, **Away**, has the sense of "depart, keep away, get away from me!" The second, **Unclean**, means ritually or ceremonially impure or defiled.

**Men cried at them** is literally "they cried to them," raising again the question of to whom the pronouns refer. The larger context gives preference to understanding "they" to refer to the people, not the priests, and so RSV has **men** and TEV "people." This is the position taken by nearly all modern translations.

**Touch not** is a command for the defiled priests not to touch the people, or, as TEV says, "Don't touch me!"

**So they became fugitives and wanderers: So** translates a Hebrew particle which RSV and TEV understand as introducing a conclusion or consequence. **They** refers to the prophets and priests who have become defiled. The English words **fugitives and wanderers** recall the case of Cain in Genesis 4.12. However, in this verse the Hebrew word translated **fugitive** is very uncertain in meaning, but probably has a similar meaning to the one translated **wanderer** (literally "they have wandered"). So we may translate, for example, "So they fled (from Jerusalem) and drifted about."

As in the first unit, where the verb is "they cried," we next have in Hebrew "they said among the nations," which is followed by a quote. There are two approaches to the understanding of the text at this point. Some join "they said" to **So they became fugitives and wanderers**. In this case the quotation in the final line of RSV is spoken by the same persons. For example AB has " 'For they have gone away and must wander,' they say. 'They shall no longer abide among the nations.' "

Others, like RSV, connect "they said" to **among the nations**. RSV translates "they said" as **men said**, referring to the people in those nations, which is then followed by what those men said: **"They** (the fugitives and wanderers) **shall stay with us no longer."** NIV with different wording follows RSV: "When they flee and wander about, people among the nations say, 'They can stay here no longer.' " TEV, which avoids using a quotation, says "So they wandered from nation to nation, welcomed by no one."

The Handbook recommends either RSV or TEV in their handling of this verse. However, translators should make every effort to avoid confusion in the use of pronouns. For example, it may be necessary in some languages to say "As a result the prophets and priests who were defiled ran away and wandered from country to country, and the people there said, 'You defiled ones cannot stay here any longer!'" or ". . . 'Get out of our country!' "

| 4.16 | RSV | TEV |
|---|---|---|

| RSV | TEV |
|---|---|
| The LORD himself has scattered them, | The LORD had no more concern for them; he scattered them himself. |
| he will regard them no more; | |
| no honor was shown to the priests, | He showed no regard for our priests and leaders. |
| no favor to the elders. | |

In this verse it is the LORD who has forced the priests to depart. The verse consists of two pairs of closely parallel half-lines.

**The LORD himself has scattered them**: NJB translates the Hebrew literally as "The face of Yahweh." However, the "face" stands for the person himself, being a case of the poetic use of a part for the whole, and so RSV is correct. FRCL translates "the LORD in person." **Scattered** translates a verb meaning distributed or divided, as is done with inheritance. But the sense here is to spread about or divide as in Genesis 49.7, "I will divide them in Jacob and scatter them in Israel." **Them** refers back to the defiled prophets and priests in verses 13 and 14.

**Regard them no more**: **regard** translates a verb meaning to look at, but in this context it is to look after, be concerned with, care for. Here it is used in a negative sense: "The LORD had no more concern" (TEV) or "he thought of them no more" (NEB). We may also say, for example, "he turned completely away from them" or "he would have nothing more to do with them." Translators should notice how TEV has placed "no more concern for" as the setting before the action "scattered them himself."

In the two parallel RSV lines beginning **no honor** and **no favor**, the Hebrew begins, as it did in the first unit, with "the faces . . . ," thus making verse 16 the only one in chapter 4 in which both units in Hebrew begin with the same letter of the alphabet. **No honor was shown to the priests** is literally "they did not lift up the faces of the priests," which is an idiom meaning to show respect. The two verbs in the second half of this verse are in the plural, and so the LORD is not the subject. Nevertheless TEV "He showed no regard . . ." does make the LORD the subject. RSV and others understand the subject to be the people and translate the verbs as passives. It is also possible in some languages to employ an impersonal subject; for example, "There was no respect for . . . no compassion for . . ." (SPCL), "One had no regard for . . ." (FRCL). **No favor** is closely parallel in meaning to **no honor** and means "one had no pity for," "had no concern for."

**Elders** is usually translated "leaders" in TEV, as it is here. In this context, however, it probably means "They had no pity even for those (of the priests) who were old."

| **4.17** | RSV | TEV |
|---|---|---|
| | Our eyes failed ever watching vainly for help; in our watching[t] we watched for a nation which could not save. | For help that never came we looked until we could look no longer. We kept waiting for help from a nation that had none to give. |

[t] Heb uncertain

With verse 17 the tone of the poem changes. The poet now identifies himself with the people who have been the subject of the verbs, switching to the first person plural. He and his companions, who may have included the king himself, judging from verse 20, are living through the days immediately before and after the fall of

Jerusalem. In this verse the sense of the two Hebrew lines or units of the verse is again closely parallel.

Some editions of TEV reverse the order of the first line, as follows: "We looked until we could look no longer for help that never came." Translators who consider using TEV as a model should use whichever word order is most appropriate in the receptor language.

The first Hebrew word in verse 17 has variants whose meanings are not certain. One probably means "we still are," and the other "they (feminine) still are." Most translations take **our eyes** as the subject and "still are" as meaning "continually, ever, still," or some other expression of continuous activity. NEB says "We strain our eyes, looking." TEV has "we looked until we could look no longer."

**Watching vainly for help: help** is literally "our help," which in this case probably refers to help from the Egyptians, who might come and defend Jerusalem from the Babylonian invaders. This half-line may also be expressed "looking for someone to help us who never came" or "watching for help that never came."

**In our watching:** the RSV footnote shows that **watching** is uncertain in Hebrew. TEV interprets it as a means of intensifying the verb itself, as does NEB "We have watched and watched." The form of the word suggests that it is a noun, so the translation of NJB and NIV "from our towers" gives a possible meaning.

**A nation that could not save:** the Hebrew text does not state that the nation (Egypt) was powerless to help, only that it did not help. A better rendering is "for the arrival of a nation that did not come to save us" (FRCL). This may have to be expressed in some languages as ". . . save us from our enemies" or "prevent our enemies from destroying us."

| **4.18** | RSV | TEV |
|---|---|---|

Men dogged our steps
  so that we could not walk in
    our streets;
our end drew near; our days
  were numbered;
for our end had come.

The enemy was watching for us;
  we could not even walk in
    the streets.
Our days were over; the end
  had come.

Where RSV has **Men** as the subject, Hebrew has the third plural suffix "they," raising again the question to whom it refers. Since this is most unlikely to refer to the priests, most take it to refer to the enemy invader. **Dogged our steps** is an English idiom meaning to follow, pursue, track, as when a dog hunts an animal. **Dogged** translates a verb meaning to hunt or lie in wait for. NEB's translation of the first unit in Hebrew, "When we go out, we take to by-ways to avoid the public streets," involves altering the verb for **dogged** to one that means "turn aside." HOTTP supports RSV, and this is recommended to translators. We may translate this half-line, for example, "The enemy watched every step we took," "The enemy spied on us," or "We were hunted down."

**So that we could not walk in our streets** is literally "from going in our open places." **Streets** is the same term used in 2.11. See there for comments. This half-line may be translated, for example, "and we could not go outside" or "so we could go nowhere."

The word translated **our end** occurs twice in the last two lines of RSV, first with the verb meaning **drew near** and then with the verb meaning **had come**. To avoid this repetition NEB omits the first reference: "Our days are all but finished, our end has come." TEV achieves much the same result by omitting the repetition and reproducing the sense: "Our days were over; the end had come." In some languages the equivalent expression may be rendered, for example, "we were about to be captured," "our lives had only a few days left," or "we had only a few days left to live."

| 4.19 | RSV | TEV |
|---|---|---|
| | Our pursuers were swifter than the vultures in the heavens; they chased us on the mountains, they lay in wait for us in the wilderness. | Swifter than eagles swooping from the sky, they chased us down. They tracked us down in the hills; they took us by surprise in the desert. |

In this verse the poet is evidently speaking of the situation following immediately upon the capture of Jerusalem by the Babylonians. He and others tried to escape, and he tells of their dangerous journey through the hills and the desert. He is probably referring to the wild, hilly country between Jerusalem and Jericho over which the king and his companions traveled in an attempt to cross the Jordan. A prose account of these events is to be found in 2 Kings 25.3-4.

**Our pursuers**, meaning the enemies who chased us, are said to be **swifter than the vultures in the heavens**. **Vultures** and "eagles" (TEV) are both included in the Hebrew term. The poet has in mind not only the swiftness of the bird but, particularly here, its eagerness to swoop down on its prey. Those trying to escape from the Babylonian army could easily liken themselves to small creatures threatened by a bird of prey such as the eagle.

Translators are free to name a bird that is best known locally as a bird of prey. In areas where both the vulture and the eagle are known, the translator's experience with the habits of these birds may confirm that "eagle" is more suitable in this context; eagles aggressively seek living prey, while vultures seek dead bodies. **In the heavens** does not designate the abode of God but only calls attention to soaring birds that locate their prey from high in the sky. We may translate, for example, "Our enemies swooped down on us like eagles out of the sky."

The second pair of half-lines, which are closely parallel in sense, describe the extent to which these people were pursued by their enemies. **Chased** translates a word which means "go in hot pursuit of." It is used in Genesis 31.36, where Jacob asks Laban "What is my sin that you have hotly pursued me?" See also 1 Samuel 17.53. NEB says "they are hot on our trail over the hills."

**Lay in wait** translates the same verb used in 3.10 and means "ambush, make a surprise attack on" someone. For **wilderness** see 4.3. In some areas people live where the land is largely flat, and "hills" and **mountains** are unknown. In such cases descriptive terms such as "land that goes up and down" or "land that is up high" may give entirely wrong impressions. In many cases an illustration serves to supplement the local expressions.

**4.20**                 RSV                                             TEV

The breath of our nostrils, the                  They captured the source of our
    LORD's anointed,                                 life, the king the LORD had
  was taken in their pits,                           chosen,
he of whom we said, "Under his                   the one we had trusted to
    shadow                                           protect us from every invad-
  we shall live among the na-                        er.
    tions."

The poet speaks on behalf of his fellow-countrymen when he describes the king as **The breath of our nostrils**. In other words, just as breath is needed to keep the body alive, so the king is the source of life for the nation. This expression is used poetically as an honorific title and is found only here in the Old Testament. It is followed by "the anointed of the LORD," which means "the one the LORD has chosen." The term **anointed** normally refers to the king, although the high priest and some prophets were also anointed.

**Was taken in their pits** means that the king was captured like an animal in a pitfall. The word translated **pits** is not the same as in 3.53,55, but the sense is the same. TEV expresses the first half of the verse well but sacrifices some of the poetic imagery: "They captured the source of our life, the king the LORD had chosen."

When rendering **The breath of our nostrils**, it will be important to identify this sentiment as applying to the king; otherwise some readers will assume it refers to God. We may say, for example, "God has chosen for us our king, and the king is the one who gives us life," ". . . and he enables us to live," or more idiomatically, ". . . and he is in every breath we draw," or ". . . and our king is as dear to us as the air we breathe."

As long as the king was alive there was hope, but with him gone all hope was lost. **He of whom we said** introduces a direct quotation of a saying which the people had used. This phrase introducing the quotation may have to be reworded to say, for example, "We had always said about our king: 'We shall live in his shadow among the nations.'" The idea of living in the **shadow** of the king means to receive his protection, and so TEV has "the one we had trusted to protect us . . . ," which makes a good translation model. Compare Judges 9.15; Isaiah 32.1-2.

**4.21**             RSV                                             TEV

Rejoice and be glad, O daughter                  Laugh on, people of Edom and
    of Edom,                                         Uz; be glad while you can.
  dweller in the land of Uz;                        Your disaster is coming too;
but to you also the cup shall                       you too will stagger naked in
    pass;                                            shame.

    you shall become drunk and
       strip yourself bare.

Verses 21-22 close the chapter with a warning to the people of Edom and Uz. Edom was situated to the southeast of Judah, and its people were thought to be descended from Esau and so were related to the people of Israel. The Book of Obadiah reflects the antagonism between the people of Judah and Edom and attacks Edom particularly for its unfriendly collaboration with Judah's enemies at the time of the fall of Jerusalem. See also Psalm 137.7-9.

**Rejoice and be glad** is satire or irony because the poet means the opposite of what he says. TEV is one of the few modern translations that has made any attempt to adjust this expression: "Laugh on . . . while you can." Languages differ greatly in their handling of irony, and in many cases adjustments will be required; for example, "You think you can rejoice and be glad . . . ," "It is too late for you to be happy," "Your rejoicing is about over . . . ."

**Daughter of Edom** carries the sense of the people or inhabitants of Edom, as do "daughter of Zion" and "daughter of Jerusalem" for those places. **Land of Uz** is not necessarily the same as the place with that name which is given as the setting for the Book of Job in Job 1.1. It appears in verse 21 to be the name of a larger area of which Edom is a part. The introduction of the people of Edom and Uz at the end of the chapter may create some confusion for the reader if there is not more identification given than in RSV and TEV. For example, we can make clear that the people of these places are, if not the main enemy, at least enemies enough to gloat over the fall of Jerusalem. We may say, for example, "you unfriendly tribes of Edom and Uz . . ." or "you people of Edom and Uz who hate us . . . ."

**But to you also the cup shall pass**: **cup** is used frequently in the Old Testament as a symbol of God's anger, as in Jeremiah 25.15-29. The symbolism passed over into the New Testament in Revelation 14.10; 16.19. The effect of drinking this **cup** is to make Edom drunk. **The cup shall pass** and TEV "Your disaster is coming" may be expressed in active terms, with God as the agent of the disaster which will strike them; for example, "God's anger will strike you too" or "when God is angry he will destroy you too." The sense of **also** is that Edom will suffer a similar fate to that which has just happened to Judah.

Edom is depicted as a woman. In her drunkenness she will strip herself naked and so make herself an object of ridicule. This parallels the picture of Jerusalem in 1.8. TEV has shifted away from the figurative language of the cup but has retained the suggestion of drunkenness in "will stagger naked."

| **4.22** | RSV | TEV |
|---|---|---|
| | The punishment of your iniquity, O daughter of Zion, is accomplished, he will keep you in exile no longer; but your iniquity, O daughter of | Zion has paid for her sin; the LORD will not keep us in exile any longer. But Edom, the LORD will punish you; he will expose your guilty acts. |

> Edom, he will punish,
> he will uncover your sins.

This verse seems to be addressed to those who had been taken into exile after the fall of Jerusalem in 587 B.C. Jeremiah 52.28-30 refers to three separate groups of exiles. The first group were taken away with King Jehoiachin, the second at the end of Zedekiah's reign, and the third some years later.

The two units of verse 22 are neatly balanced in the Hebrew. The first half of the verse speaks of the punishment of Jerusalem as being over, and that is matched in the second half by the punishment of Edom yet to come. In the first half Jerusalem's exile is over, and in the second half Edom's sin is yet to be made public.

**Punishment of your iniquity** is one word, "your iniquity," in Hebrew. As in 3.39, **iniquity** refers to the consequence of wrongdoing, and so, when used with **is accomplished** (or, "completed"), means **punishment**. In many languages these nouns must be changed to verbs; for example, "The LORD will not punish you any more for the evil you have done" or "You people of Jerusalem have been punished for your wrongdoing, and it is ended." For **daughter of Zion** see comments on 1.6. TEV "paid for her sin" is an English idiom which means "She has suffered for her sin" or "She has been punished for her sin."

**Will keep you in exile no longer**: literally "will not add to your exile." This statement may be translated in two ways: as a promise that Jerusalem's people will not be forced into another exile again, or as a promise that the exile will soon end, will not be prolonged. Translations that understand it to refer to no more exiles are FRCL, SPCL, GECL, NJB, Mft, TOB, and NEB. For example, NEB translates "and never again shall you be carried into exile." NIV, NAB, and NJV join RSV and TEV in referring to not prolonging the present exile. Translators may follow the NEB model or that of RSV and TEV. If we follow the NEB model we may adapt it to say, for example, "he will never send you away into exile again," "God will not send you away to live as prisoners in foreign lands," or ". . . as prisoners in other tribes."

Many translations show the contrast between the first and second halves of this verse by using a contrasting word such as **but**. We may also say, for example, "as for you people of Edom . . . ."

**He will punish** is literally "he will visit," that is, come for the purpose of punishing. See also Exodus 32.34; Hosea 8.13; 9.9. **Daughter of Edom** follows the pattern used throughout the book, in which Zion, Judah, and Jerusalem have been addressed directly as a woman. The reference is again to the people of Edom.

Translators may find it natural to begin both units of this verse with the address forms and so maintain the matching patterns between the units in the verse. TEV keeps "Zion" and "Edom" at the beginning of each half of the verse, but only "Edom" is kept as an address form.

**Iniquity** in relation to Edom is the same word in Hebrew as in the first unit. The two half-lines of the second unit are parallel in sense, so that "punish your iniquity" is matched by **uncover your sins**. **Uncover** translates the same Hebrew word rendered "exposing" by TEV in 2.14. The sense is to reveal or make known, or as FRCL says, "He will unmask your crimes." In some language areas **uncover your sins** may be expressed "God will bring your sins out into the open" or "The evil things you have done will be seen by everybody."

# Chapter 5

Chapter 5 is unlike all of the earlier chapters in that it is not an alphabetical acrostic. In the Hebrew Bible each verse consists of two half-lines of approximately the same length, each being a sentence. There are, as in chapters 1, 2, and 4, twenty-two verses.

The chapter may be divided into three parts based upon the poet's use of the first person plural pronoun. In the first part (verses 1-10) the poet speaks in terms of "us" and "our." In the second (verses 11-14) the reference shifts to such nouns as women, virgins, princes, and young and old men without identifying them as "ours." Finally in verses 15-22 the author again speaks of "us" and "our."

The theme of verses 1-18 is the sufferings of the people of Jerusalem. In two verses (7 and 16) the poet recognizes that sin has been the cause of Jerusalem's fall.

Verse 19 introduces a contrast with all that goes before. The closing verses (19-22), which serve as a climax to chapter 5 and a conclusion to the book as a whole, consist of: (19) a statement of trust in God's eternal rule; (20) a question "Why have you abandoned us?"; (21) a plea or prayer to be restored to the situation of former times; and (22) a final expression of the LORD's rejection of his people.

## 5.1-22

| RSV | TEV |
|---|---|
| | *A Prayer for Mercy* |
| 1 Remember, O LORD, what has befallen us;<br>behold, and see our disgrace! | 1 Remember, O LORD, what has happened to us.<br>Look at us, and see our disgrace. |
| 2 Our inheritance has been turned over to strangers,<br>our homes to aliens. | 2 Our property is in the hands of strangers;<br>foreigners are living in our homes. |
| 3 We have become orphans, fatherless;<br>our mothers are like widows. | 3 Our fathers have been killed by the enemy,<br>and now our mothers are widows. |
| 4 We must pay for the water we drink,<br>the wood we get must be bought. | 4 We must pay for the water we drink;<br>we must buy the wood we need for fuel. |
| 5 With a yoke on our necks we are hard driven;<br>we are weary, we are given no rest. | 5 Driven hard like donkeys or camels,<br>we are tired, but are allowed no rest. |
| 6 We have given the hand to Egypt,<br>and to Assyria, to get bread enough. | 6 To get food enough to stay alive,<br>we went begging to Egypt and Assyria. |
| 7 Our fathers sinned, and are no more;<br>and we bear their iniquities. | |
| 8 Slaves rule over us;<br>there is none to deliver us from their hand. | |
| 9 We get our bread at the peril of our lives, | |

because of the sword in the wilderness.

10 Our skin is hot as an oven
with the burning heat of famine.

11 Women are ravished in Zion,
virgins in the towns of Judah.

12 Princes are hung up by their hands;
no respect is shown to the elders.

13 Young men are compelled to grind at the
mill;
and boys stagger under loads of wood.

14 The old men have quit the city gate,
the young men their music.

15 The joy of our hearts has ceased;
our dancing has been turned to
mourning.

16 The crown has fallen from our head;
woe to us, for we have sinned!

17 For this our heart has become sick,
for these things our eyes have grown
dim,

18 for Mount Zion which lies desolate;
jackals prowl over it.

19 But thou, O LORD, dost reign for ever;
thy throne endures to all generations.

20 Why dost thou forget us for ever,
why dost thou so long forsake us?

21 Restore us to thyself, O LORD, that we
may be restored!
Renew our days as of old!

22 Or hast thou utterly rejected us?
Art thou exceedingly angry with us?

7 Our ancestors sinned, but now they are
gone,
and we are suffering for their sins.

8 We are ruled by men who are no better
than slaves,
and no one can save us from their
power.

9 Murderers roam through the countryside;
we risk our lives when we look for
food.

10 Hunger has made us burn with fever
until our skin is as hot as an oven.

11 Our wives have been raped on Mount
Zion itself;
in every Judean village our daughters
have been forced to submit.

12 Our leaders have been taken and hanged;
our old men are shown no respect.

13 Our young men are forced to grind grain
like slaves;
boys go staggering under heavy loads
of wood.

14 The old people no longer sit at the city
gate,
and the young people no longer make
music.

15 Happiness has gone out of our lives;
grief has taken the place of our dances.

16 Nothing is left of all we were proud of.
We sinned, and now we are doomed.

17 We are sick at our very hearts
and can hardly see though our tears,

18 because Mount Zion lies lonely and deserted,
and wild jackals prowl through its
ruins.

19 But you, O LORD, are king forever
and will rule to the end of time.

20 Why have you abandoned us so long?
Will you ever remember us again?

21 Bring us back to you, LORD! Bring us
back!
Restore our ancient glory.

> 22    Or have you rejected us forever?
>        Is there no limit to your anger?

## Section Heading

TEV's heading, "A prayer for mercy," if used in some languages, will require adjustment by saying, for example, "The people of Jerusalem ask the LORD to be merciful to them," "Bring us back to you, LORD," "We pray that the LORD will restore us." SPCL and NJB have "Fifth lament," NEB "A prayer for remembrance and restoration," TOB "The grace of conversion," GECL and FRCL "Bring us back to you."

| 5.1 | RSV | TEV |
|---|---|---|
| | Remember, O LORD, what has befallen us; behold, and see our disgrace! | Remember, O LORD, what has happened to us. Look at us, and see our disgrace. |

This chapter begins, not with a contrast between past and present, but with an appeal to the LORD to keep in mind the sufferings of his people. It is the scorn and mockery resulting from defeat and failure that the poet is thinking of at this point, rather than physical suffering. The same attitude is found in Psalm 79.4; 123.3-4.

**Remember, O LORD** is a plea or prayer for mercy. A similar plea was voiced in 3.19; but unlike there, the imperative here is very emphatic. The poet is asking that God keep in mind and not forget the suffering of Jerusalem's people. GECL and FRCL express this plea as a negative: "LORD, do not forget . . . ." We may also translate, for example, "O LORD, think about . . . ," or idiomatically in some languages, "O LORD, do not let go . . . ," or "O LORD, keep tied tightly . . . ." **Befallen** means "happened": "what has happened to us" (TEV), or "what the enemy has done to us."

The second line of RSV matches **our disgrace** with the more general expression **what has befallen us** of the first line. **Disgrace** translates a word meaning insult, shame, reproach. In Genesis 30.23 it applies to Rachel's shame for having no children, "God has taken away my reproach." Here it refers to the offense or shame of being conquered and insulted by a pagan nation. The nature of the disgrace is spelled out from verse 2 to 18. **Behold, and see** translates the same verbs used in 1.11; however, the verbs are in the reverse order here. The double use of verbs of seeing serves to emphasize the force of the poet's plea for the LORD to recognize, acknowledge, be aware of what has happened to his people.

The expression **see our disgrace** may require some adjustment in translation, because "disgrace" is an abstract term, and it may not be possible to speak of seeing it. In some languages **disgrace** will have to be changed to a verb; for example, "look at us and see how our enemies have shamed us" or "look how much our enemies have insulted us." Also in some languages **see our disgrace** must be expressed idiomatically; for example, "see how our faces are hot" or ". . . how we have turned away our eyes."

**5.2**
        RSV
                         TEV

> **Our inheritance has been turned
> over to strangers,
> our homes to aliens.**

> **Our property is in the hands of
> strangers;
> foreigners are living in our
> homes.**

In this verse we are to understand that God is the one who has caused **our inheritance** to be **turned over to strangers. Inheritance** generally means inherited property, or property and possessions that are passed on to a dead person's survivors. However, the word is often used in the Old Testament as referring to the land promised to Abraham and his descendants (Deut 26.1): "the land which the LORD your God gives you for an inheritance." In Jeremiah 2.7 "heritage" is used in parallel with "land" (of Israel); see the same usage in Jeremiah 3.18. Many translators use **inheritance** or "heritage" in this half-line, but "our land" is more likely to be the meaning here and is a more suitable translation. It is also possible to use, for example, "country" or "nation," meaning the land of Judah.

In some languages the passive **has been turned over** must be reworded as active; for example, "The land you gave us you have now given to foreigners" or "You have taken our country from us and given it to foreigners."

The second part of the verse has no verb, and **has been turned over** serves for both halves. The more general **Our inheritance** in the first half is matched in the second by **our homes** as a particular example of the inheritance, a poetic device that calls attention to the matching pair of words.

The two Hebrew words translated as **strangers** and **aliens** are virtually identical in meaning. **Strangers** probably refers not to the Babylonians but to the people from neighboring countries such as Edom. In some languages distinctions are made between those who are native to the community and those who have become incorporated into it, but were originally from another tribe or area. Another distinction is between members of the community and the group of outsiders who are totally alien to the community in question. It is this second distinction which is referred to here; and sometimes it is helpful to say, for example, "people from other tribes are living in our houses" or "people who do not belong to us have taken over our houses."

**5.3**
        RSV
                         TEV

> **We have become orphans, father-
> less;
> our mothers are like widows.**

> **Our fathers have been killed by
> the enemy,
> and now our mothers are wid-
> ows.**

**Orphans** and **widows** were traditionally looked upon in Israel as the members of society who were most in need of protection. Here the poet emphasizes the lack of protection for the people living in Jerusalem. The men have either been killed in battle or been taken away into captivity. So those left behind are **orphans** in the sense that they have lost their fathers.

TEV and others expand what is in Hebrew "no fathers" to a statement which explains the reason for their being **orphans**: "Our fathers have been killed . . . ." FRCL is better because it retains **orphans**: "Our fathers are no longer there, and so we are orphans."

In some languages the word **orphan** does not apply to a child who has lost only the father—both parents are understood to be dead. In other languages a child is called an **orphan** only until he or she reaches a certain age. In cases where there is no term at all for **orphan**, it will often be necessary to say, for example, "We are children without a father," or "We are children without fathers because the enemy killed them," or ". . . the enemy has taken them away."

This restructuring also gives the reason for the **mothers** being **widows**. However, the expression **like widows** raises the question whether the husbands have been killed (as in TEV) or are no longer there (as in FRCL). Some interpreters take **like widows** to mean that perhaps the husbands and fathers are still living but are in exile, and so the women are left without the help and protection of their men. However, the Hebrew preposition used here probably has the same function as in 1.20, where it means not "like death" but "there is death."

**5.4**            RSV                                    TEV

We must pay for the water we          We must pay for the water we
  drink,                                     drink;
  the wood we get must be                we must buy the wood we need
  bought.                                    for fuel.

In the days before the conquest of Jerusalem by the Babylonians, there was no question of paying for water or for firewood. The inhabitants were able to use the wells and forests to supply their own needs. According to Deuteronomy 29.11 foreigners could cut wood and carry water for the people of Israel; but now all that was changed, and foreigners made the people pay for what had been theirs by right. No indication is given in the text of the way in which payment was enforced.

The Hebrew for this verse is literally "Our water for silver we drink, and our wood for a price comes." The two parts of this verse are parallel in form, in that the order of words in both half-lines in Hebrew is: noun phrase ("our water . . . our wood"), means ("for silver . . . for a price"), subject with verb ("we have drunk . . . it comes"). Translators may prefer to keep the two half-lines closely parallel in structure. But in some languages translators may find it more natural to use only a single verb; for example, "We have to pay for the water we drink and for the wood we burn." In many languages the term for "firewood" is distinct from the one for wood that is used for construction.

**5.5**            RSV                                    TEV

With a yoke[u] on our necks we         Driven hard like donkeys or
  are hard driven;                       camels,
  we are weary, we are given no          we are tired, but are allowed

**rest.**                                              **no rest.**

<sup>u</sup> Symmachus: Heb lacks *with a yoke*

As the RSV footnote shows, the words **With a yoke** are not found in the Hebrew text, which says literally "Upon our necks we are pursued . . . ." The poet probably communicated clearly by sound and context that he was speaking of a yoke. The word translated "upon" is similar in form to the Hebrew word meaning **yoke**, and scholars believe that one of these two words, "upon" or "yoke," may have been accidentally dropped. One ancient Greek translation has a word meaning **yoke**, and so RSV, NEB, and others translate **with a yoke on our necks** . . . . TEV also has assumed that the original sentence included the Hebrew word for **yoke**, and has therefore translated "Driven hard like donkeys or camels."

Some translations take **on our necks** to mean "follow in hot pursuit," and so NJV has "We are hotly pursued." NIV has "Those who pursue us are at our heels." FRCL says "Our pursuers are on our backs." It is also possible that the expression may refer to the ancient practice of a victor placing his foot on the neck of an enemy to symbolize complete submission (see Joshua 10.24 for instance). Translators may follow this suggestion or any of the above models of NIV, NJV, FRCL, or RSV. For translation suggestions regarding **yoke** see 1.14.

The phrase translated **we are weary** may also mean "We work hard" or, as Mft says, "We toil." In some languages it may be necessary to make clear that the enemy is the one causing these conditions; for example, "The enemy is hotly pursuing us; we are tired, but they do not let us rest."

**5.6**              RSV                              TEV

**We have given the hand to Egypt,**          **To get food enough to stay alive,**
**    and to Assyria, to get bread**             **    we went begging to Egypt and**
**    enough.**                                  **    Assyria.**

The two countries **Egypt** and **Assyria** are named in the two parallel half-lines of this verse; but this does not mean that the content of the first half-line applies only to Egypt and that of the second only to Assyria. Instead the statements in both half-lines apply to both countries, as in TEV.

In the past Israel's rulers had made treaties with Egypt and Assyria, not only for military protection but also for material gain. At the time of the fall of Jerusalem to the Babylonians, the Assyrian empire had already been destroyed. The poet is therefore thinking chiefly in terms of the political activities of a previous generation, as the next verse suggests. But the present generation cannot consider itself entirely free of blame for the sins of earlier generations, as the poet suggests by the use of the first person plural here.

**We have given the hand** is interpreted in various ways. One sense is seen by comparing this expression with that in 2 Kings 10.15, in which Jehu makes a pact with Jehonadab by "giving his hand." In this case the two men make a pact with each other as equals. A different sense of the same expression is found in Jeremiah 50.15, which speaks of the fall of Babylon. Here "give her hand" is translated by both RSV and TEV as "surrendered." The context of verse 6 makes clear that Jerusalem is in need of food and therefore is reaching out to a foreign nation for help or, as TEV says, "went begging." NIV has "We submitted to Egypt and Assyria," Mft "we surrendered to the foe."

In translation it is important to use an expression which shows that one party to the agreement is under pressure (in this case forced by starvation) to submit or make concessions in order to gain its objective. For example, we may say "In order to get food from them we bowed down to the . . . ," ". . . we agreed to their demands," ". . . we promised to call them 'boss,' " "We laid our necks out for them (to chop off)," or "We tied our hands and feet for them."

For **bread** see comments on 1.11.

| 5.7 | RSV | TEV |
|---|---|---|
| | Our fathers sinned, and are no more; <br> and we bear their iniquities. | Our ancestors sinned, but now they are gone, <br> and we are suffering for their sins. |

It may be that there is a connection in the poet's mind between the political alliances with Egypt and Assyria in verse 6 and the recollection of the sins of bygone **fathers** in this verse. Those belonging to a previous generation had **sinned** but were no longer alive to suffer for their sins. So, in accordance with the principles expressed in Exodus 20.5, their descendants were suffering for their sins.

In the light of Exodus 20.5; Jeremiah 16.10-13; 31.29-30; and Ezekiel 18, it is unlikely that the **fathers** are the immediate fathers of the survivors, who were either killed or are now in exile in Babylonia, although this cannot be ruled out. Most likely **Our fathers** means "Our ancestors" (TEV), those who lived before us. **And are no more** is a phrase which means they are no longer living, or they are now dead.

**Bear their iniquities** means "bear the burden of their sins" or "suffer the punishment for their sins." In some languages it may be necessary to say, for example, "We suffer now because they sinned" or "They sinned and now we suffer because of their sins."

| 5.8 | RSV | TEV |
|---|---|---|
| | Slaves rule over us; <br> there is none to deliver us <br> from their hand. | We are ruled by men who are no better than slaves, <br> and no one can save us from their power. |

**Slaves rule over us: Slaves** most likely refers here to minor Babylonian officials whom the people had to deal with, and who could act insultingly and cruelly. This verse recalls Proverbs 30.21-22, which speaks of the intolerable conditions resulting when a slave becomes a ruler. TEV attempts to add a modifier to the term

**Slaves** with "men who are no better than slaves." GECL says "slaves who have become lords over us."

In some cases the term **Slaves** in this context would be inappropriate, because it would be difficult for the reader to imagine how slaves could wield such power. Therefore it is preferable to connect these people to the ruling class of the invaders; for example, "The ones who rule over us are the slaves of those who destroyed us" or "The slaves who rule us are the servants of our enemies."

**None to deliver us from their hand** is an idiom meaning "no one who can save us from their power" (TEV) or "no one who can free us from them."

### 5.9

| RSV | TEV |
|---|---|
| We get our bread at the peril of our lives, because of the sword in the wilderness. | Murderers roam through the countryside; we risk our lives when we look for food. |

The first line in RSV states the fact, the second states the reason. **Bread** is again the main item of food and is used to represent all food, produce, crops. **At the peril of our lives** is literally "With our souls we bring in our bread." The sense here is "we risk our lives" (TEV). We may also say, for example, "We put our lives in danger to get food."

**Because of the sword in the wilderness** is literally "from the face of the sword in the wilderness," which means "from the presence of the sword . . . ." However, in this context **sword** probably refers to people who use their swords to rob, and therefore, as in FRCL, to "armed bands," or in SPCL, to "desert warriors." NEB finds the expression **sword in the wilderness** too odd, and so alters one vowel in the Hebrew to get "heat" and translates "in the scorching heat." Mft takes the expression to refer to Arabs who carried swords, and translates "Arabs of the desert." TEV says "Murderers." The Handbook recommends an expression like that of FRCL, SPCL, or TEV. **Wilderness** is the same word used in 4.3, but here it refers to the outlying areas in the country away from the city, and presumably to places where crops may grow or where wild plants may be available for food.

Note that TEV and others reverse the order of the statements in this verse so that the situation is named first, followed by the consequence. We may also translate, for example, "Because armed people wander through the countryside, we risk our lives when we go there in search of food."

### 5.10

| RSV | TEV |
|---|---|
| Our skin is hot as an oven with the burning heat of famine. | Hunger has made us burn with fever until our skin is as hot as an oven. |

In this verse the meaning of the expression translated **hot as an oven** is not certain. AB and NEB say something like "black as an oven," in which the Hebrew word rendered **hot** by RSV is associated with one of the words meaning "darkness" in Job 3.5. Another possibility is "shriveled," favored by the Septuagint and Syriac. The Handbook recommends that translators follow RSV and TEV.

**The burning heat of famine** is taken by most translators to mean fever brought on by hunger. NEB, however, takes it as a figurative expression and translates more generally "the ravages of starvation." The word translated **burning heat** occurs also in Psalm 11.6 ("scorching"); 119.53 ("hot indignation"). In order to make this verse clear, in some languages it may be necessary to restructure it. For example, "Hunger causes us to burn with fever, and our skin has become hot like an oven." FRCL says "Hunger gnaws on us so much that our skin burns as if we were inside an oven." These, as well as TEV, are suitable translation models.

| 5.11 | RSV | TEV |
|------|-----|-----|
| | Women are ravished in Zion, virgins in the towns of Judah. | Our wives have been raped on Mount Zion itself; in every Judean village our daughters have been forced to submit. |

In verses 11-14 in the Hebrew text, the use of the first person plural is replaced by the third person, in which the poet speaks of women, virgins, princes, elders, and young and old men. "We" and "our" will be resumed again in verse 15 and will continue to the end. Translators will note that, while RSV reflects the Hebrew usage, TEV uses first person plural pronouns ("we," "our," "us") throughout chapter 5. The reason for this is that, even though the Hebrew omits these pronouns in verses 11-14, all references are still to the same people of Jerusalem and Judah who have been included in the first person plural pronouns. TEV's consistent use of first person plural makes the persons in verses 11-14 more clearly part of the suffering people in the rest of the chapter. Translators should consider following TEV.

The Hebrew of this verse need not be understood as literally as in RSV. The poet is not trying to make a distinction between the two kinds of victims, as though only **virgins** were raped in the towns. The two parallel half-lines refer to a single situation, so that the sense is that women both married and unmarried have been raped both in Jerusalem and in the surrounding towns. There is only one verb in the Hebrew verse, and it is an active verb with no actor expressed, though the actor is fairly clearly the enemy.

**Ravished** translates a verb which has the general sense of doing violence, humiliating, oppressing, and in this context it refers to a man forcing a woman to have sex. RSV translates as a passive what in Hebrew is "They raped." Translators may not be able to use the passive; and in such cases it may be possible to use an indefinite subject or, more directly, "the enemies," "the invaders," "those who invaded us," or "our enemies."

Two places are named; the first is **Zion**, which also means Jerusalem, although on this occasion TEV has translated "Mount Zion," which is the location of the

Temple. This particular reference hardly seems necessary or appropriate in this context. The other place is **the towns of Judah**.

The word **virgins** is the same Hebrew term as is found in 1.4 ("maidens"). There it was pointed out that **virgins** was inappropriate in some languages, because its central meaning in English is often young women or girls who have not had sexual experience. In this context, however, that element of meaning is central, and so **virgins** is a suitable translation. However, the translation of **virgins** can be a problem in some languages. The Hebrew term refers to young women who have not had sexual relations with men, but also who are approaching or are already of marriageable age. However, in some societies a girl called a "virgin" is one who before marriage participates in ritual sexual relations. In others a "virgin" is a woman who has not married after passing a certain age. In some languages a woman who has not married because of physical or mental handicaps is called a "virgin." If serious problems are encountered in the translation of this term, it will often be better to use a less technical word such as "young women" or "girls."

In some languages it may be best to reduce the parallelism of verse 11 to a single line; for example, "Our women have been raped in Jerusalem and in the towns of Judah" or "The enemy troops have raped our women in . . . ." Terms for rape are often euphemisms or roundabout expressions which refer to violence; for example, "They did harm to the bodies of . . ." or "They put disgrace on the women . . . ." In languages in which only a descriptive expression will make clear what happened to these women, we may sometimes say, for example, "forced to have sex" or "made to sleep with." Whatever expression is used, it should be acceptable for public reading.

**5.12**

| RSV | TEV |
|---|---|
| Princes are hung up by their hands; no respect is shown to the elders. | Our leaders have been taken and hanged; our old men are shown no respect. |

In this verse the poet turns his attention to **princes** and **elders**, respected people who are now disgraced by the invaders.

**Princes** translates the same word used in 1.6. See there for comments. **Hung up by their hands** is ambiguous, since **by their hands** can mean "the hands of the enemies hung them" or that the enemies hung the princes by tying their hands above their heads as a form of torture. The latter seems to be the interpretation of RSV. TEV "Our leaders have been taken and hanged" follows the first thought. From the information available there is no way to decide between these interpretations, and so either may be used. If the translator follows TEV, it may be necessary to shift to the active; for example, "The enemy has hanged our leaders."

In language areas where hanging is unknown, it is often necessary to specify the manner and purpose. For example, "The enemy has put our leaders to death by hanging them with ropes around their necks."

**No respect is shown to the elders** is literally "The faces of the elders were not honored." "Faces of the elders" is an idiom and means "the elders" and not just their faces. As in the first half of the verse, those who fail to respect or honor these people are the enemies of Jerusalem. For a discussion of **elders** see 1.19; 2.10. Although TEV and some others take **elders** to mean "old men," in the light of 1.19 and 2.10 it is possible to understand both **Princes** and **elders** as representing one body of rulers or leaders. If the enemy has been made the subject in the first half of the verse, the same subject can serve in the second half, often without repeating the subject; for example, "The enemy has hanged our leaders and shown them no respect." If, however, the translator wishes to retain the poetic form of parallelism, it may be best to show the subject in both parts.

**5.13**  RSV  TEV

Young men are compelled to  Our young men are forced to
grind at the mill;  grind grain like slaves;
and boys stagger under loads  boys go staggering under
of wood.  heavy loads of wood.

**Young men** (as in 1.18, where the word is associated with its female counterpart) normally refers to fully developed youths who are unmarried. But if in this context it has the same meaning as **boys** in the second part of the verse, it may refer to youths who have not yet developed their full strength. **Compelled to grind at the mill** has lent itself to various interpretations. The best sense is to assume that the enemy forced young men to operate a grinding mill, which consisted of two huge stones often called "millstones" (See Mark 9.42). The lower stone was stationary, and the grinder turned the upper stone to grind the grain between the two. Grinding was often the work of an animal, a prisoner, or servants and slaves. TEV has emphasized the aspect of forced labor by saying "forced to grind grain like a slave." (See Exo 11.5; Judges 16.21.)

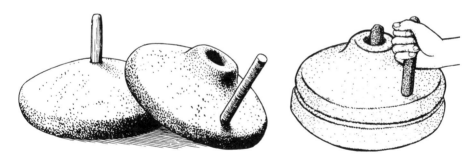

SMALL MILLSTONES

**Grind at the mill** must often be expressed in terms of the local equipment used for grinding such things as corn or rice to make flour. This may involve using a small cylindrical stone on a flat stone surface in which the grinder works in a kneeling position. In some language areas the grinding of grain will be rendered by the terms used for crushing grains with a pestle in a mortar; for example, "Young men are forced to pound grain in a mortar."

**Boys** translates a noun which has the same sense as **Young men** in the previous half-line. It is therefore difficult to argue that the poet is focusing on a younger group in the second part of the verse. These **boys** or "young men" are said to **stagger under loads of wood**. That is, because they are forced to carry loads which are too heavy for them, they stumble or stagger as they struggle under their burdens.

**5.14**        RSV                                    TEV

The old men have quit the city          The old people no longer sit at
   gate,                                           the city gate,
the young men their music.              and the young people no lon-
                                   ger make music.

**Old men** translates the same term used for "elders" in verse 12. However, the term is used here in a more general sense, referring to the old men who were responsible for settling legal disputes and advising in family matters. **Have quit the city gate** can be taken as an idiomatic phrase meaning "no longer give their advice" or "have ceased their counseling." The fact that these old men carried on their discussions at **the city gate** is of secondary importance.

In 1.4 the poet laments that "the city gates stand empty" (TEV), and here it is especially the **old men** who are no longer to be found there. In the past the space near the **city gate** had been the place in which business was conducted, as in Ruth 4.1-12, and where old men gave legal decisions, as in Job 29.7-10.

The expression **city gate** or "doors of the city" will have little meaning for most readers unacquainted with the way a biblical city was built. Even where gates are known, the reader is apt to think of the gate which leads to a particular house, rather than the gate which leads into a city. Since the primary reference is not to the gate itself but to the area of meeting and carrying on business, it will often be clearer to say, for example, "The old men have left the meeting place inside the city gates," or "The old men are no longer found sitting in the town square," or, as suggested above, "The old men have ceased to give advice to people."

In the same way the **young men** (this is the same word as in the first half of verse 13) have given up **their music**. The verb in the first half-line, **have quit**, serves also for the second half-line. The poet is saying that the normal, happy routine of life, with old men conversing in the square and young people making music to entertain the people, has ceased. Although the Hebrew word for **music** refers to music made on stringed instruments, the attention is drawn to the absence of music. TEV has kept the two halves of the verse parallel, with "no longer sit" and "no longer make." In a similar manner we may say, for example, "We no longer hear the old men talking in the square, nor do we hear the music played by the young people there."

> The joy of our hearts has
>     ceased;
>   our dancing has been turned
>     to mourning.

> Happiness has gone out of our
>     lives;
>   grief has taken the place of
>     our dances.

The poet now speaks again for the whole community. Since community life is so totally disrupted that the old men have ceased to advise, and the young men to play their instruments, **The joy of our hearts** translates the Hebrew literally and clearly for English. **Heart** is here taken as the center of emotions. The expression refers to the feeling of happiness. **Ceased** translates the same verb used in "old men have quit" in verse 14. TEV says this effectively: "Happiness has gone out of our lives," or FRCL "Our hearts have ceased to be happy."

The expression **our dancing has been turned to mourning** may have to be expressed differently in some languages, particularly where dancing is associated with particular occasions or purposes such as healing or rain making, but not principally with the celebration of happiness. Accordingly we may sometimes say, for example, "We used to dance because we were happy; now we only mourn because we are sad."

> The crown has fallen from our
>     head;
>   woe to us, for we have
>     sinned!

> Nothing is left of all we were
>     proud of.
>   We sinned, and now we are
>     doomed.

**The crown has fallen from our head** is a literal translation. A **crown** in the Old Testament is sometimes a symbol of royalty, as in 2 Samuel 12.30; Psalm 21.3; Jeremiah 13.18. But a **crown** of flowers is mentioned in Isaiah 28.1,3 as a sign of festivity and celebration, just as the removal of his crown in Job 19.9 means that Job's former position of dignity had ceased. So here the fact that the **crown** has fallen from Jerusalem's head may possibly be a reference to the end of the royal line of David. However, in the context which speaks of misery taking the place of past glory, the poet is probably saying "The joyful celebrations are over." TEV expresses this in slightly different language by saying "Nothing is left of all we were proud of," and NEB attempts to retain something of the figurative language, with "The garlands have fallen from our heads." FRCL says "It is the end of our dignity." The sense of this half-line may also be translated figuratively in some languages; for example, "No one holds his face up any more" or "The eyes of everybody look downward now."

**Woe to us** translates an interjection of grief, sadness, doom, which TEV translates "we are doomed." This cry is used many times in the Old Testament, and its sense is expressed in many languages by a repetition of sound suggesting wailing or weeping. The reason for this lament is **for we have sinned**, which repeats the confession of 3.42. This half of the verse may sometimes be translated, for example,

"We have done wrong and so ay, ay, ay!" or "We have sinned and now evil (curse, damnation, suffering, doom) has taken hold of us!"

**5.17**  RSV  TEV

> For this our heart has become
> sick,
> for these things our eyes
> have grown dim,

> We are sick at our very hearts
> and can hardly see though
> our tears,

The first half of verse 17 begins in Hebrew with "Because of this," and the second half begins with "because of these." Here again interpreters differ in regard to whether **this** and **these things** point back to verse 16 or forward to verse 18. In favor of linking back to verse 16, it is difficult to see how **these things** can refer ahead to the single condition of the destruction of the Temple, unless **these** refers to both "Mount Zion lies desolate" and "jackals prowl." However, the vast majority of modern translations link verse 17 with verse 18, since this agrees with the outlook of the poet expressed elsewhere, that the greatest disaster of all is the destruction of the Temple. The link forward is made in a variety of ways.

The Handbook encourages translators to link verse 17 to verse 18, but the manner in which they do this may be quite different from that in RSV and others. For example, it may be necessary to state the conditions without any forward reference: (17) "Our hearts have become sick and our eyes have grown dim," (18) "because Mount Zion lies desolate and jackals prowl over it."

**Sick** translates the same word as in 1.13, which RSV translates as "faint" and TEV "in constant pain." The thought expressed by **heart . . . sick** is a feeling of being hopeless, discouraged, defeated. The expression **heart has become sick**, with the sense of hopelessness, may sometimes be rendered by means of other metaphors; for example, "our livers have vanished," "our breath is gone," or "our insides have no strength."

**Grown dim** translates a verb which generally means to become dark and is applied to the eyes in such passages as Psalm 69.23; the idea is that the vision is partially lost or blurred. TEV says "We . . . can hardly see through our tears," and FRCL ". . . our eyes are veiled with tears."

**5.18**  RSV  TEV

> for Mount Zion which lies
> desolate;
> jackals prowl over it.

> because Mount Zion lies lonely
> and deserted,
> and wild jackals prowl
> through its ruins.

Since verse 18 provides the reason for the conditions described in verse 17, some translators place a colon after the final word in 17. On the other hand, some express both halves of 17 as "if" clauses; for example, FRCL says "If our hearts . . . if our eyes . . . ," and then begins verse 18 with "it is because . . . ." TEV places a comma after "tears" in verse 17 and begins verse 18 "because Mount Zion . . . ." If the reason must be placed before the consequence, the order of verses 17 and 18 will be reversed, and in that case their numbers must also be adjusted.

**Mount Zion** is the hill on which the Temple stood. Here it refers only to the Temple location and not to Jerusalem as a whole. **Lies desolate** may be translated "abandoned, deserted." The desolation of the former site of the Temple is emphasized by the mention of the defiling presence of unclean animals there, as in Isaiah 13.19-22; 34.11-17; Zephaniah 2.13-15.

With the exception of AB, which has "fox," modern translations prefer to translate the Hebrew term here as **jackals**. This is not the same Hebrew word used in 4.3; there are three terms used in the Old Testament in reference to the fox and the jackal, and apparently these words were used interchangeably. See *Fauna and Flora of the Bible,* pages 31-32. For translation suggestions see 4.3.

### Section Heading

Although translations do not seem to use a heading for the closing of Lamentations, some recognize a break before verse 19 by inserting white space. See RSV, NEB. For translators who wish to use a heading here, we suggest "Why have you forgotten us?" or "Bring us back to you."

| 5.19 | RSV | TEV |
|---|---|---|
| | But thou, O LORD, dost reign for ever; thy throne endures to all generations. | But you, O LORD, are king forever and will rule to the end of time. |

The poet now reaches the closing phase of the book. Verse 19 is a statement of trust in God, in which the two half-lines are parallel in meaning. For a similar recognition of God's eternal rule in laments, see Psalm 44.1-8; 74.12-17; 80.1-2; 89.1-18. Although the Hebrew does not have a contrast word like **But**, such a connection is implied by the placement of "you" at the opening of the verse. The ancient versions understood the contrast in the same way.

**Reign** translates the same term as used in 2.10, where it means "sit." When used, as here, in parallel with **throne**, the sense is clearly that of "reign, rule, govern." TEV and FRCL say "you . . . are king." The word translated **for ever** can either refer back to the beginning of time or forward to the end of time, as in Psalm 90.2: "from everlasting to everlasting thou art God." In this context the poet is looking to the future, and so translators should indicate this.

**Thy throne** is a symbol of God's rule, or of God's being the ruler. **Endures to all generations** is literally "to generation and generation," which means "from one generation to another" (NEB), or continually, without ceasing. God's eternal kingly rule was an article of faith for the psalmists, as is clear from such passages as Psalm 9.7; 29.10; 93.2; 102.12. **For ever** and **to all generations** may sometimes be rendered as "going on and on," or negatively as "having no end"; for example, "LORD, you will go on and on ruling and you will rule us for ever."

**5.20**  RSV  TEV

> Why dost thou forget us for
> ever,
> why dost thou so long for-
> sake us?

> Why have you abandoned us so
> long?
> Will you ever remember us
> again?

Having expressed his faith in God's eternal rule, the poet now questions God's faithfulness. Each half of verse 20 consists of a "Why?" question. The first asks God the reason for his failure to remember his people, as though to repeat the appeal made in 5.1. The thought that God was capable of forgetting is expressed elsewhere in the Old Testament. For example, the psalmist asks in Psalm 13.1 "How long, O LORD? Wilt thou forget me for ever? How long wilt thou hide thy face from me?" In Psalm 42.9 we read "Why hast thou forgotten me?" and in Psalm 74.1 "O God, why dost thou cast us off for ever?" The poet is afraid that God's forgetfulness will last indefinitely, so in the agony of his lament he pursues these two parallel questions. Translators will note that TEV has switched the two verbs. Although this is not necessary in English, the TEV wording in the second half gives a greater sense of being forgotten.

**Forget us for ever: forget** has the sense of neglecting, putting out of mind, ceasing to think about, and so, ceasing to care for. **For ever** refers to an indefinite future. **So long** in the second half-line translates "length of days" and refers to a long period of time. Here the reference is most likely to the years of suffering experienced by the people of Jerusalem, and so Mft translates "all these years." **Forsake** here has the sense of God deserting someone (Israel) who has been formerly under his care and protection, and in some languages this may be translated "Why have you left us like orphaned children?" or "Why have you gone away and left us behind?"

In some languages the first line of RSV may be rendered "Why do you go on and on forgetting us?" and the second line as "Why do you go on and on abandoning us?" Since these are so closely parallel, the verse may also be translated "Why do you go on and on forgetting and abandoning us?"

**5.21**  RSV  TEV

> Restore us to thyself, O LORD,
> that we may be restored!
> Renew our days as of old!

> Bring us back to you, LORD!
> Bring us back!
> Restore our ancient glory.

The verbs in the two parts of this verse are imperatives, pleas that the LORD will restore or bring the people of Jerusalem back again to himself.

**Restore us** is a prayer, plea, or request that recognizes the separation between God and his people. TEV says "Bring us back to you." We may also say, for example, "Cause us to return to you" or "Take us back again." The second form of the same word, translated **that we may be restored** may mean "and we will return" (AB) and may also be expressed "so that we may return to you." In other words, the only hope for the people is that God himself will enable them to do what they cannot do by themselves, and will make them come back to serve him.

In the second half of the verse the poet appeals for the situation in Jerusalem to be once again what it had been before the invasion by the enemy; that is, he appeals for the restoration of worship in the Temple and political freedom from oppression.

**Renew our days** is a plea for the LORD to cause the people to be as they were in former times. In a general sense **our days** can mean "our lives." TEV makes it refer to the former situation of the people, with "our ancient glory," that is, "the glory that we used to have." We may also translate, for example, "Make us as great as we were before the enemy defeated us" or, more generally, "Cause us to live again as we lived in former times."

In translating these imperatives as pleas or prayers, it may be necessary to say "We ask you to restore us . . . ," "We pray that you will take us back again," or "We pray that you will make us as great as we were . . . ."

**5.22**            RSV                                    TEV

Or hast thou utterly rejected            Or have you rejected us forev-
  us?                                          er?
Art thou exceedingly angry               Is there no limit to your an-
  with us?                                     ger?

The final verse of the book appears to question God's relation to his people. If this is not despair, it certainly is not hope. The verse is difficult to interpret, and translations tend to be divided between those like RSV and TEV, which make questions of each half-line, and those like NEB, NIV, and AB, which translate as statements of some kind.

The basis for the difficulty is the interpretation of the first two Hebrew words *ki 'im*, which RSV translates as **Or**. Literally these words, if taken separately, mean "for if," which is expected to be followed by a condition leading to a consequence. An example is NEB, "For if thou hast utterly rejected us, then great indeed has been thy anger against us." For a similar handling of these introductory words, see Exodus 8.21. This rendering suggests that the poet cannot really accept that God has rejected his people.

Another wording which likewise implies unwillingness to believe that God has abandoned his people is expressed by NJB, "Unless you have utterly rejected us, in an anger which knows no limit." Those who defend this wording claim support in Genesis 32.26, in which Jacob says to his adversary "I will not let you go, unless you bless me."

AB, which argues against translating as a question (as in RSV, TEV), as well as a condition followed by a consequence (as in NEB), and against "unless" (NJB), favors translating as a statement which contrasts or opposes the thought of verse 21: "But instead you have completely rejected us; you have been very angry with us." This is also a traditional interpretation which is followed by the Vulgate, Luther, and KJV.

Gordis translates the opening words of the verse as "even though" and refers to Isaiah 10.22 and Amos 5.22 as further examples of the same construction. So he translates verses 21 and 22 as "Turn us to yourself, O LORD, and we shall return; renew our days as of old, even though you had despised us greatly and were very angry with us." It may be noted that in the other examples of this construction the "even though" clause comes before the main clause and so differs from this example, where it follows the main clause.

That verse 22 ends on a pessimistic note is confirmed, at least in the Jewish liturgical reading of this book, by the habit of repeating verse 21 after verse 22. NJV follows this tradition in its text. There is a similar tradition concerning the conclusion of Isaiah, Malachi, and Ecclesiastes.

Many translators will come to their own conclusion regarding the best way to handle this verse. However, the Handbook has attempted to evaluate the choices and accordingly recommends that translators give serious consideration to the interpretation proposed by AB.

We must now consider how best to make this contrastive statement clear in translation. For example, "But instead" (AB) suggests here that God has not done what was requested of him in verse 21; rather he has done something different. Therefore the contrast may have to be made clearer than with "But instead." For example, we may say "Instead of doing what we have asked, you have completely rejected us . . . ," or "You have not done what we asked, you have rejected us completely," or "You have not brought us back to you, instead you have rejected us completely."

Another solution which may be particularly suitable for some languages is to switch the order of verses 21 and 22, so that the sense is "22 is true, but in spite of 22, 21 is also true." In this case we are following the order of the Jewish liturgical reading, not for theological reasons but rather for translational reasons. Accordingly we may join these final two verses and number them as 21-22: "Have you rejected us forever, and is there no limit to your anger? In spite of your rejecting us, LORD, we pray that you will take us back again and we will return to you. We pray that you will make us as great as we were in former times."

In the final half-line **exceedingly** matches **utterly** in the first half-line. It may be necessary to supply "and" to create a coordinate thought, "and you have been so very angry with us," or, as an exclamation, "and how great your anger toward us has been!" In some languages the final half-line will be rendered idiomatically; for example, "and your heart has been hot against us."

# Selected Bibliography

## Bible Texts and Versions Cited

### Texts

*Biblia Hebraica Stuttgartensia.* 1966/77, 1983. Edited by K. Elliger and W. Rudolph. Stuttgart: Deutsche Bibelgesellschaft.

*Septuaginta: Id est Vetus Testamentum graece iuxta LXX interpretes.* 1935. Edited by Alfred Rahlfs. Stuttgart: Württembergische Bibelanstalt. (Cited as Septuagint.)

### Versions

*Die Bibel in heutigem Deutsch: Die Gute Nachricht des Alten und Neuen Testaments.* 1982. Stuttgart: Deutsche Bibelgesellschaft. (Cited as GECL, German common language version.)

*The Bible: A New Translation.* 1926. James Moffatt, translator. London: Hodder & Stoughton. (Cited as Mft.)

*La Bible de Jérusalem.* 1973. Paris: Éditions du Cerf. (Cited as BJ.)

*La Bible en français courant.* 1982. Paris: Société biblique française. (Cited as FRCL, French common language version.)

*Dios Habla Hoy: La Biblia con Deuterocanónicos. Versión Popular.* 1979. New York: Sociedades Biblicas Unidas. (Cited as SPCL, Spanish common language version.)

*Good News Bible: The Bible in Today's English Version.* 1976, 1979. New York: American Bible Society. British edition, 1976. London: British and Foreign Bible Societies. (Cited as TEV.)

*The Holy Bible* (Authorized or King James Version). 1611. (Cited as KJV.)

*The Holy Bible: New International Version.* 1987. New York: New York International Bible Society. (Cited as NIV.)

*The Holy Bible: Revised Standard Version.* 1952, 1971, 1973. New York: Division of Christian Education of the National Council of the Churches of Christ in the United States of America. (Cited as RSV.)

*The Living Bible.* 1971. Translated by Kenneth Taylor. Wheaton, Illinois: Tyndale House.

*The New American Bible.* 1970. New York: P.J. Kenedy & Sons. (Cited as NAB.)

*The New English Bible.* 1961, 1970. London: Oxford University Press; and Cambridge: Cambridge University Press. (Cited as NEB.)

*The New Jerusalem Bible.* 1985. Garden City, NY: Doubleday. (Cited as NJB.)

*TANAKH: A New Translation of the Holy Scriptures According to the Traditional Hebrew Text.* 1985. Philadelphia: Jewish Publication Society. (Cited as NJV, New Jewish Version.)

*Traduction œcuménique de la Bible.* 1972, 1975, 1977. Paris: Société biblique française et Éditions du Cerf. (Cited as TOB.)

## General Bibliography

### Commentaries

Gordis, Robert. 1954, 1968, 1974. *The Song of Songs and Lamentations: A Study, Modern Translation, and Commentary.* Revised and Augmented Edition. New York: KTAV Publishing House.

Gottwald, Norman K. 1962. *Studies in the Book of Lamentations* (Studies in Biblical Theology, No. 14). Revised edition. London: ???

Hillers, Delbert R. 1972. *Lamentations: Introduction, Translation, and Notes* (The Anchor Bible). Garden City, New York: Doubleday. (Cited as AB.)

Meek, Theophile J., and William Pierson Merrill. 1956. "The Book of Lamentations." In *The Interpreter's Bible,* Volume 6, pages 1-38. New York and Nashville: Abingdon Press.

### Special Studies

Alter, Robert. 1985. *The Art of Biblical Poetry.* New York: Basic Books.

Berlin, Adele. 1985. *The Dynamics of Biblical Parallelism.* Bloomington: Indiana University Press.

Budde, Karl. 1882. "Das hebräische Klagelied," *Zeitschrift für die altestamentliche Wissenschaft* 2.1-52.

Collins, T. 1979. *Line-Forms in Hebrew Poetry.* Rome: Biblical Institute Press.

Greenstein, Edward L. 1982. "How does parallelism mean?" In *A Sense of Text: The Art of Language in the Study of Biblical Literature.* Papers from a Symposium on Literature, Language and the Study of the Bible at the Dropsie College. Winona Lake, Indiana: Eisenbrauns.

Kugel, James L. 1981. *The Idea of Biblical Poetry: Parallelism and Its History.* New Haven: Yale University Press.

O'Connor, M. 1980. *Hebrew Verse Structure.* Winona Lake, Indiana: Eisenbrauns.

Watson, W.G.E. 1984. *Classical Hebrew Poetry: A Guide to Its Techniques.* Journal for the Study of the Old Testament, Supplement Series 26. Sheffield, England.

## Other Works

Barthélemy, Dominique; A.R. Hulst; Norbert Lohfink; W.D. McHardy; H.P. Rüger; and James A. Sanders. 1979. *Preliminary and Interim Report on the Hebrew Old Testament Text Project,* Volume 4, *Prophetical Books I, Isaiah, Jeremiah, Lamentations.* New York: United Bible Societies. (Cited as HOTTP.)

Brown, Francis; Samuel R. Driver; and Charles A. Briggs. 1968. *A Hebrew and English Lexicon of the Old Testament.* London: Oxford University Press. (Cited as BDB.)

*Fauna and Flora of the Bible.* 1972, 1980. New York: United Bible Societies. (Cited as *Fauna and Flora.*)

Holladay, William L. 1971. *A Concise Hebrew and Aramaic Lexicon of the Old Testament.* Grand Rapids, Michigan: Eerdmans.

Koehler, Ludwig, and Walter Baumgartner, editors. *Lexicon in Veteris Testamenti Libros.* Two volumes. Leiden: E.J. Brill; and Grand Rapids, Michigan: Eerdmans. (Cited as K-B.)

Robinson, David, editor. 1983. *Concordance to the Good News Bible.* Swindon: The British and Foreign Bible Society.

Whitaker, Richard E., and James E. Goehring, compilers. 1988. *The Eerdmans Analytical Concordance to the Revised Standard Version of the Bible.* Grand Rapids, Michigan: Eerdmans.

# Glossary

This Glossary contains terms that are technical from an exegetical or a linguistic viewpoint. Other terms not defined here may be referred to in a Bible dictionary.

**ABSTRACT** refers to terms which designate the qualities and quantities (that is, the features) of objects and events but which are not objects or events themselves. For example, "red" is a quality of a number of objects but is not a thing in and of itself. Typical abstracts include "goodness," "beauty," "length," "breadth," and "time."

**ACROSTIC** refers to a style of writing lines, usually poetic lines, in such a way that the first letter of every line will combine with the other first letters to form the letters of the alphabet in their order, or else to form a phrase or a message.

**ACTIVE.** See **VOICE.**

**ACTOR.** See **AGENT.**

**ADJECTIVE** is a word which limits, describes, or qualifies a noun. In English, "red," "tall," "beautiful," and "important" are adjectives.

**AGENT** (or, **ACTOR**) is that which accomplishes the action in a sentence or clause, regardless of whether the grammatical construction is active or passive. In "John struck Bill" (active) and "Bill was struck by John" (passive), the agent in either case is John.

**AMBIGUOUS** describes a word or phrase which in a specific context may have two or more different meanings. For example, "Bill did not leave because John came" could mean either (1) "the coming of John prevented Bill from leaving" or (2) "the coming of John was not the cause of Bill's leaving." It is often the case that what is ambiguous in written form is not ambiguous when actually spoken, since features of intonation and slight pauses usually make clear which of two or more meanings is intended. Furthermore, even in written discourse, the entire context normally serves to indicate which meaning is intended by the writer.

**ANCIENT VERSIONS.** See **VERSIONS.**

**ANIMATE** identifies objects which are regarded as alive and normally able to move voluntarily. "Man," "dog," and "fish" are animate objects, but "tree" is not.

151

**ARTICLE** is a grammatical class of words, often obligatory, which indicate whether the following word is definite or indefinite. In English the **DEFINITE ARTICLE** is "the," and the **INDEFINITE ARTICLE** is "a" or ("an").

**ASPECT** is a grammatical category which specifies the nature of an action; for example, whether the action is completed, uncompleted, repeated, begun, continuing, increasing in intensity, decreasing in intensity, etc. "Was built" indicates completed aspect, while, "was running" indicates continuing aspect.

**BORROWED** term refers to a foreign term that is used in another language. For example, "matador" is a Spanish word that has been borrowed by English speakers for "bullfighter."

**CAUSATIVE** relates to events and indicates that someone or something caused something to happen, rather than that the person or thing did it directly. In "John ran the horse," the verb "ran" is a causative, since it was not John who ran, but rather it was John who caused the horse to run.

**CENTRAL MEANING** is the meaning of a word which is generally understood when the word is given with no context. This is also called the "unmarked meaning."

**CHIASMUS** is a reversal of words or phrases in an otherwise parallel construction. For example: "I (1) / was shapen (2) / in iniquity (3) // in sin (3) / did my mother conceive (2) / me (1)."

**CLAUSE** is a grammatical construction, normally consisting of a subject and a predicate. An **INDEPENDENT CLAUSE** may stand alone. The **MAIN CLAUSE** is that clause in a sentence which could stand alone as a complete sentence, but which has one or more dependent or subordinate clauses related to it. A **SUBORDINATE CLAUSE** is dependent on the main clause, but it does not form a complete sentence.

**CLIMAX** is the point in a discourse, such as a story or speech, which is the most important, or the turning point, or the point of decision.

**COLLECTIVE** refers to a number of things (or persons) considered as a whole. In English, a collective noun is considered to be singular or plural, more or less on the basis of traditional usage; for example, "The crowd is (the people are) becoming angry."

**COMMAND.** See **IMPERATIVE**.

**CONNECTIVE** is a word or phrase which connects other words, phrases, clauses, etc.

**CONSEQUENCE** is that which shows the result of a condition or event.

**CONSONANTS** are symbols representing those speech sounds which are produced by obstructing, blocking, or restricting the free passage of air from the lungs through the mouth. They were originally the only spoken sounds recorded in the Hebrew system of writing; **VOWELS** were added later as marks associated with the **CONSONANTS**. See also **VOWELS**.

**CONSTRUCTION.** See **STRUCTURE**.

**CONTEXT** is that which precedes and/or follows any part of a discourse. For example, the context of a word or phrase in Scripture would be the other words and phrases associated with it in the sentence, paragraph, section, and even the entire book in which it occurs. The context of a term often affects its meaning, so that a word does not mean exactly the same thing in one context that it does in another context.

**COORDINATE** structure is a phrase or clause joined to another phrase or clause, but not dependent on it. Coordinate structures are joined by such conjunctions as "and" or "but," as in "the man and the boys" or "he walked but she ran"; or they are paratactically related, as in "he walked; she ran."

**DEFINITE ARTICLE.** See **ARTICLE**.

**DESCRIPTIVE** is said of a word or phrase which characterizes or describes another term.

**DIRECT ADDRESS, DIRECT DISCOURSE, DIRECT QUOTATION, DIRECT SPEECH.** See **DISCOURSE**.

**DISCOURSE** is the connected and continuous communication of thought by means of language, whether spoken or written. The way in which the elements of a discourse are arranged is called **DISCOURSE STRUCTURE**. **DIRECT DISCOURSE** (or, **DIRECT ADDRESS, DIRECT QUOTATION, DIRECT SPEECH**) is the reproduction of the actual words of one person quoted and included in the discourse of another person; for example, "He declared 'I will have nothing to do with this man.'" **INDIRECT DISCOURSE** (or, **INDIRECT SPEECH**) is the reporting of the words of one person within the discourse of another person, but in an altered grammatical form rather than as an exact quotation; for example, "He said he would have nothing to do with that man."

**EMPHASIS (EMPHATIC)** is the special importance given to an element in a discourse, sometimes indicated by the choice of words or by position in the sentence. For example, in "Never will I eat pork again," "Never" is given emphasis by placing it at the beginning of the sentence.

**EQUIVALENCE (EQUIVALENT)** is a very close similarity in meaning, as opposed to similarity in form. It contrasts with **FORMAL CORRESPONDENCE**.

**EXEGESIS (EXEGETICAL)** is the process of determining the meaning of a text (or the result of this process), normally in terms of "who said what to whom under what circumstances and with what intent." A correct exegesis is indispensable before a passage can be translated correctly.

**FEMININE** is one of the genders expressed in the grammar of many languages. See **GENDER**.

**FIGURE, FIGURE OF SPEECH,** or **FIGURATIVE EXPRESSION** involves the use of words in other than their literal or ordinary sense, in order to bring out some aspect of meaning by means of comparison or association. For example, "raindrops dancing on the street," or "his speech was like thunder." **METAPHORS** and **SIMILES** are figures of speech.

**FINITE VERB** is any verb form which distinguishes person, number, tense, mode, or aspect. It is usually referred to in contrast to an **INFINITIVE** verb form, which indicates the action or state without specifying such things as agent or time.

**FIRST PERSON.** See **PERSON**.

**FIRST PERSON PLURAL** includes the speaker and at least one other person: "we," "us," "our," "ours."

**FIRST PERSON SINGULAR** is the speaker: "I," "me," "my," "mine."

**FOCUS** is the center of attention in a discourse or in any part of a discourse.

**FORMAL CORRESPONDENCE** (or, **FORMAL RENDERING, FORMAL TRANSLATION**) is a type of translation in which the features of form in the source text have been more or less mechanically reproduced in the receptor language.

**FUTURE TENSE.** See **TENSE**.

**GENDER** is any of three grammatical subclasses of nouns and pronouns (called **MASCULINE, FEMININE,** and **NEUTER**), which determine agreement with and selection of other words or grammatical forms.

**GENERAL.** See **GENERIC**.

**GENERIC** has reference to a general class or kind of objects, events, or abstracts; it is the opposite of **SPECIFIC**. For example, the term "animal" is generic in relation to "dog," which is a specific kind of animal. However, "dog" is generic in relation to the more specific term "poodle."

**GRAMMATICAL** refers to grammar, which includes the selection and arrangement of words in phrases, clauses, and sentences.

**GREEK** was the language spoken in Greece, corresponding to the Roman province of Achaia in New Testament times. The language was in use especially in the eastern part of the Roman Empire, and the **SEPTUAGINT VERSION** was the translation of the Hebrew Bible into Greek.

**HEBREW** is the language in which the Old Testament was written. It belongs to the Semitic family of languages. By the time of Christ, many Jewish people no longer used Hebrew as their common language.

**HONORIFIC** is a form used to express respect or deference. In many languages such forms are obligatory in talking to or about royalty and persons of social distinction.

**IDIOM,** or **IDIOMATIC EXPRESSION,** is a combination of terms whose meanings cannot be understood by adding up the meanings of the parts. "To hang one's head," "to have a green thumb," and "behind the eightball" are American English idioms. Idioms almost always lose their meaning or convey a wrong meaning when translated literally from one language to another.

**IMPERATIVE** refers to forms of a verb which indicate commands or requests. In "Go and do likewise," the verbs "Go" and "do" are imperatives. In most languages imperatives are confined to the grammatical second person; but some languages have corresponding forms for the first and third persons. These are usually expressed in English by the use of "must" or "let"; for example, "We must not swim here!" or "They must work harder!" or "Let them eat cake!"

**IMPERFECT** is a form of a Hebrew verb that expresses the action as ongoing, continuative, or incomplete, regardless of the time of the action in relation to the time of speaking or writing.

**IMPERSONAL VERB** is a usage of the verb which denotes an action by an unspecified agent. It may involve the use of the third person singular, as in "It is raining" or "One normally prefers cake," or in some languages the use of the third person plural, as in "They say . . . ," or in still other languages the use of the first person plural, as in "We cook this way," meaning "People cook this way."

**IMPLICIT (IMPLY, IMPLIED)** refers to information that is not formally represented in a discourse, since it is assumed that it is already known to the receptor, or evident from the meaning of the words in question. For example, the phrase "the other son" carries with it the implicit information that there is a son in addition to the one mentioned.

**INCLUSIVE** first person plural includes both the speaker and the one(s) to whom that person is speaking.

**INDIRECT SPEECH.** See **DISCOURSE.**

**INFINITIVE** is a verb form which indicates an action or state without specifying such factors as agent or time; for example, "to mark," "to sing," or "to go." It is in

155

contrast to **FINITE VERB** form, which often distinguishes person, number, tense, mode, or aspect; for example "marked," "sung," or "will go." See **FINITE VERB**.

**INTERJECTIONS** are exclamatory words or phrases, invariable in form, usually used to express emotion. "Hey!" or "Oh!" and "Indeed!" are examples of interjections.

**INTERPRETATION** of a text is the exegesis of it. See **EXEGESIS**.

**IRONY** is a sarcastic or humorous manner of discourse in which what is said is intended to express its opposite; for example, "That was a smart thing to do!" when intended to convey the meaning, "That was a stupid thing to do!"

**LEVEL** refers to the degree of difficulty characteristic of language usage by different constituencies or in different settings. A translation may, for example, be prepared for the level of elementary school children, for university students, for teen-agers, or for rural rather than urban people. Differences of level also are involved as to whether a particular discourse is formal, informal, casual, or intimate in nature.

**LINGUISTIC** refers to qualities of language, especially the formal structure of language.

**LITERAL** means the ordinary or primary meaning of a term or expression, in contrast with a figurative meaning. A **LITERAL TRANSLATION** is one which represents the exact words and word order of the source language; such a translation is frequently unnatural or awkward in the receptor language.

**LITURGICAL** refers to liturgy, that is, public worship.

**MAIN CLAUSE.** See **CLAUSE**.

**MANUSCRIPTS** are books, documents, or letters written or copied by hand. A **SCRIBE** is one who copies a manuscript. Thousands of manuscript copies of various Old and New Testament books still exist, but none of the original manuscripts. See **TEXT**.

**MARKERS (MARK, MARKING)** are features of words or of a discourse which signal some special meaning or some particular structure. For example, words for speaking may mark the onset of direct discourse, a phrase such as "once upon a time" may mark the beginning of a fairy story, and certain features of parallelism are the dominant markers of poetry. The word "body" may require a marker to clarify whether a person, a group, or a corpse is meant.

**MASCULINE** is one of the genders. See **GENDER**.

**MASORETIC TEXT** is the traditional Hebrew text of the Old Testament which was established by Hebrew scholars by the time of the eighth and ninth centuries **A.D.**

**METAPHOR** is likening one object, event, or state to another by speaking of it as if it were the other; for example, "flowers dancing in the breeze" compares the movement of flowers with dancing. Metaphors are the most commonly used figures of speech and are often so subtle that a speaker or writer is not conscious of the fact that he or she is using figurative language. See **SIMILE**.

**METER**, in Hebrew poetry, refers to the measured number of accented words in a line. In most Hebrew poetry, a regular pattern is formed.

**MODIFY (MODIFIER)** is to affect the meaning of another part of the sentence, as when an adjective modifies a noun or an adverb modifies a verb.

**NONFIGURATIVE**. See **FIGURE, FIGURATIVE**.

**NOUN** is a word that names a person, place, thing, or idea, and often serves to specify a subject or topic of discussion.

**NOUN PHRASE**. See **PHRASE**.

**OBJECT** of a verb is the goal of an event or action specified by the verb. In "John hit the ball," the object of "hit" is "ball."

**ORTHOGRAPHY (ORTHOGRAPHIC)** refers to a system of writing and is often used in speaking of a similarity or difference in spelling.

**PARAGRAPH** is a distinct segment of discourse dealing with a particular idea, and usually marked with an indentation on a new line.

**PARALLEL, PARALLELISM**, generally refers to some similarity in the content and/or form of a construction; for example, "The man was blind, and he could not see." The structures that correspond to each other in the two statements are said to be parallel.

**PARTICLE** is a small word whose grammatical form does not change. In English the most common particles are prepositions and conjunctions.

**PARTICULAR** is the opposite of **GENERAL**. See **GENERIC**.

**PASSAGE** is the text of Scripture in a specific location. It is usually thought of as comprising more than one verse, but it can be a single verse or part of a verse.

**PASSIVE**. See **VOICE**.

**PAST TENSE**. See **TENSE**.

**PERFECT** is a form of a Hebrew verb that expresses the action as a unit, or as a complete, total action, regardless of the time of the action in relation to the time of speaking or writing.

**PERSON**, as a grammatical term, refers to the speaker, the person spoken to, or the person or thing spoken about. **FIRST PERSON** is the person(s) speaking (such as "I," "me," "my," "mine," "we," "us," "our," or "ours"). **SECOND PERSON** is the person(s) or thing(s) spoken to (such as "thou," "thee," "thy," "thine," "ye," "you," "your," or "yours"). **THIRD PERSON** is the person(s) or thing(s) spoken about (such as "he," "she," "it," "his," "her," "them," or "their"). The examples here given are all pronouns, but in many languages the verb forms have affixes which indicate first, second, or third person and also indicate whether they are **SINGULAR** or **PLURAL**.

**PERSONIFICATION** is a reference to an inanimate object or an abstract idea in terms that give it a personal or a human nature; as in "Wisdom is calling out," referring to wisdom as if it were a person.

**PHRASE** is a grammatical construction of two or more words, but less than a complete clause or a sentence. A phrase is usually given a name according to its function in a sentence, such as "noun phrase," "verb phrase," or "prepositional phrase."

**PLURAL** refers to the form of a word which indicates more than one. See **SINGULAR**.

**POINT OF VIEW**. See **VIEWPOINT**.

**PREFIX** is a part of a word which cannot stand alone and which is positioned at the beginning of the word to which it belongs; for example, "*im-* possible," or "*re-* structure."

**PREPOSITION** is a word (usually a particle) whose function is to indicate the relation of a noun or pronoun to another noun, pronoun, verb, or adjective. Some English prepositions are "for," "from," "in," "to," and "with."

**PRESENT TENSE, PRESENT PERFECT TENSE**. See **TENSE**.

**PRONOUNS** are words which are used in place of nouns, such as "he," "him," "his," "she," "we," "them," "who," "which," "this," or "these."

**PROPER NAME** or **PROPER NOUN** is the name of a unique object, as "Jerusalem," "Joshua," "Jordan." However, the same name may be applied to more than one object; for example, "John" (the Baptist or the Apostle) and "Antioch" (of Syria or Pisidia).

**PROSE** is the ordinary form of spoken or written language, without the special forms and structure of meter and rhythm which are characteristic of poetry.

**QUOTATION** is the reporting of one person's speech by another person. See **DISCOURSE**.

**READ, READING,** frequently refers to the interpretation of the written form of a text, especially under the following conditions: if the available text appears to be defective; or if differing versions of the same text are available; or if several alternative sets of vowels may be understood as correct in languages such as biblical Hebrew, in which only the consonants were written. See also **TEXT, TEXTUAL.**

**RECEPTOR** is the person(s) receiving a message. The **RECEPTOR LANGUAGE** is the language into which a translation is made. For example, in a translation from Hebrew into German, Hebrew is the source language and German is the receptor language.

**RENDERING (RENDER)** is the manner in which a specific passage is translated from one language to another.

**RESTRUCTURE.** See **STRUCTURE.**

**RHETORICAL QUESTION** is an expression which is put in the form of a question but which is not intended to ask for information. Rhetorical questions are usually employed for the sake of emphasis.

**ROOT** is the minimal base of a derived or inflected word. For example, "friend" is the root of "friendliness."

**SARCASM (SARCASTIC)** is an ironical and frequently contemptuous manner of discourse in which what is said is intended to express its opposite; for example, "What a brilliant idea!" when intended to convey the meaning, "What a ridiculous idea!"

**SATIRE** is a form or style of **DISCOURSE** that ridicules the subject it discusses, often by the use of **IRONY** or **SARCASM.**

**SCRIBE, SCRIBAL.** See **MANUSCRIPT.**

**SECOND PERSON.** See **PERSON.**

**SENTENCE** is a grammatical construction composed of one or more clauses and capable of standing alone.

**SEPTUAGINT** is a translation of the Hebrew Old Testament into Greek, begun some two hundred years before Christ. It is often abbreviated as LXX.

**SIMILE** (pronounced SIM-i-lee) is a **FIGURE OF SPEECH** which describes one event or object by comparing it to another, using "like," "as," or some other word to mark or signal the comparison. For example, "She runs like a deer," "He is as straight as an arrow." Similes are less subtle than metaphors in that metaphors do not mark the comparison with words such as "like" or "as." See **METAPHOR.**

**SINGULAR** refers to the form of a word which indicates one thing or person, in contrast to **PLURAL,** which indicates more than one. See **PLURAL.**

**SPECIFIC** refers to the opposite of **GENERAL, GENERIC.** See **GENERIC.**

**STRUCTURE** is the systematic arrangement of the elements of language, including the ways in which words combine into phrases, phrases into clauses, clauses into sentences, and sentences into larger units of discourse. Because this process may be compared to the building of a house or bridge, such words as **STRUCTURE** and **CONSTRUCTION** are used in reference to it. To separate and rearrange the various components of a sentence or other unit of discourse in the translation process is to **RESTRUCTURE** it.

**STYLE** is a particular or a characteristic manner in discourse. Each language has certain distinctive **STYLISTIC** features which cannot be reproduced literally in another language. Within any language, certain groups of speakers may have their characteristic discourse styles, and among individual speakers and writers, each has his or her own style.

**SUBJECT** is one of the major divisions of a clause, the other being the predicate. In "The small boy walked to school," "The small boy" is the subject. Typically the subject is a noun phrase. It should not be confused with the semantic "agent," or **ACTOR.**

**SUBORDINATE CLAUSE.** See **CLAUSE.**

**SUFFIX** is a letter or one or more syllables added to the end of a word, to modify the meaning in some manner. For example, "-s" suffixed to "tree" changes the word from singular to plural, "trees," while "-ing" suffixed to "sing" changes the verb to a participle, "singing."

**SYMBOL** is a form, whether linguistic or nonlinguistic, which is arbitrarily and conventionally associated with a particular meaning. For example, the word "cross" is a linguistic symbol, referring to a particular object. Similarly, within the Christian tradition, the cross as an object is a symbol for the death of Jesus.

**SYNONYMS** are words which are different in form but similar in meaning, such as "boy" and "lad." Expressions which have essentially the same meaning are said to be **SYNONYMOUS.** No two words are completely synonymous.

**SYNTAX** is the selection and arrangement of words in phrases, clauses, and sentences.

**SYRIAC** is the name of a Semitic language, a part of the Aramaic family, used in Western Asia, into which the Bible was translated at a very early date (the **SYRIAC VERSION**).

**TABOO** refers to something set apart as sacred by religious custom and is therefore forbidden to all but certain persons or uses (**POSITIVE TABOO**), or something which is regarded as evil and therefore forbidden to all by tradition or social usage (**NEGATIVE TABOO**).

**TENSE** is usually a form of a verb which indicates time relative to a discourse or some event in a discourse. The most common forms of tense are past, present, and future.

**TEXT, TEXTUAL,** refers to the various Greek and Hebrew manuscripts of the Scriptures. **TEXTUAL EVIDENCE** is the cumulative evidence for a particular form of the text. **TEXTUAL PROBLEMS** arise when it is difficult to reconcile or to account for conflicting forms of the same text in two or more manuscripts. Ancient texts that resemble each other may be said to belong to a specific **TEXTUAL TRADITION**. See also **MANUSCRIPTS**.

**THEME** is the subject of a discourse.

**THIRD PERSON**. See **PERSON**.

**TONE** is the spirit, character, or emotional effect of a passage or discourse.

**TRANSITION** in discourse involves passing from one thought-section or group of related thought-sections to another.

**TRANSLATION** is the reproduction in a receptor language of the closest natural equivalent of a message in the source language, first, in terms of meaning, and second, in terms of style. A translator may seem to be following an inferior textual reading (see **TEXTUAL**) when he is simply adjusting the rendering to the requirements of the receptor language, that is, for a **TRANSLATIONAL** reason.

**TRANSLITERATE** is to represent in the receptor language the approximate sounds or letters of words occurring in the source language, rather than translating their meaning; for example, "Amen" from the Hebrew, or the title "Christ" from the Greek.

**VERBS** are a grammatical class of words which express existence, action, or occurrence, such as "be," "become," "run," or "think."

**VERBAL** has two meanings. (1) It may refer to expressions consisting of words, sometimes in distinction to forms of communication which do not employ words ("sign language," for example). (2) It may refer to word forms which are derived from verbs. For example, "coming" and "engaged" may be called verbals, and participles are called verbal adjectives.

**VERSIONS** are translations. The ancient, or early, versions are translations of the Bible, or of portions of the Bible, made in early times; for example, the Greek Septuagint, the ancient Syriac, or the Ethiopic versions.

**VIEWPOINT (POINT OF VIEW)** is the place or situation or circumstance from which a speaker or writer presents a message. If, for example, the **VIEWPOINT PLACE** is the top of a hill, movement in the area will be described differently from the way one would describe it from the bottom of a hill. If the **VIEWPOINT PERSON** is a priest, he will speak of the temple in a way that differs from that of a common person.

**VOICE** in grammar is the relation of the action expressed by a verb to the participants in the action. In English and many other languages, the **ACTIVE VOICE** indicates that the subject performs the action ("John hit the man"), while the **PASSIVE VOICE** indicates that the subject is being acted upon ("The man was hit").

**VOWELS** are symbols representing the sound of the vocal cords, produced by unobstructed air passing from the lungs though the mouth. They were not originally included in the Hebrew system of writing; they were added later as marks associated with the consonants. See also **CONSONANTS**.

**VULGATE** is the Latin version of the Bible translated and/or edited originally by Saint Jerome. It has been traditionally the official version of the Roman Catholic Church.

# Index

This Index includes concepts, key words, and terms for which the Handbook contains a discussion useful for translators. Hebrew and Greek terms have been transliterated and occur in English alphabetical order.

'adam 92
'adonai 9
Affliction 26
Ah 64
Aliens 133
Altar 53
Anointed 126
Appointed feasts 19
Approve 91

Babies 58
Bars 56
Bear 80
Befallen 132
Behold 37, 103
Bend
    bent his bow 49, 50
Bereave 38
    bereft 83
Betray 17
Bitterly 16
Bitterness 78, 82
Blood 121
Booth 52
Bosom 59
Bow
    bent his bow 49, 50
Bowed down 85
Bread 27, 59, 137
Broken down 52
Bronze 79

Captives 21
Captivity 36
Cause 92, 102
Chains 79
Chastisement 114
chesed 86
Children 21
City 15
    city gate 141
Clamor 54

Clap
    clap their hands 62
Comfort 17, 34
    comforter 25
Compassionate 118
Congregation 27
Coral 116
Courage 34
Cower 83
Crown 142
Cup 127
Curse 105
Cut down 48

Dainties 113
Dancing 142
Dandle 71
Darkness 79
Daughter
    daughter of Edom 128
    daughter of my people 58, 112
    daughter of Zion 22
    daughters of my city 99
    virgin daughter of Judah 33
    virgin daughter of Zion 60
Day
    day of his anger 46
    day of the LORD 29, 64
    the day 39
Deal 40
Death 38
Defiled 121
Desolate 19, 34, 81
Despised 28
Destroy 47, 51, 71
Devices 102
Disgrace 132, 133
Dishonor 48
Disown 53
Distress 37
Dogged our steps 125
Doom 25

Downfall 24

Eagles 125, 126
Earth
    earthen pots 111
    of the earth 91
'el 9, 95
Elders 37, 57, 123, 140, 141
'elyon 9, 92
Enduring 84
Evil 93
Exile
    gone into exile 18
Eye
    pride of our eyes 50

Face
    in the face of the enemy 49
Faint 30, 58
Fall
    fall by the sword 69
Fathers 136
Favor 123
Feasts
    appointed feasts 19
    Filthy 24, 35
Flout 32
Footstool 46
For ever 145
Forget 145
Forgiven 95
Forsake 145
Fortune
    restore your fortunes 61
Fruit 68
Fugitive 122

Gall 84
Garden 52
Gate 55, 56
    city gate 141
    gates 19
Gave me into the hands of 32
geber 76
Gloat 23
Glory 84
Gnash their teeth 64
God 9, 95
    'el 9, 95
    'elyon 9, 92
    the Most High 9
Gold 109, 110
    pure gold 109
Good 88
goyim 15
Grievously 24
Grind 140

Habitation
    habitations of Jacob 47
Hand
    clap their hands 62
    fell into the hand 23
    gave me into the hands of 32
    give the hand 136
    lift your hands 67
    right hand 48
    stretched out his hands over 26
    stretches out her hands 35
    turn his hand against 77
Hart 22
Head
    wag their heads 62
Heart 40, 81, 142
    heart is poured out 58
    pour out your heart 67
Hewn stones 80
Hills 126
Hiss 62, 64
Holy
    holy stones 110
Honor 123
Hope 87
Horn 48, 65

Infants 58
Inheritance 133
Iniquity 128
    bear their iniquities 136

Jackals 111, 112, 144
Jacob 35
    habitations of Jacob 47
Jerusalem 19
Judge 102

ki 26, 40
Kidneys 81
kurios 9

Laid in ruins 51
Lamentation 51
Languish 55
Lapis lazuli 116
Laughingstock 81
Law 56
Lay in wait 126
Life
    life is poured out 59
Lift
    lift your hands 67
Line
    mark off by line 54
Lion 80
Lips 103

Lord
    *'adonai* 9
    *kurios* 9
    LORD 9, 21
    *Yahweh* 9
    *yhwh* 9, 21
Love
    steadfast love 86
Lovers 16, 17, 37

Maiden 20
    maidens of my city 99
Majesty 22
Man 76, 92
    *'adam* 92
    *geber* 76
    mighty men 32
    old men 141
    young men 69
Mark 81
    mark off by line 54
Mercies 86
Mercy
    without mercy 47, 70
Might 48
    mighty men 32
Mill 140
Mocking 24
Most High 9, 92
Mountains 126
Mourning 51
Music 141

Name 100
Nations 15, 18, 26
*nazir* 115
Nazirites 115
*nefesh* 59, 88
Neighbors 35
Net 30
Nursling 113

Offscouring 96
Offspring 68
Old men 141
Oracle 61
Orphans 134
Ostrich 112

Palace 51
Path
    crooked path 80
Peace 83
Pined away 118
Pit 100, 126
    pitfall 97
Pity
    without pity 96

Pots
    earthen pots 111
Pour
    heart is poured out 58
    life is poured out 59
    pour out your heart 67
    poured out his fury 50
Precious 111
    precious things 26
Prevailed 34
Pride
    pride of our eyes 50
Priest 20
Prince 22, 56, 115, 140
Princess 15
Prophet 56, 61
Punishment 114
    punishment of your iniquity 128
Purple 114
Pursue 105
    pursuers 18

Quiver 81

Rail 63
    rail against 64
Rampart 55
Ravish 139
Rebel 36
    rebellious 38
Redeem 102
Refuse 96
Regard 123
Reign 144
Remember
    has not remembered 46
Renew 146
Requite 104
Resting place 18
Restore 146
    restore your fortunes 61
Revive 37
Right 92
    in the right 36
    right hand 48
Righteous 121
Rod
    rod of his wrath 77
Ruins
    laid in ruins 51

Sabbath 52
Sackcloth 57
Salvation 88
Sanctuary 26, 27
Sapphire 116
Scatter 123
Scorn 53

INDEX

Sea  60
See
    see affliction  77
Seek  88
Shadow  127
*shalom*  83
Sheol  38, 79
Sick  143
Sin  24
    sins  94
Skirts  25
Slaughter  70
Slaves  137
Son
    sons of men  90
    sons of Zion  111
Soot  116, 117
Soul  87, 88
    soul is in tumult  38, 58
Splendor  46
Steadfast love  86
Stones
    hewn stones  80
    holy stones  110
Strangers  133
Street  58, 67
    in the street  38
Stretch
    stretched out his hands over  26
    stretches out her hands  35
Stricken  118
Stronghold  47
Stunned  30
Surely  77
Sword  38, 137
    fall by the sword  69

Taunts  103
Temple  19, 26, 27
Tent  50
Terror  70
    terrors on every side  70
Throne  145
*tob*  88
*torah*  56
Transgression  21
Treacherous
    dealt treacherously  17

Treasures  27
Tribulation  78
Triumph  26
Trouble  39
Tumult
    soul is in tumult  58
Turn aside  92

Unclean  122
    uncleanness  25
Uncover  129

Vassal  16
Vengeance  102
Vent
    gave full vent to  119
Virgin  33, 139
    virgin daughter of Judah  33
    virgin daughter of Zion  60
Visage  116
Vision  56, 57, 61
Vultures  125, 126

Wag
    wag their heads  62
Wall  55
Wanderer  122
Watches  67
Ways  94
Widow  15, 134
Wilderness  112, 126, 137
Wine  59
    wine press  32
Woe  143
Word
    his word  36
Wormwood  82, 84
Wrath
    rod of his wrath  77

*Yahweh*  9
*yhwh*  9, 21
Yoke  31, 88, 135
Young men  36, 69

Zion  19
    daughter of Zion  22
    Mount Zion  144

PRINTED IN THE UNITED STATES OF AMERICA